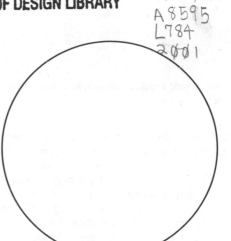

D0573066

ASTRONAUTS IN TROUBLE
LIVE FROM THE MOON
LARRY YOUNG . CHARLIE ADLARD . MATT SMITH

AiT/PLANET LAR
SAN FRANCISCO

comic book trade paperbacks available from
AiT/Planet Lar

Astronauts in Trouble: Live From the Moon
by Larry Young, Matt Smith, and Charlie Adlard
            The Making of Astronauts in Trouble
                by Larry Young
        Astronauts in Trouble: Space 1959
                by Larry Young and Charlie Adlard
Astronauts in Trouble: One Shot, One Beer
by Larry Young and Charlie Adlard
            nobody
                    by Alex Amado, Sharon Cho, and Charlie Adlard
        Channel Zero
                by Brian Wood
Space Beaver Volume One and Volume Two
by Darick Robertson
            Sky Ape
                    by Amara, McCarney, Russo, and Jenkins
The Foot Soldiers Volume One and Volume Two
by Jim Krueger and Mike Oeming/Jim Krueger and Phil Hester
        Come in Alone
                by Warren Ellis

Astronauts in Trouble: Live From the Moon
by Larry Young, Matt Smith, and Charlie Adlard

Published by
AiT/Planet Lar
2034 47th Avenue
San Francisco, CA 94116

First edition November 1999
Second edition June 2001

0 10 9 8 7 6 5 4 3 2

Cover design by Brian Wood
Cover art by Darick Robertson
Back cover art by Charlie Adlard, Matt Smith and Aman Chaudhary
Back cover color by Matt Hollingsworth and Aman Chaudhary

ISBN: 0-9676847-1-4

Printed and bound in Canada by Quebecor Printing, Inc.

for Mimi, who understands

Okay, I admit it. I'm queer for Saturn Fives.

My favourite toy as a very young kid was a detailed
scale model of the Apollo 11 Saturn V stack that my dad
made from an Airfix kit. I was talking to Niki about this
just the other day: if I close my eyes, I can see the
damned thing in my head still. You could unscrew each
section of the stack to see the engine bells, and the
CSM, and the LEM, and even the little escape rocket.
Must've sent Dad half blind, painting all those little
cylinders and struts with Humbrol enamel paints. He
probably did it during the nights of the first three years
of my charmed life, when I was reportedly being
hyperactively sleepless in my cot-cum-cage, in an
attempt to keep himself half-sane. It didn't work. My
Dad put space travel away long ago, and now devotes
his crazed energies to horrible and convoluted schemes
to eradicate the snail and slug from the entire
biosphere.

Point being, I've always had a thing for space
exploration.

I was a young teenager when the first Shuttle went up,
so I didn't see the STS program for what it is, then.

INTRODUCTION
WARREN ELLIS

I was just delighted to see a spacecraft that looked like a spacecraft banging off the pad, even if it was strapped to what looked like a copper boiler with delusions of grandeur and two fireworks. (The latter were the Solid Rocket Boosters, designated SRB, which was also the brand name of a hot dog sold in British cinemas, indivisible from NASA's SRBs in terms of taste, texture and consistency.) The first launch was screened live on British TV, and they set a TV up in the main hall at school so we could watch it. I put off beating up Michael Wood that day so I could watch it.

So I'm talking to Larry Young one day. Odds are I was talking to him in his day-job office of Wise And Terrible Minister Of Propaganda at the world's best comics store, Comix Experience in San Francisco. Anyway. Larry makes mention of the fact that he's planning to write and otherwise cause to have produced a five-issue comics story. This pleased me no end, if only because of the suffering and pain it would cause him. Because, frankly, I'm a bit of a bastard. What's it about?, I ask him.

And he tells me: The richest man in the world decides to go back to the moon...

And that's it. I'm hooked. Because I was born the year before human space exploration reached its climax. Because my earliest memory is of, at seventeen months old, being held up in front of our little Philco black and white television by my mother and being told, "Look at this, this is history, this is" as Neil and Buzz bring her down on the moon. Because human spaceflight was essentially dead before I could read. Because last night my daughter looked up at the night sky and said, "I'd like to go to the moon tomorrow, Daddy" and I had to say no... and that, in 1999, is wrong.

ASTRONAUTS IN TROUBLE concludes its first chapter with the money shot for all of us who grew up in the twilight of crewed spaceflight. Three crew-rated spacecraft lifting off in formation, on direct transLunar injection trajectories. By then, I needed this book like it was crack.

It combines spaceflight, you see, with another of my favourite things; journalism. And it holds all that within what first appears to be the structure of a summer blockbuster. But it's a Trojan Horse of a structure, for within its middle it contains plain old oral storytelling. Your actual people sitting down talking about themselves, their lives and their culture, a quiet mindbomb in the centre of the more literal explosions. A David Mamet pause in the middle of a Michael Bay movie. A beautifully measured structure that shows off both sides of Larry as a writer -- the one who waves his beer at *Armageddon* and the one who thinks long and hard before he begins his pen portraits of people as real as he can make them.

The artwork, by Matt Smith and Charlie Adlard, is more suggestive than representative in its depictions of the technology and materiel, which is fair enough -- the mind's eye of the late 20th Century human fills in the unrendered gaps anyway. It's not important, because Matt and Charlie's very human, expressive marks bring the people to life, which is by far the more vital task.

Because, ultimately, AiT isn't about the big spaceships and walking on the moon and the stylish distractions of the action-movie rough and tumble that Larry handles so deftly. Ultimately, like all worthwhile pieces of fiction, AiT is about the people.

Yeah, okay, I can hear you saying it: "It's about the astronauts in trouble. Couldn't have worked that out for myself, eh?" Shut up. This is an introduction. Introductions are all about people like me stating the sodding obvious so you people don't have to get a nosebleed doing it all for yourself.

AiT is a summer tentpole action movie with a brain. It's a play that you can dance to. It's one of the most entertaining and compelling pieces of fiction in comics that this year produced. And it's a book I can hand to my daughter in ten years and say; "This came out at the same time I bought you that 'Future Martian" t-shirt you used as a nightie for ages. I wrote the introduction the night after you asked me if we could go to the moon together.

"ASTRONAUTS IN TROUBLE was as close as we ever got, sweetheart. Give it a read, and you'll see that that's not so bad."

Warren Ellis
Southend
October 1999

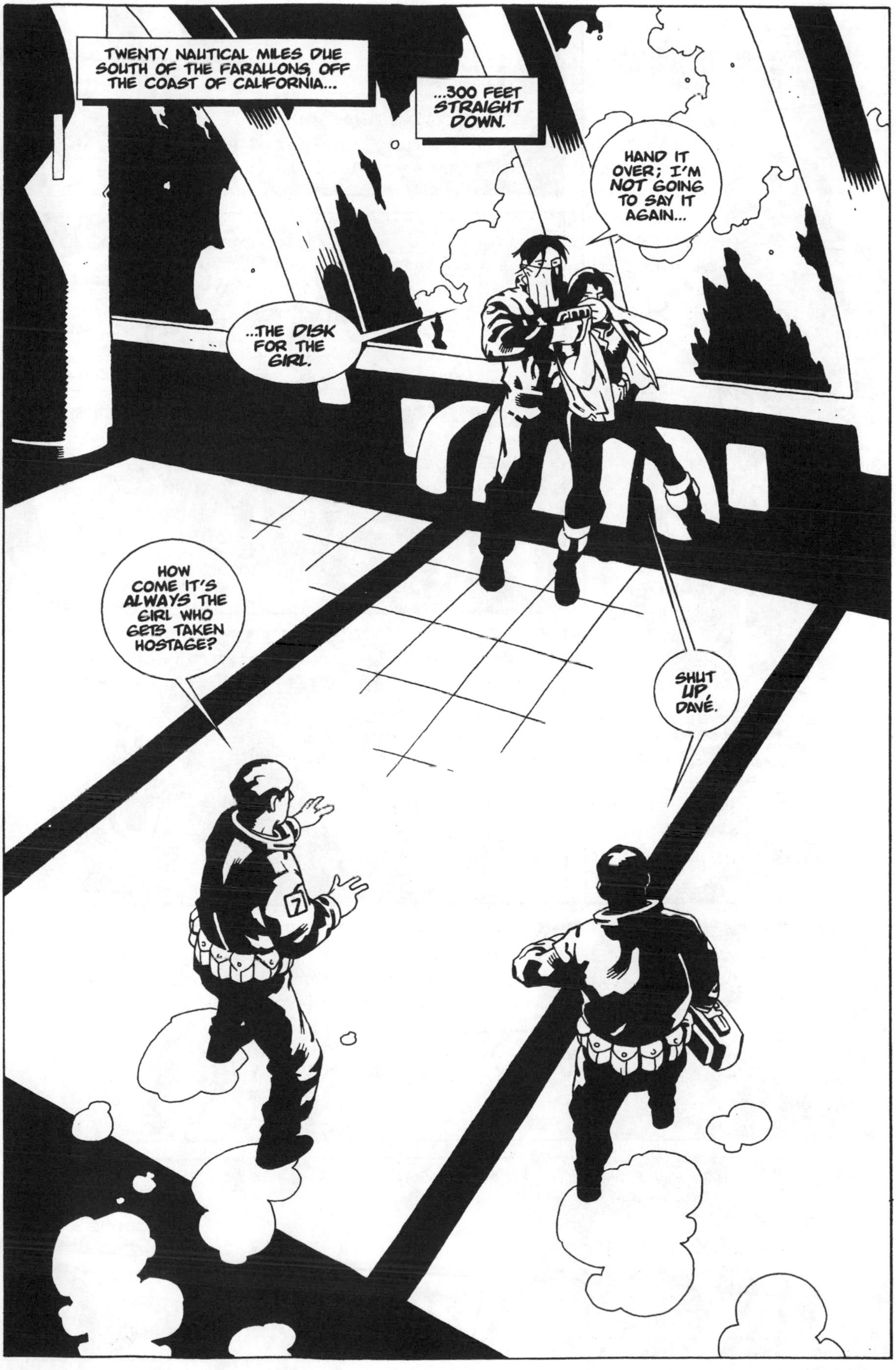
TWENTY NAUTICAL MILES DUE SOUTH OF THE FARALLONS, OFF THE COAST OF CALIFORNIA...
...300 FEET STRAIGHT DOWN.
HAND IT OVER; I'M NOT GOING TO SAY IT AGAIN...
...THE DISK FOR THE GIRL.
HOW COME IT'S ALWAYS THE GIRL WHO GETS TAKEN HOSTAGE?
SHUT UP, DAVE.

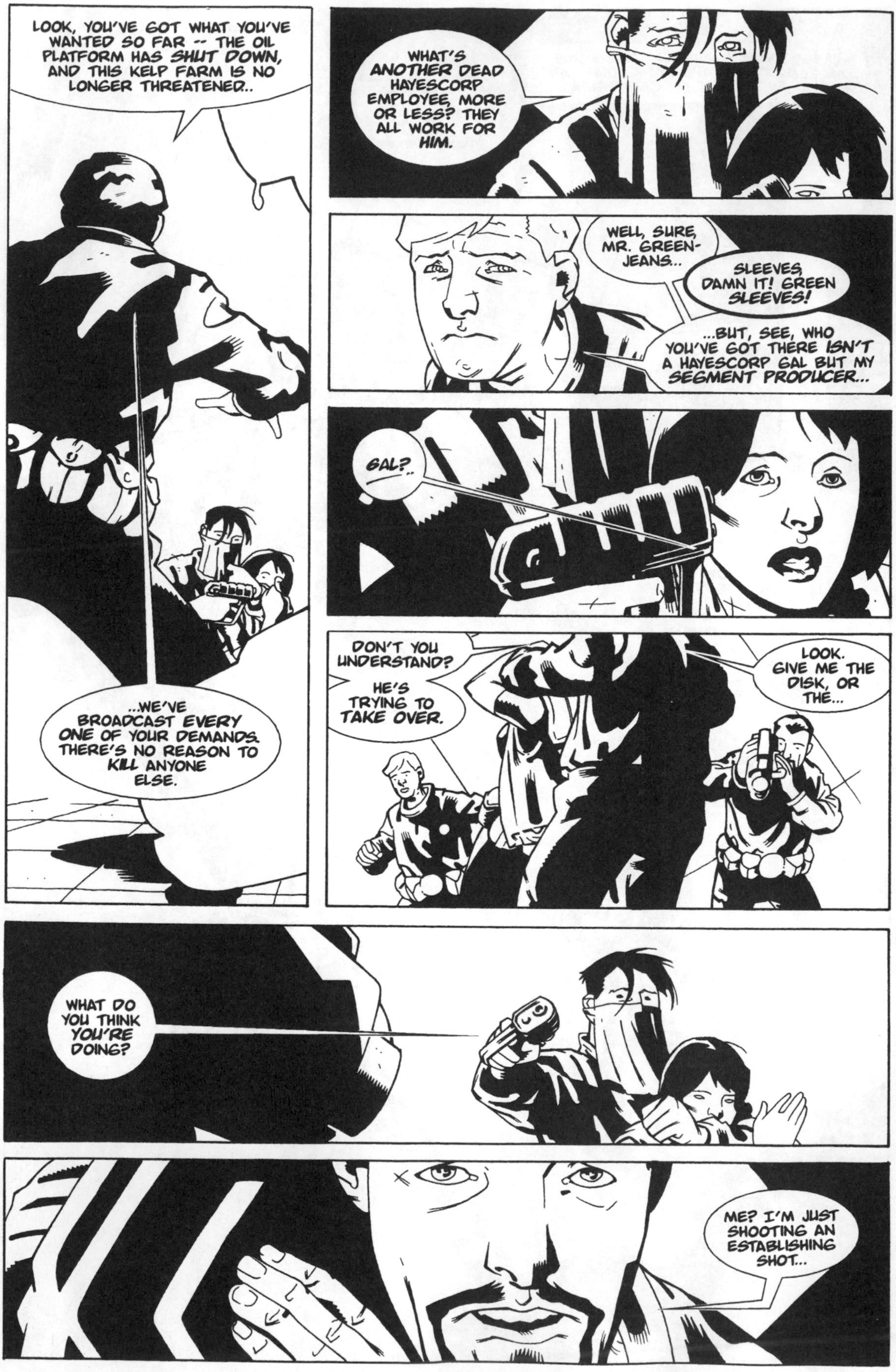
LOOK, YOU'VE GOT WHAT YOU'VE WANTED SO FAR -- THE OIL PLATFORM HAS SHUT DOWN, AND THIS KELP FARM IS NO LONGER THREATENED..
...WE'VE BROADCAST EVERY ONE OF YOUR DEMANDS. THERE'S NO REASON TO KILL ANYONE ELSE.
WHAT'S ANOTHER DEAD HAYESCORP EMPLOYEE, MORE OR LESS? THEY ALL WORK FOR HIM.
WELL, SURE, MR. GREEN-JEANS...
SLEEVES, DAMN IT! GREEN SLEEVES!
...BUT, SEE, WHO YOU'VE GOT THERE ISN'T A HAYESCORP GAL BUT MY SEGMENT PRODUCER...
GAL?..
DON'T YOU UNDERSTAND?
HE'S TRYING TO TAKE OVER.
LOOK. GIVE ME THE DISK, OR THE...
WHAT DO YOU THINK YOU'RE DOING?
ME? I'M JUST SHOOTING AN ESTABLISHING SHOT...

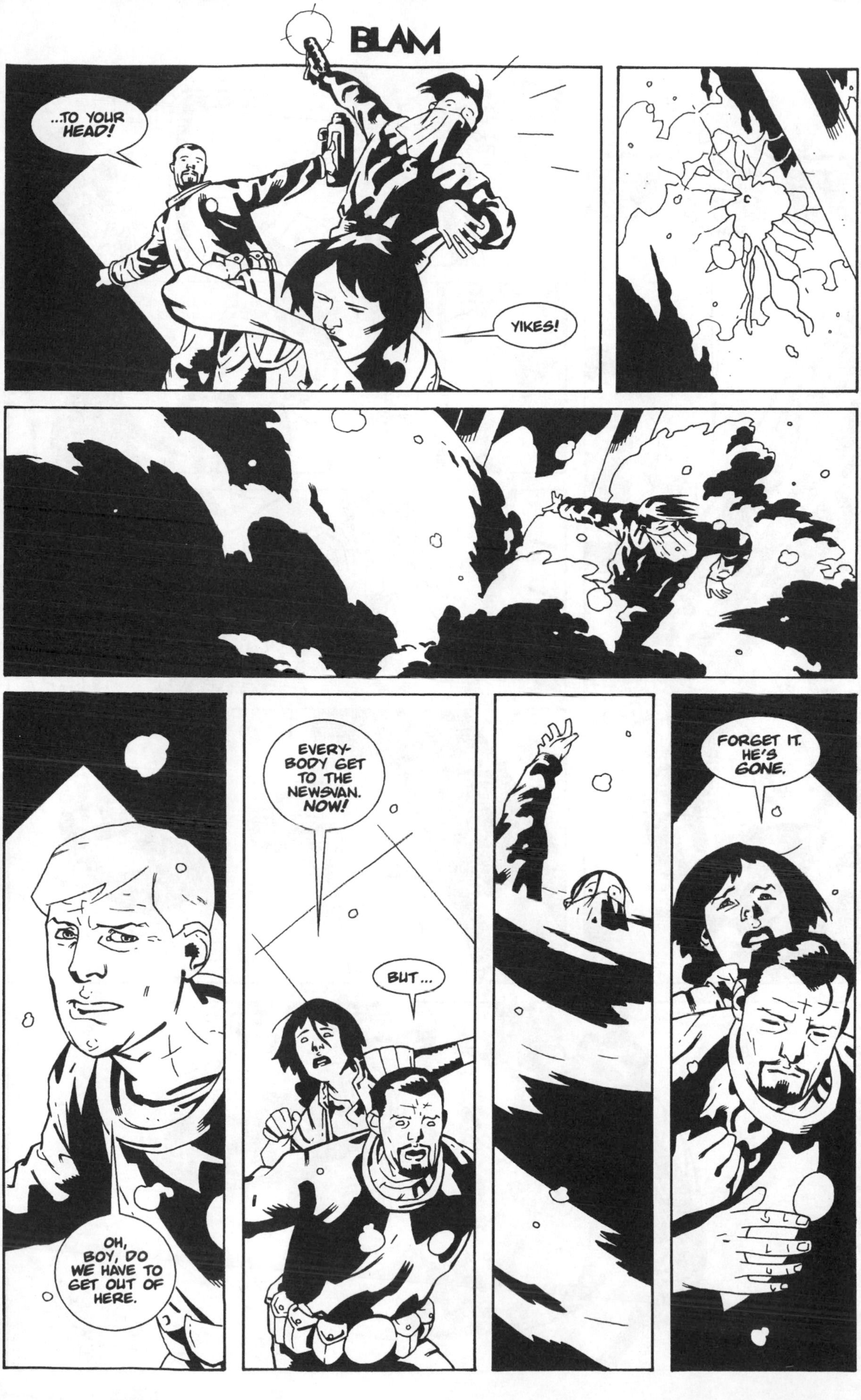
BLAM
...TO YOUR HEAD!
YIKES!
OH, BOY, DO WE HAVE TO GET OUT OF HERE.
EVERY-BODY GET TO THE NEWSVAN. NOW!
BUT...
FORGET IT. HE'S GONE.

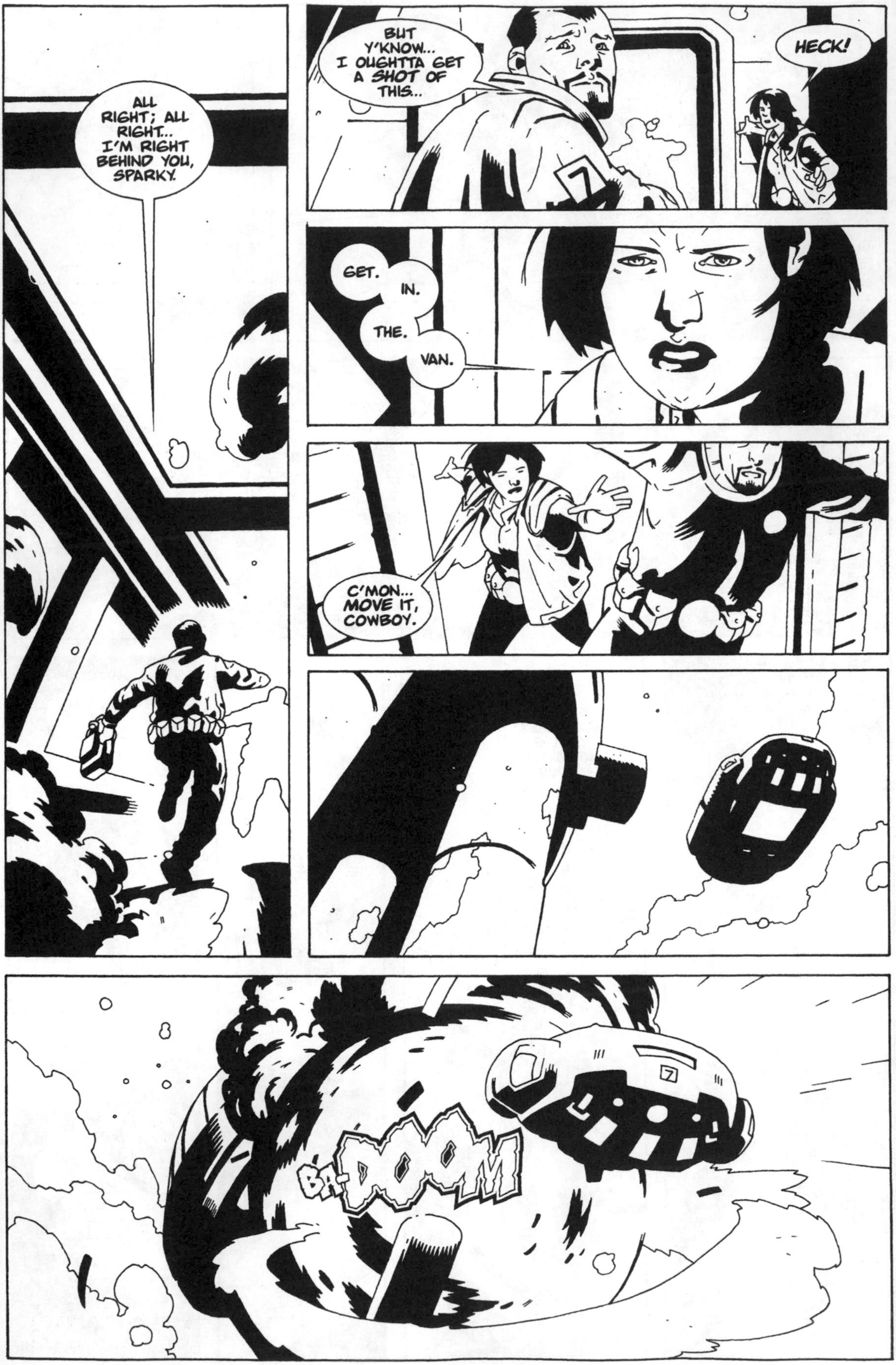
ALL RIGHT; ALL RIGHT... I'M RIGHT BEHIND YOU, SPARKY.
BUT Y'KNOW... I OUGHTTA GET A SHOT OF THIS...
HECK!
GET.
IN.
THE.
VAN.
C'MON... MOVE IT, COWBOY.
BA-DOOM

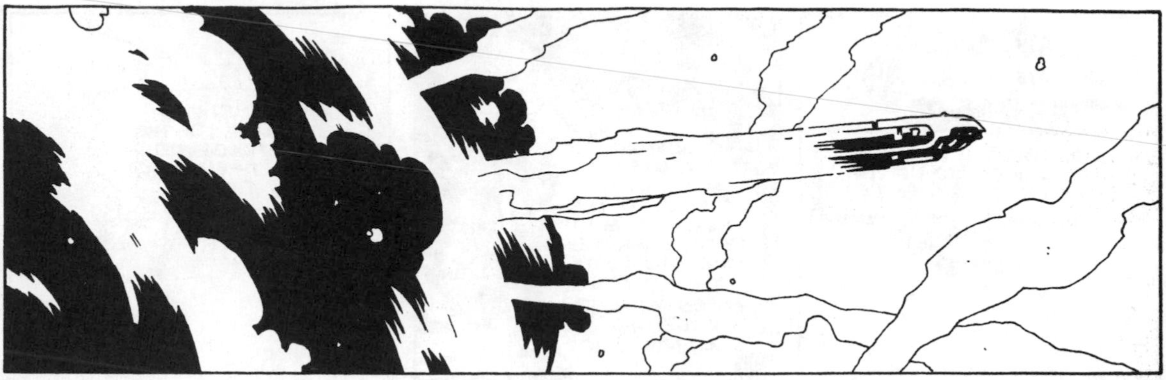

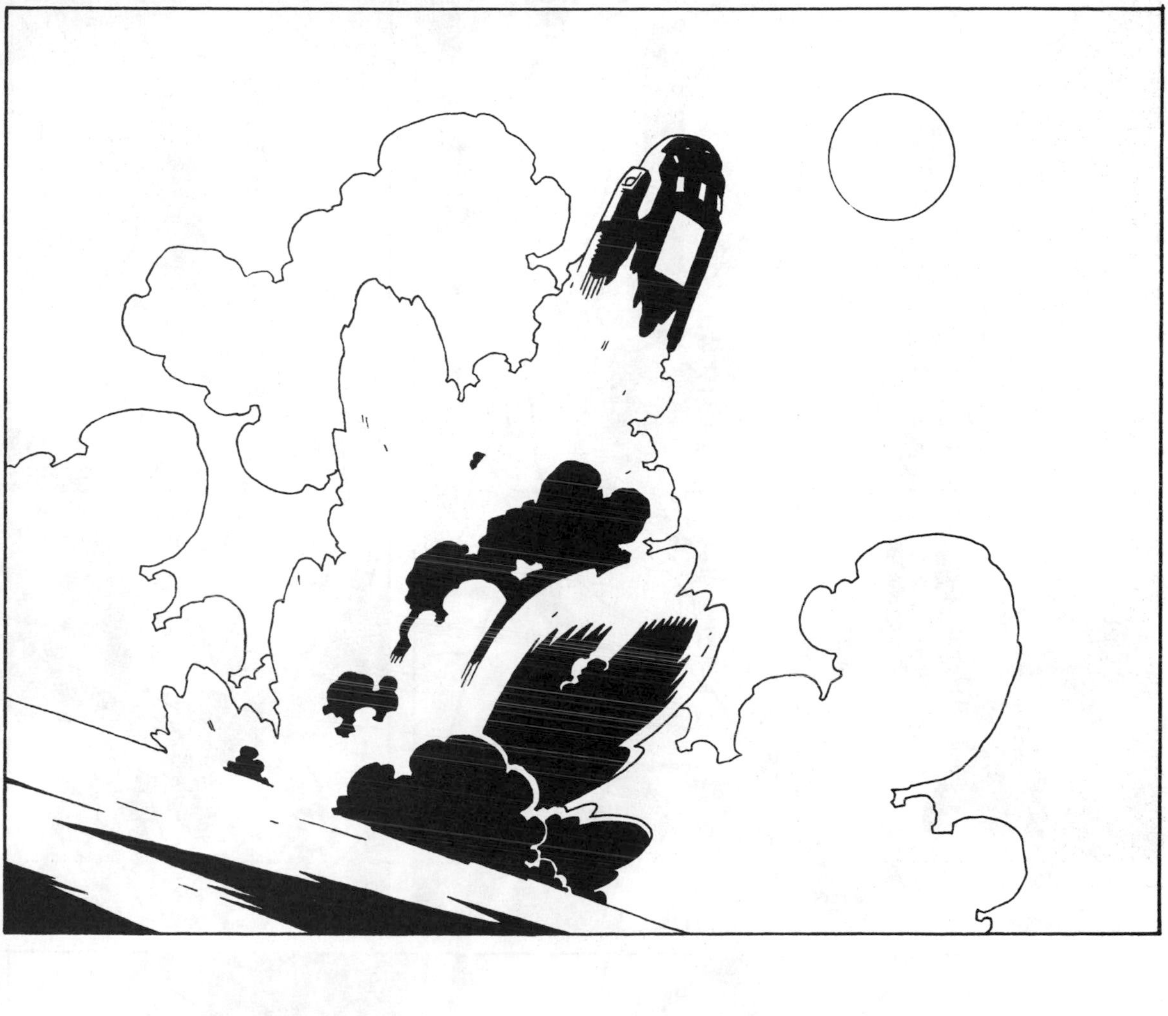

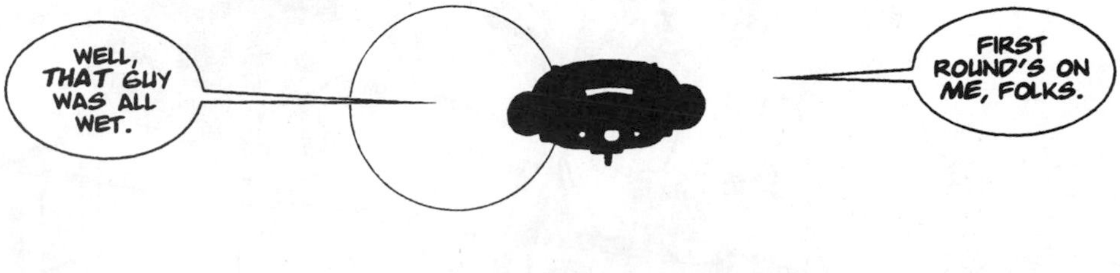

WELL, THAT GUY WAS ALL WET.
FIRST ROUND'S ON ME, FOLKS.

ASTRONAUTS IN TROUBLE : LIVE FROM THE MOON IS BROUGHT TO YOU BY :

LARRY YOUNG — WRITER CREATOR

MATT SMITH — ARTIST

MIMI ROSENHEIM — EDITOR

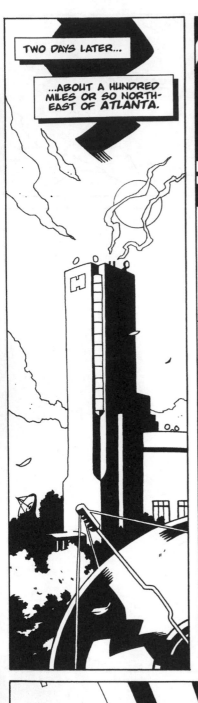

TWO DAYS LATER...

...ABOUT A HUNDRED MILES OR SO NORTH-EAST OF ATLANTA.

WHAT NOW?

JOANNE HAS YOU MEETING THE CHANNEL SEVEN NEWS TEAM IN FIFTEEN MINUTES, AND THEN WITH THE NATIONAL SALES MANAGER OF GEORGIA MARBLE AT TWO-THIRTY.

WHAT'S GEORGIA MARBLE WANT?

SOMETHING TO DO WITH THE SELENOLOGISTS IN NORTH-BUILDING THREE.

YES, SIR; IN THREE DAYS.

ARE WE STILL GO?

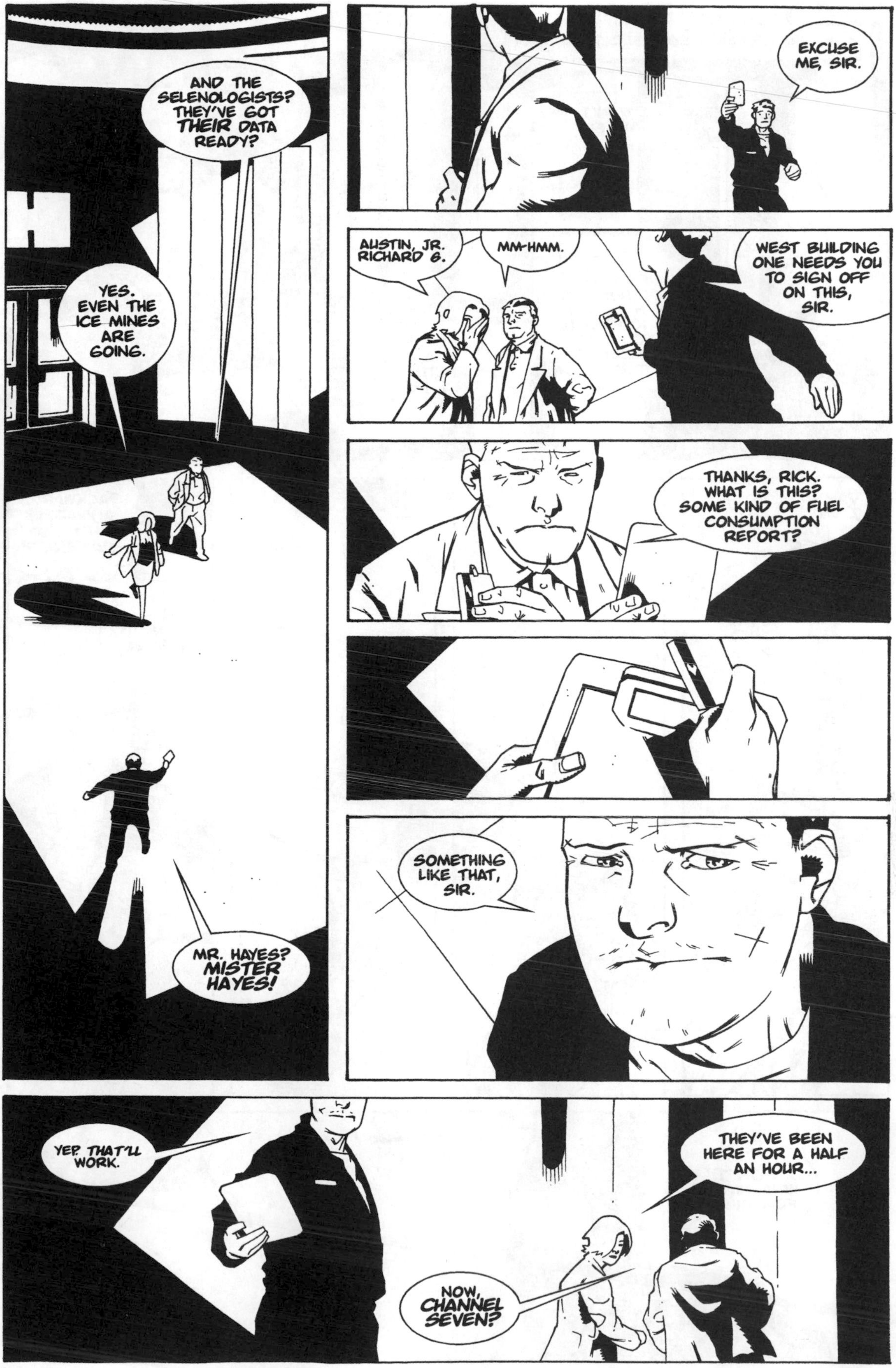
AND THE SELENOLOGISTS? THEY'VE GOT THEIR DATA READY?
YES. EVEN THE ICE MINES ARE GOING.
MR. HAYES? MISTER HAYES!
EXCUSE ME, SIR.
AUSTIN, JR. RICHARD 6.
MM-HMM.
WEST BUILDING ONE NEEDS YOU TO SIGN OFF ON THIS, SIR.
THANKS, RICK. WHAT IS THIS? SOME KIND OF FUEL CONSUMPTION REPORT?
SOMETHING LIKE THAT, SIR.
YEP. THAT'LL WORK.
THEY'VE BEEN HERE FOR A HALF AN HOUR...
NOW, CHANNEL SEVEN?

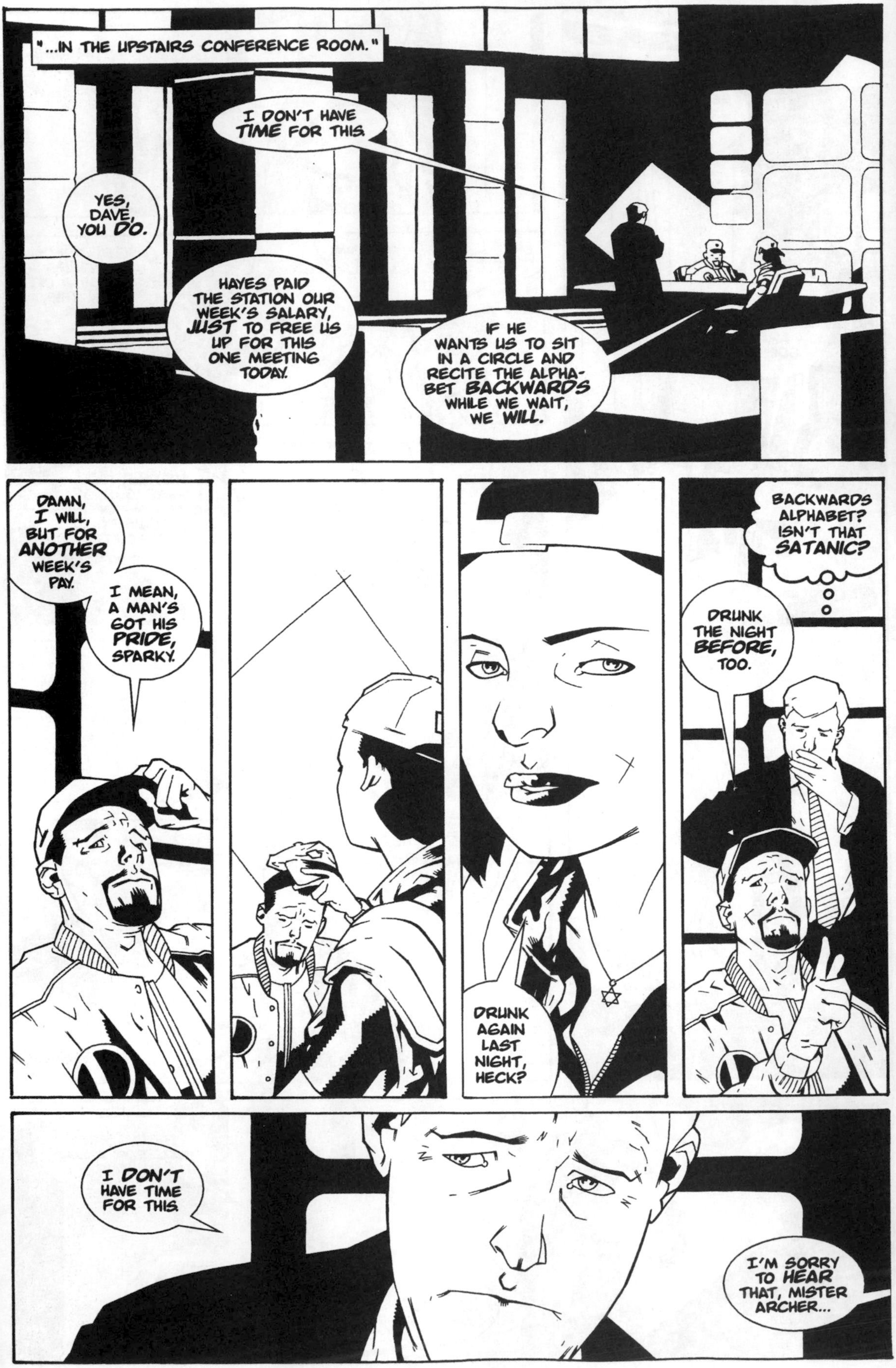
"...IN THE UPSTAIRS CONFERENCE ROOM."
I DON'T HAVE TIME FOR THIS.
YES, DAVE, YOU DO.
HAYES PAID THE STATION OUR WEEK'S SALARY, JUST TO FREE US UP FOR THIS ONE MEETING TODAY.
IF HE WANTS US TO SIT IN A CIRCLE AND RECITE THE ALPHA-BET BACKWARDS WHILE WE WAIT, WE WILL.
DAMN, I WILL, BUT FOR ANOTHER WEEK'S PAY.
I MEAN, A MAN'S GOT HIS PRIDE, SPARKY.
DRUNK AGAIN LAST NIGHT, HECK?
BACKWARDS ALPHABET? ISN'T THAT SATANIC?
DRUNK THE NIGHT BEFORE, TOO.
I DON'T HAVE TIME FOR THIS.
I'M SORRY TO HEAR THAT, MISTER ARCHER...

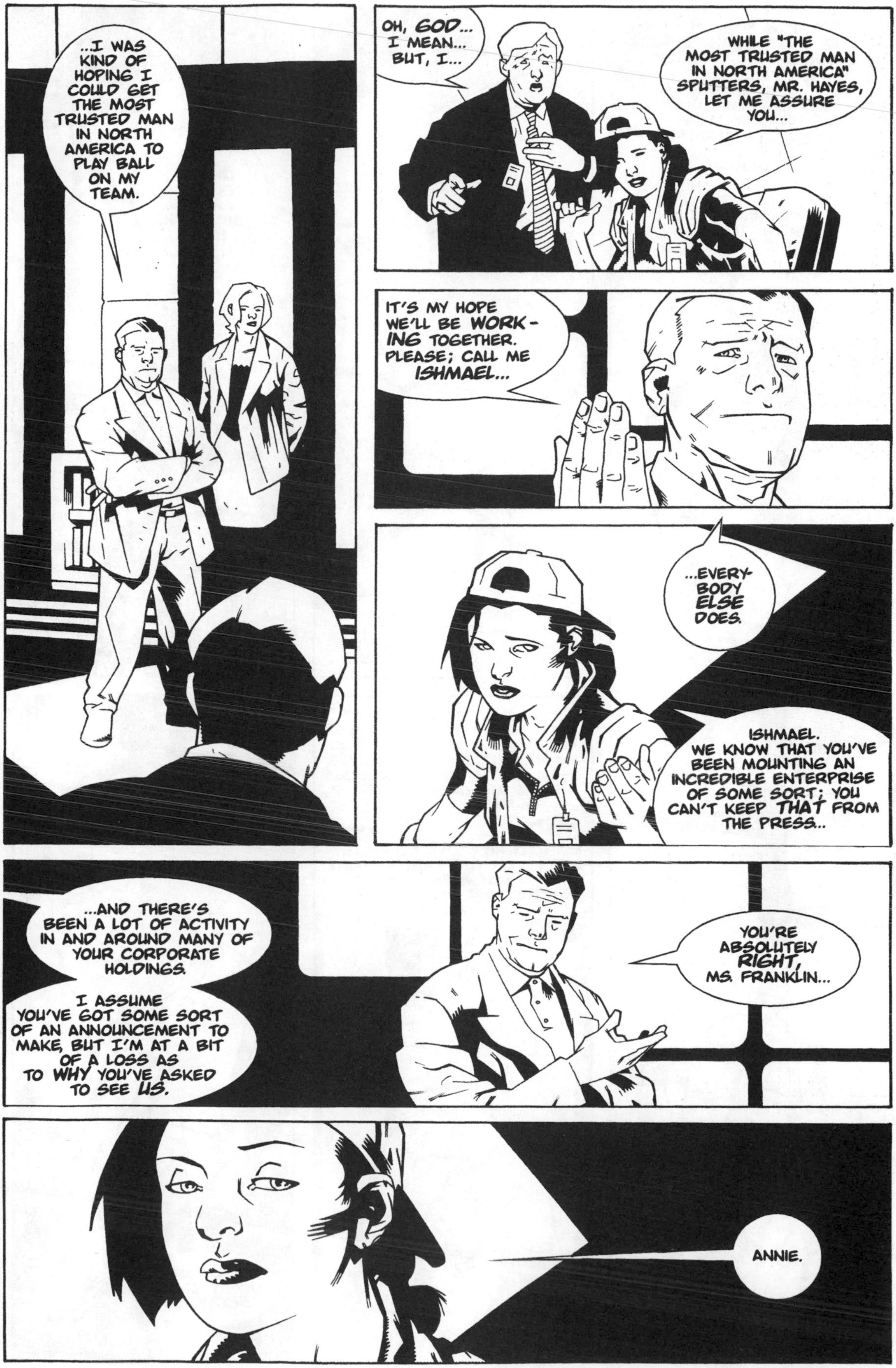
...I WAS KIND OF HOPING I COULD GET THE MOST TRUSTED MAN IN NORTH AMERICA TO PLAY BALL ON MY TEAM.
OH, GOD... I MEAN... BUT, I...
WHILE "THE MOST TRUSTED MAN IN NORTH AMERICA" SPUTTERS, MR. HAYES, LET ME ASSURE YOU...
IT'S MY HOPE WE'LL BE WORKING TOGETHER. PLEASE; CALL ME ISHMAEL...
...EVERYBODY ELSE DOES.
ISHMAEL. WE KNOW THAT YOU'VE BEEN MOUNTING AN INCREDIBLE ENTERPRISE OF SOME SORT; YOU CAN'T KEEP THAT FROM THE PRESS...
...AND THERE'S BEEN A LOT OF ACTIVITY IN AND AROUND MANY OF YOUR CORPORATE HOLDINGS.
I ASSUME YOU'VE GOT SOME SORT OF AN ANNOUNCEMENT TO MAKE, BUT I'M AT A BIT OF A LOSS AS TO WHY YOU'VE ASKED TO SEE US.
YOU'RE ABSOLUTELY RIGHT, MS. FRANKLIN...
ANNIE.

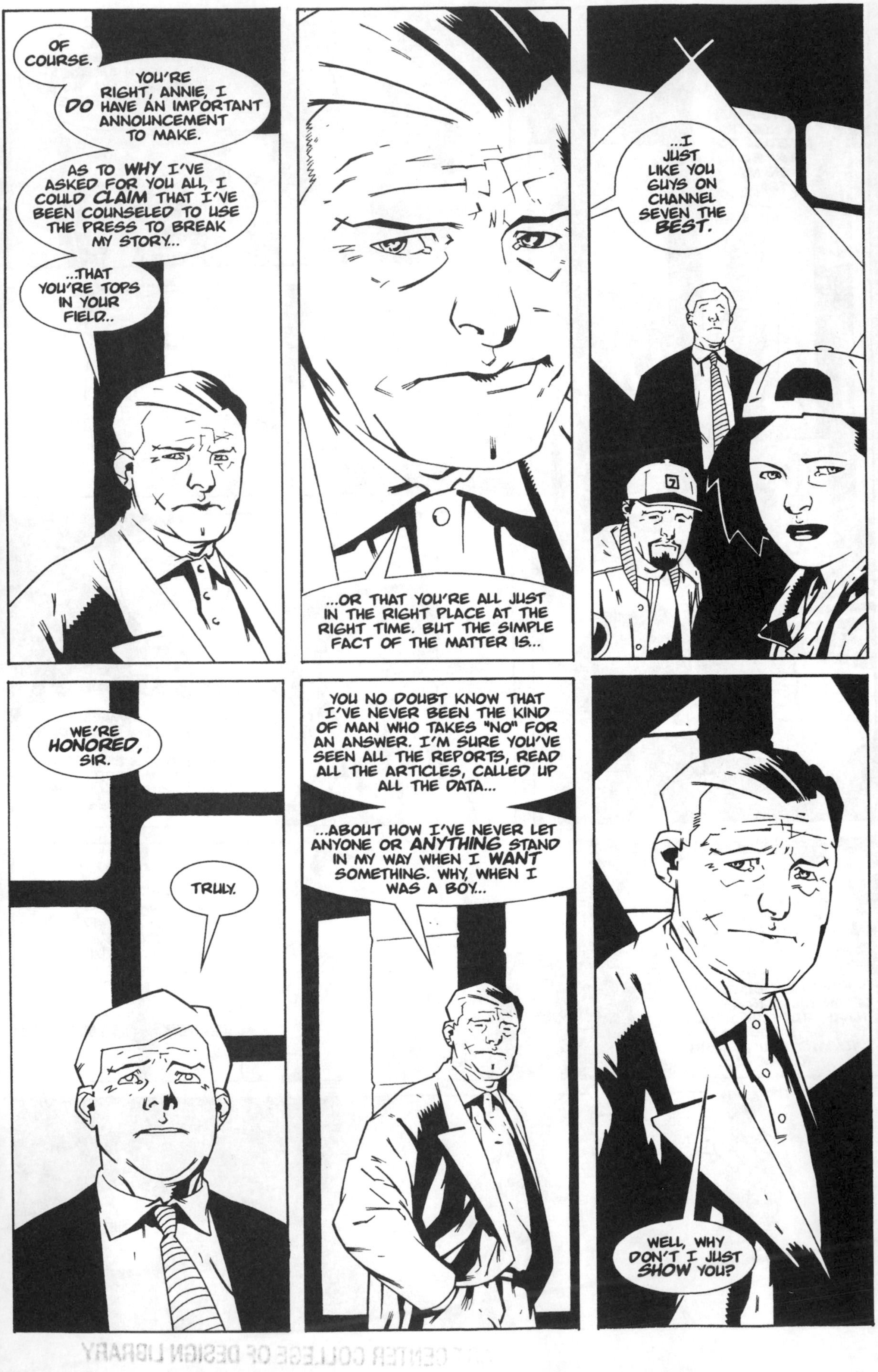
OF COURSE.
YOU'RE RIGHT, ANNIE, I DO HAVE AN IMPORTANT ANNOUNCEMENT TO MAKE.
AS TO WHY I'VE ASKED FOR YOU ALL, I COULD CLAIM THAT I'VE BEEN COUNSELED TO USE THE PRESS TO BREAK MY STORY...
...THAT YOU'RE TOPS IN YOUR FIELD..
...OR THAT YOU'RE ALL JUST IN THE RIGHT PLACE AT THE RIGHT TIME. BUT THE SIMPLE FACT OF THE MATTER IS...
...I JUST LIKE YOU GUYS ON CHANNEL SEVEN THE BEST.
WE'RE HONORED, SIR.
TRULY.
YOU NO DOUBT KNOW THAT I'VE NEVER BEEN THE KIND OF MAN WHO TAKES "NO" FOR AN ANSWER. I'M SURE YOU'VE SEEN ALL THE REPORTS, READ ALL THE ARTICLES, CALLED UP ALL THE DATA...
...ABOUT HOW I'VE NEVER LET ANYONE OR ANYTHING STAND IN MY WAY WHEN I WANT SOMETHING. WHY, WHEN I WAS A BOY...
WELL, WHY DON'T I JUST SHOW YOU?

NOBODY'S GOING ANYWHERE...

NO, SIR. THIS MORNING'S PERIMETER BREACH.

I TOOK CARE OF IT.

SECURITY? CHANNEL SEVEN?

NOWHERE, THAT IS, UNTIL *I* SAY SO.

A LITTLE *BEHIND SCHEDULE* TODAY, BENNETT?

-:CLEAR.:-

OK. THEY'VE BEEN *PASSED*. *NOW* YOU CAN GO.

WELL, THEN, MY NEWS TEAM, I HAVE *SUCH* A SIGHT TO SHOW YOU.

I'M GOING ON A TRIP, AND I WANT *YOU* TO WITNESS THE JOURNEY.

"THERE IS SOMETHING *HAUNTING* IN THE LIGHT OF THE MOON; IT HAS ALL THE DISPASSIONATENESS OF THE DISEMBODIED SOUL..."

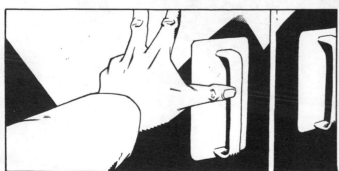

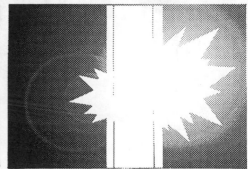

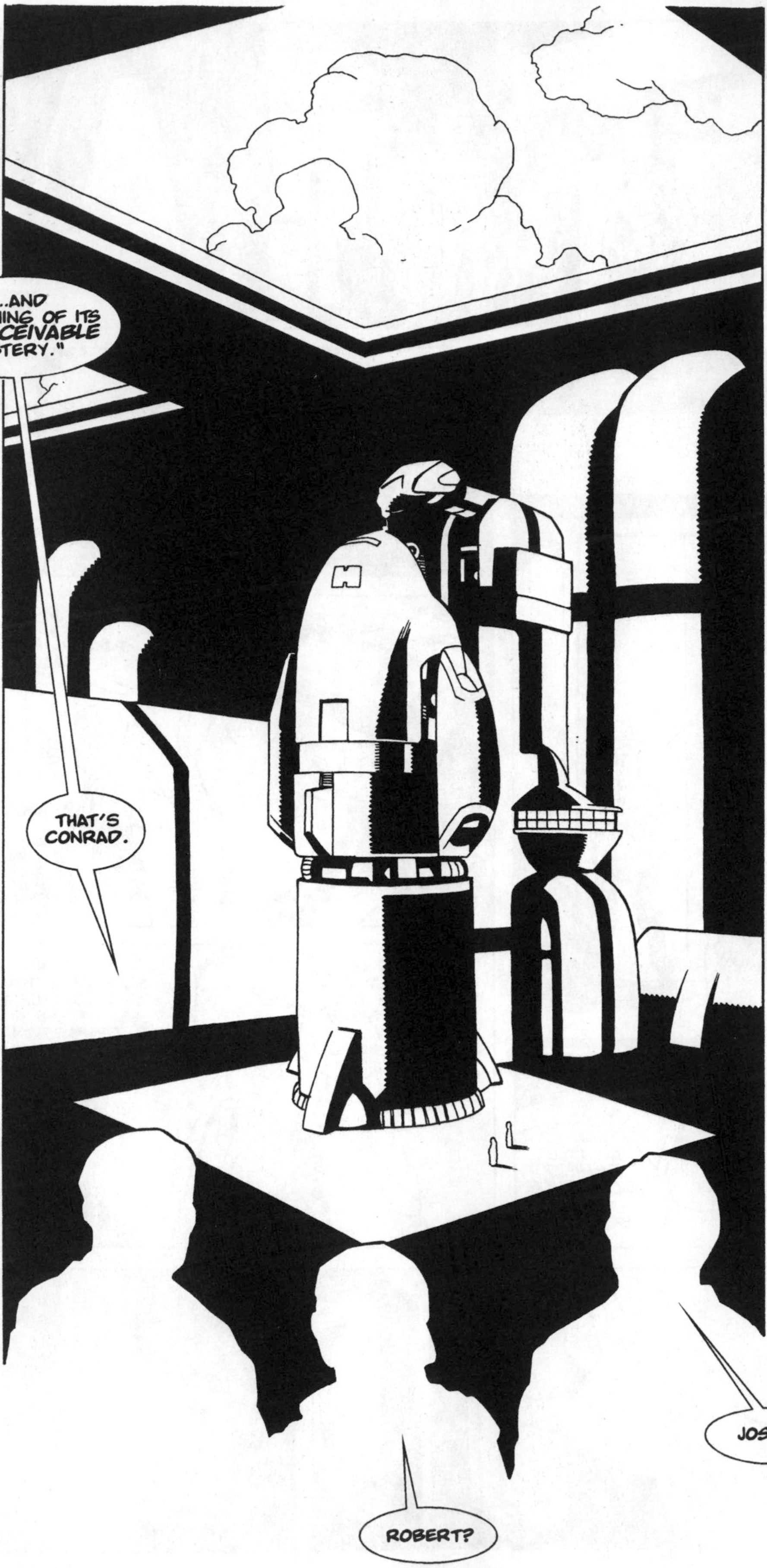
"...AND SOMETHING OF ITS INCONCEIVABLE MYSTERY."
THAT'S CONRAD.
JOSEPH.
ROBERT?

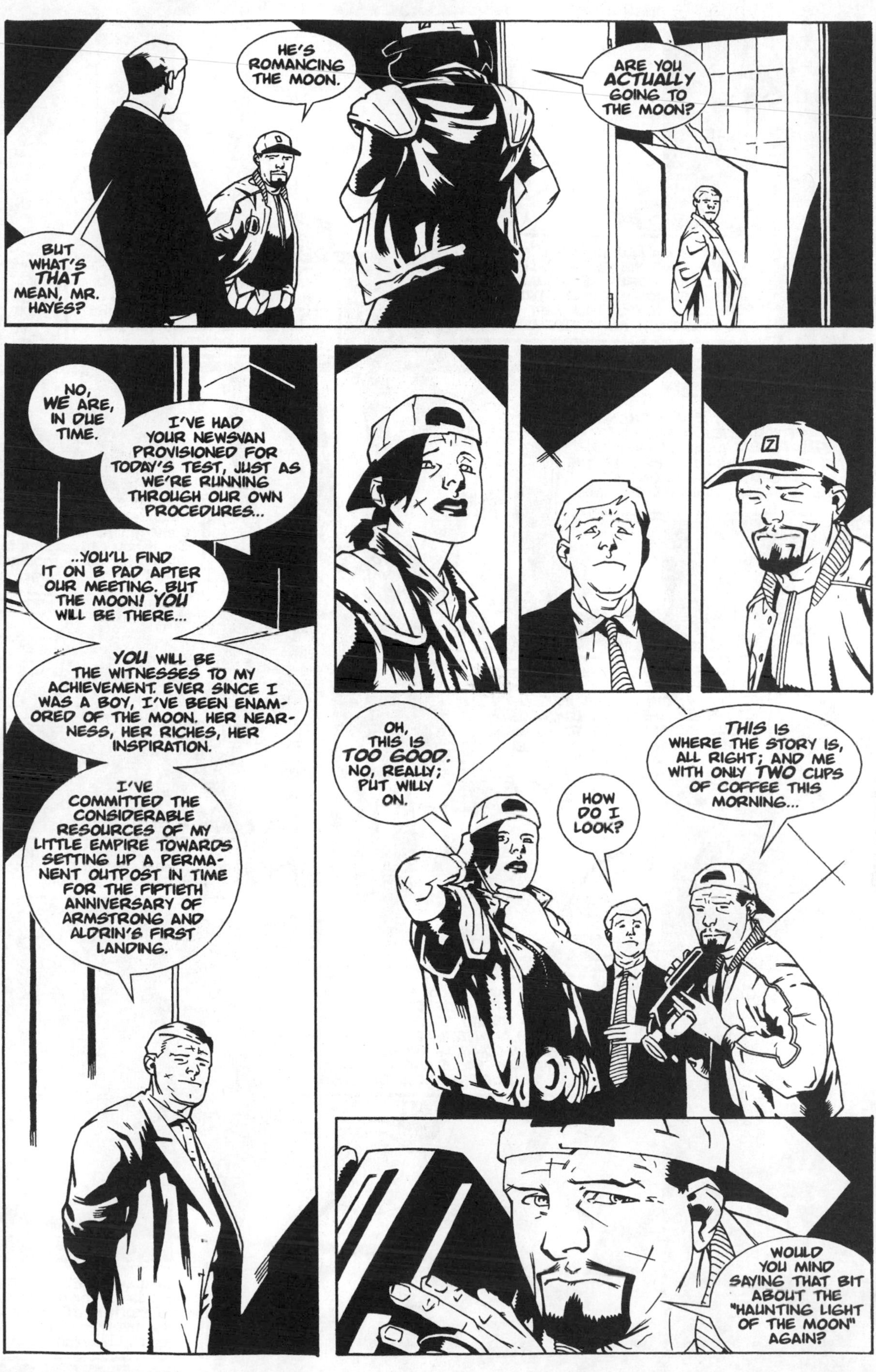
HE'S ROMANCING THE MOON.
ARE YOU ACTUALLY GOING TO THE MOON?
BUT WHAT'S THAT MEAN, MR. HAYES?
NO, WE ARE, IN DUE TIME.
I'VE HAD YOUR NEWSVAN PROVISIONED FOR TODAY'S TEST, JUST AS WE'RE RUNNING THROUGH OUR OWN PROCEDURES...
...YOU'LL FIND IT ON B PAD AFTER OUR MEETING. BUT THE MOON! YOU WILL BE THERE...
YOU WILL BE THE WITNESSES TO MY ACHIEVEMENT. EVER SINCE I WAS A BOY, I'VE BEEN ENAMORED OF THE MOON. HER NEARNESS, HER RICHES, HER INSPIRATION.
I'VE COMMITTED THE CONSIDERABLE RESOURCES OF MY LITTLE EMPIRE TOWARDS SETTING UP A PERMANENT OUTPOST IN TIME FOR THE FIFTIETH ANNIVERSARY OF ARMSTRONG AND ALDRIN'S FIRST LANDING.
OH, THIS IS TOO GOOD. NO, REALLY; PUT WILLY ON.
HOW DO I LOOK?
THIS IS WHERE THE STORY IS, ALL RIGHT; AND ME WITH ONLY TWO CUPS OF COFFEE THIS MORNING...
WOULD YOU MIND SAYING THAT BIT ABOUT THE "HAUNTING LIGHT OF THE MOON" AGAIN?

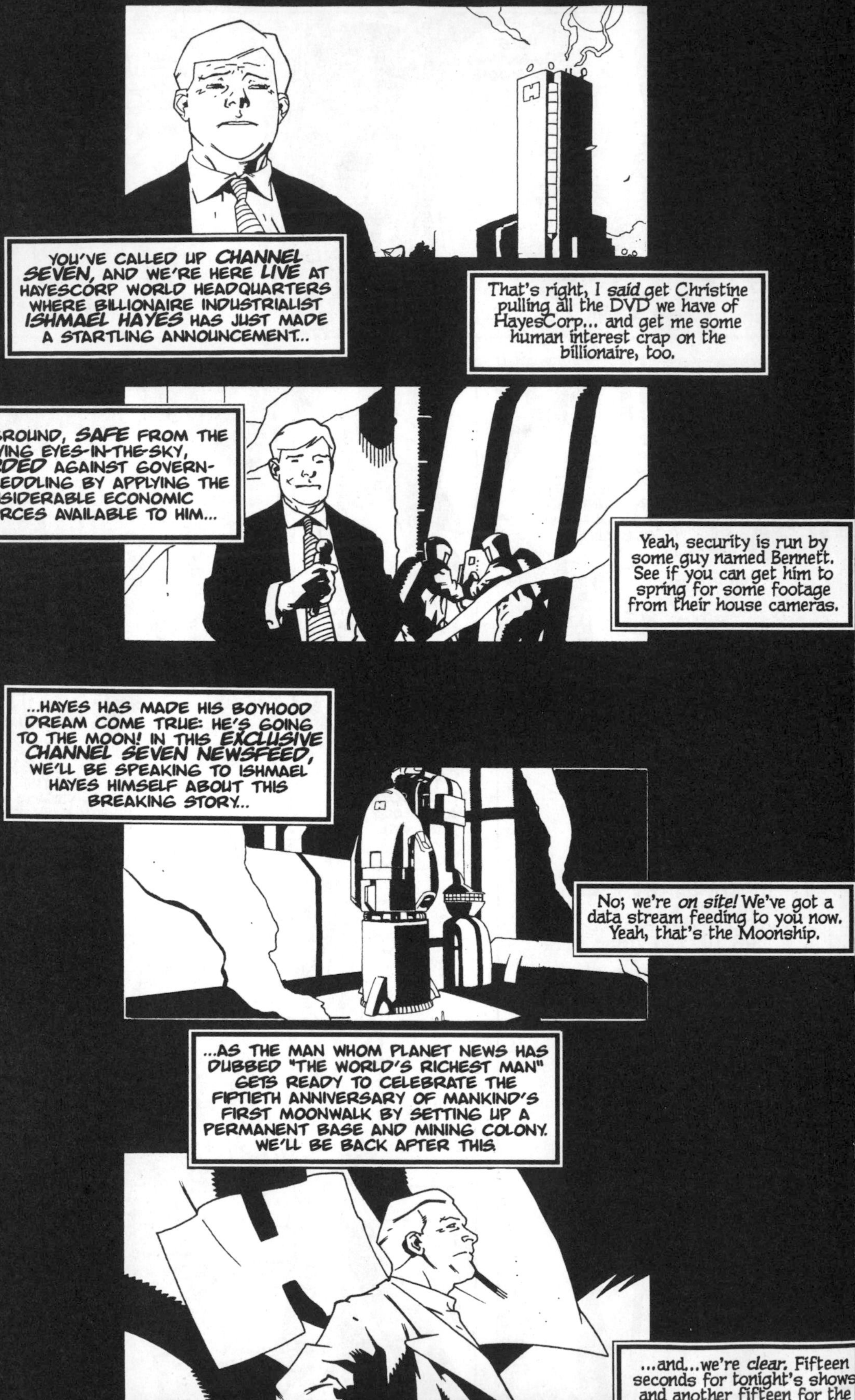
YOU'VE CALLED UP CHANNEL SEVEN, AND WE'RE HERE LIVE AT HAYESCORP WORLD HEADQUARTERS WHERE BILLIONAIRE INDUSTRIALIST ISHMAEL HAYES HAS JUST MADE A STARTLING ANNOUNCEMENT...
That's right, I said get Christine pulling all the DVD we have of HayesCorp... and get me some human interest crap on the billionaire, too.
UNDERGROUND, SAFE FROM THE PRYING EYES-IN-THE-SKY, GUARDED AGAINST GOVERNMENT MEDDLING BY APPLYING THE CONSIDERABLE ECONOMIC RESOURCES AVAILABLE TO HIM...
Yeah, security is run by some guy named Bennett. See if you can get him to spring for some footage from their house cameras.
...HAYES HAS MADE HIS BOYHOOD DREAM COME TRUE: HE'S GOING TO THE MOON! IN THIS EXCLUSIVE CHANNEL SEVEN NEWSFEED, WE'LL BE SPEAKING TO ISHMAEL HAYES HIMSELF ABOUT THIS BREAKING STORY...
No; we're on site! We've got a data stream feeding to you now. Yeah, that's the Moonship.
...AS THE MAN WHOM PLANET NEWS HAS DUBBED "THE WORLD'S RICHEST MAN" GETS READY TO CELEBRATE THE FIFTIETH ANNIVERSARY OF MANKIND'S FIRST MOONWALK BY SETTING UP A PERMANENT BASE AND MINING COLONY. WE'LL BE BACK AFTER THIS.
...and...we're clear. Fifteen seconds for tonight's shows and another fifteen for the shills, and then we're back on again. Get ready, Dave.

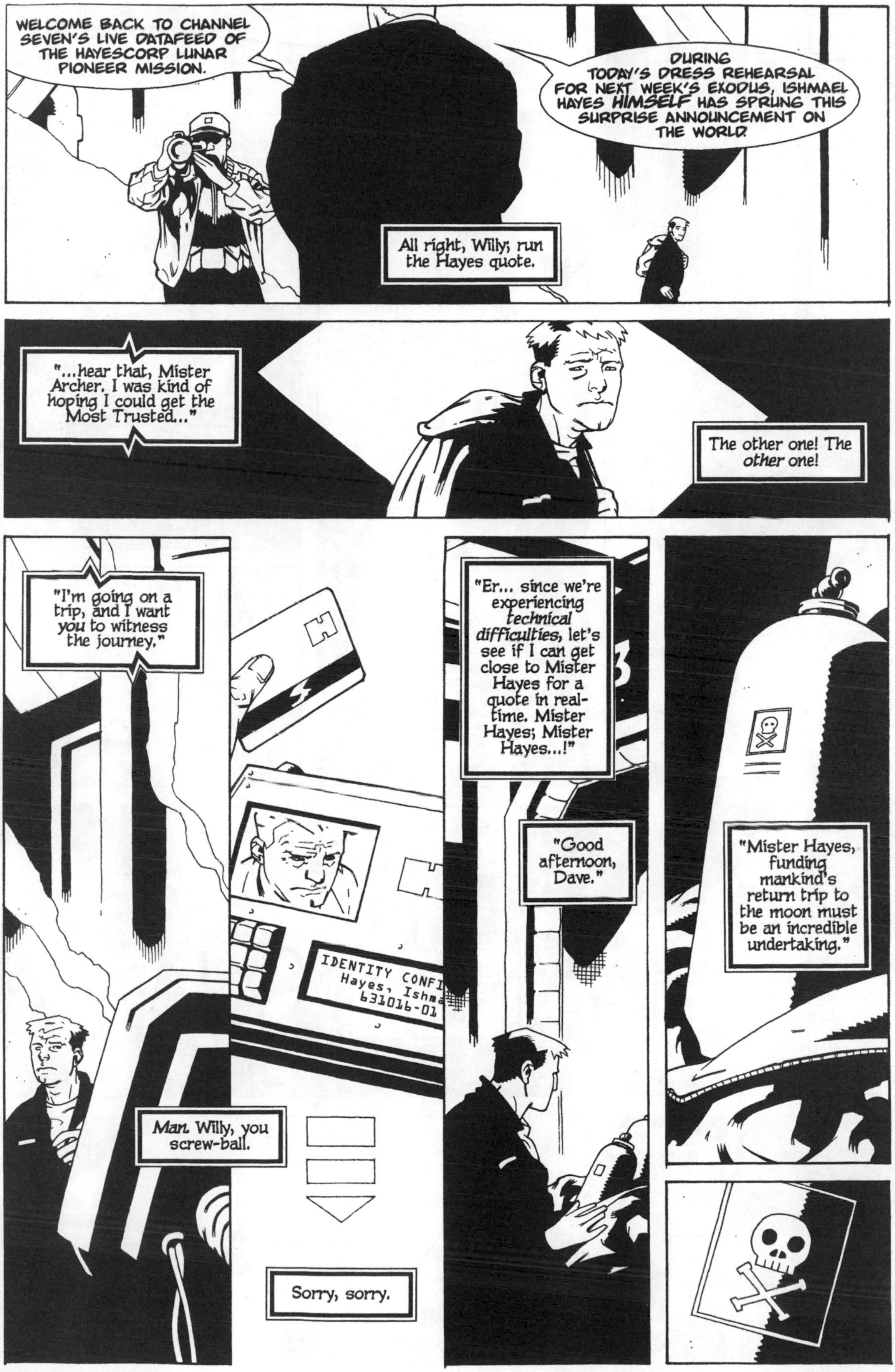
WELCOME BACK TO CHANNEL SEVEN'S LIVE DATAFEED OF THE HAYESCORP LUNAR PIONEER MISSION.
DURING TODAY'S DRESS REHEARSAL FOR NEXT WEEK'S EXODUS, ISHMAEL HAYES HIMSELF HAS SPRUNG THIS SURPRISE ANNOUNCEMENT ON THE WORLD.
All right, Willy; run the Hayes quote.
"...hear that, Mister Archer. I was kind of hoping I could get the Most Trusted..."
The other one! The other one!
"I'm going on a trip, and I want you to witness the journey."
IDENTITY CONFI
Hayes, Ishma
631016-01
Man. Willy, you screw-ball.
Sorry, sorry.
"Er... since we're experiencing technical difficulties, let's see if I can get close to Mister Hayes for a quote in real-time. Mister Hayes; Mister Hayes...!"
"Good afternoon, Dave."
"Mister Hayes, funding mankind's return trip to the moon must be an incredible undertaking."

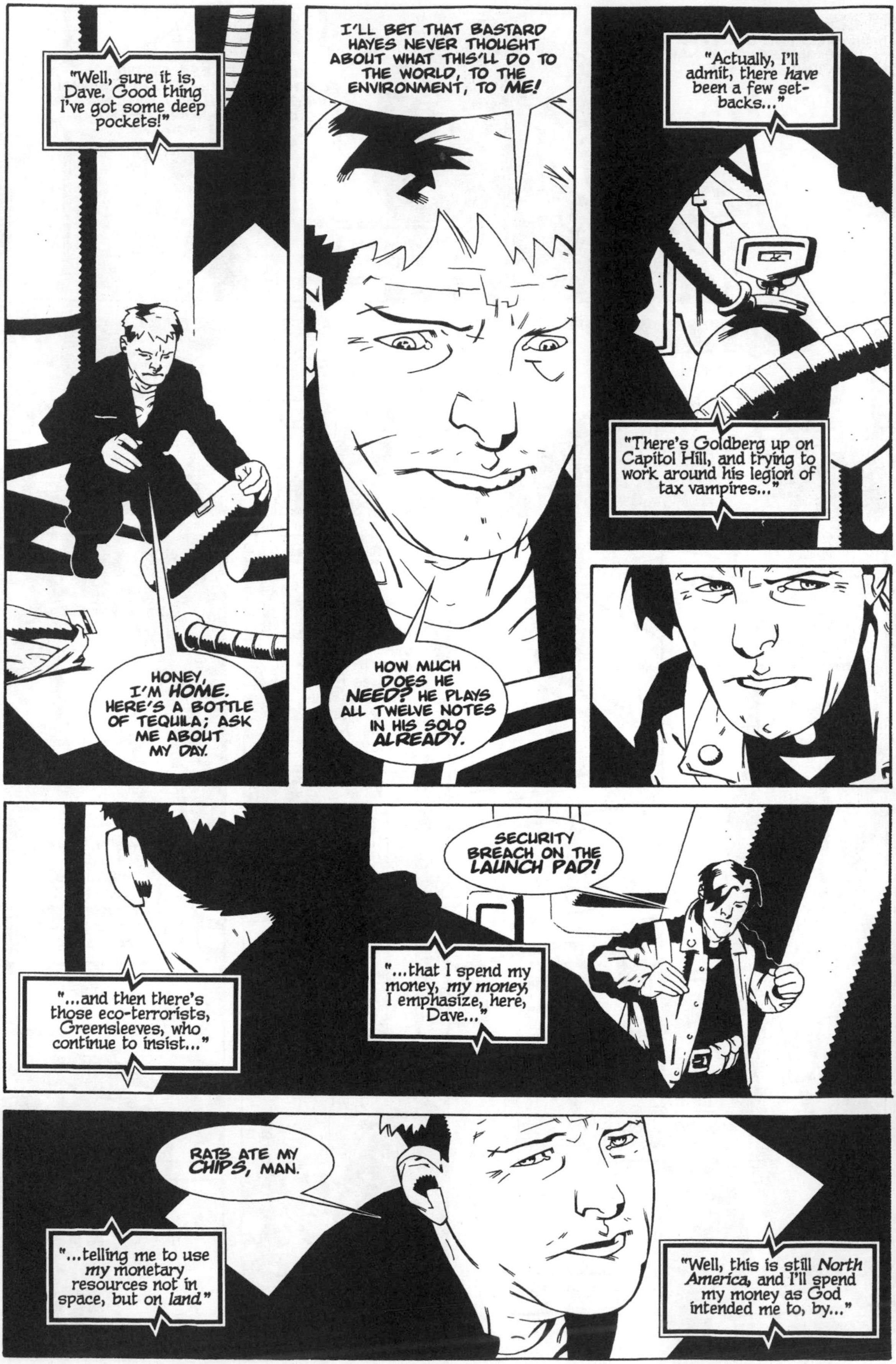
"Well, sure it is, Dave. Good thing I've got some deep pockets!"
HONEY, I'M HOME. HERE'S A BOTTLE OF TEQUILA; ASK ME ABOUT MY DAY.
I'LL BET THAT BASTARD HAYES NEVER THOUGHT ABOUT WHAT THIS'LL DO TO THE WORLD, TO THE ENVIRONMENT, TO ME!
HOW MUCH DOES HE NEED? HE PLAYS ALL TWELVE NOTES IN HIS SOLO ALREADY.
"Actually, I'll admit, there have been a few set-backs..."
"There's Goldberg up on Capitol Hill, and trying to work around his legion of tax vampires..."
"...and then there's those eco-terrorists, Greensleeves, who continue to insist..."
"...that I spend my money, my money, I emphasize, here, Dave..."
SECURITY BREACH ON THE LAUNCH PAD!
"...telling me to use my monetary resources not in space, but on land."
RATS ATE MY CHIPS, MAN.
"Well, this is still North America, and I'll spend my money as God intended me to, by..."

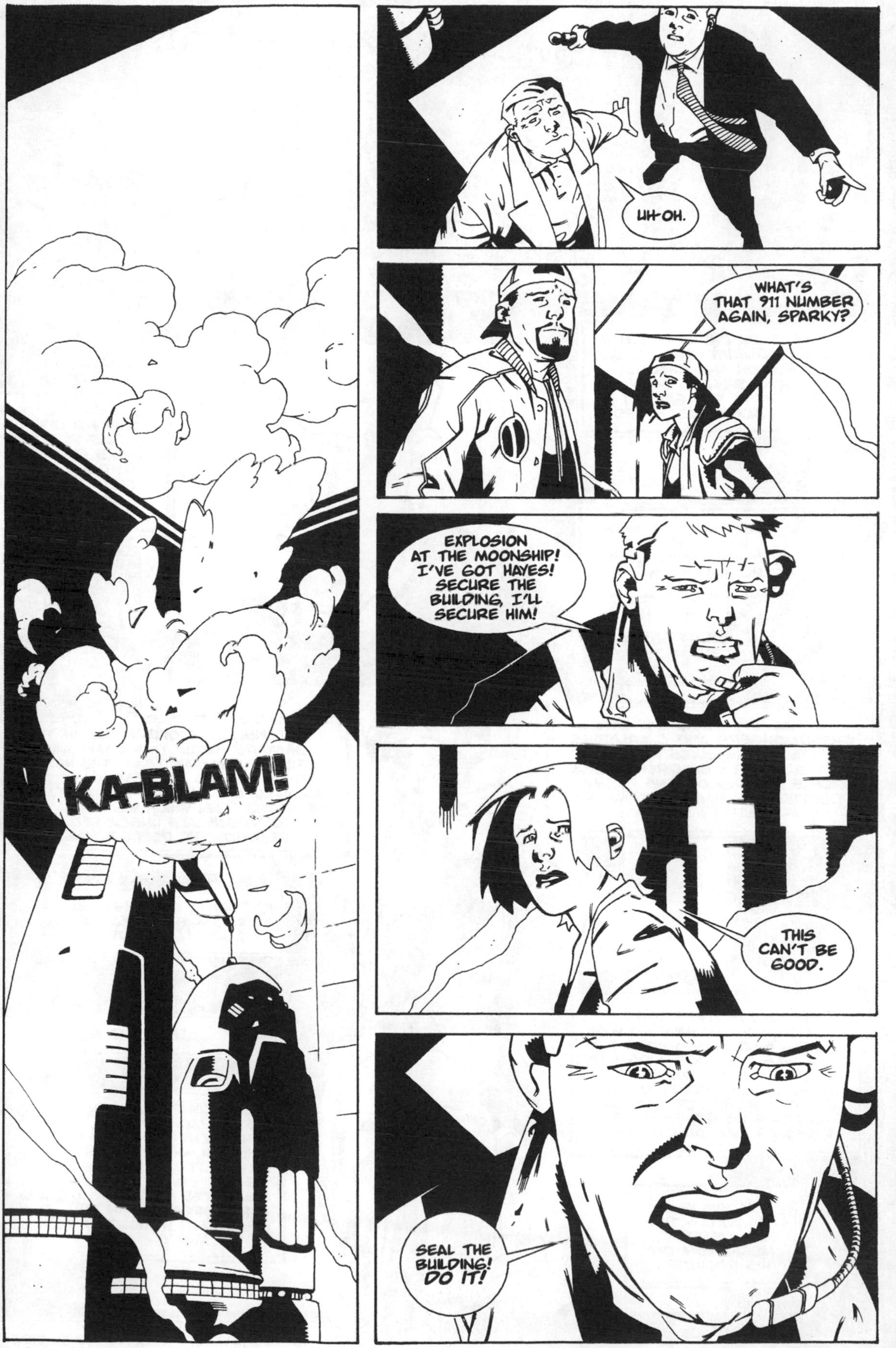
KA-BLAM!
UH-OH.
WHAT'S THAT 911 NUMBER AGAIN, SPARKY?
EXPLOSION AT THE MOONSHIP! I'VE GOT HAYES! SECURE THE BUILDING, I'LL SECURE HIM!
THIS CAN'T BE GOOD.
SEAL THE BUILDING! DO IT!

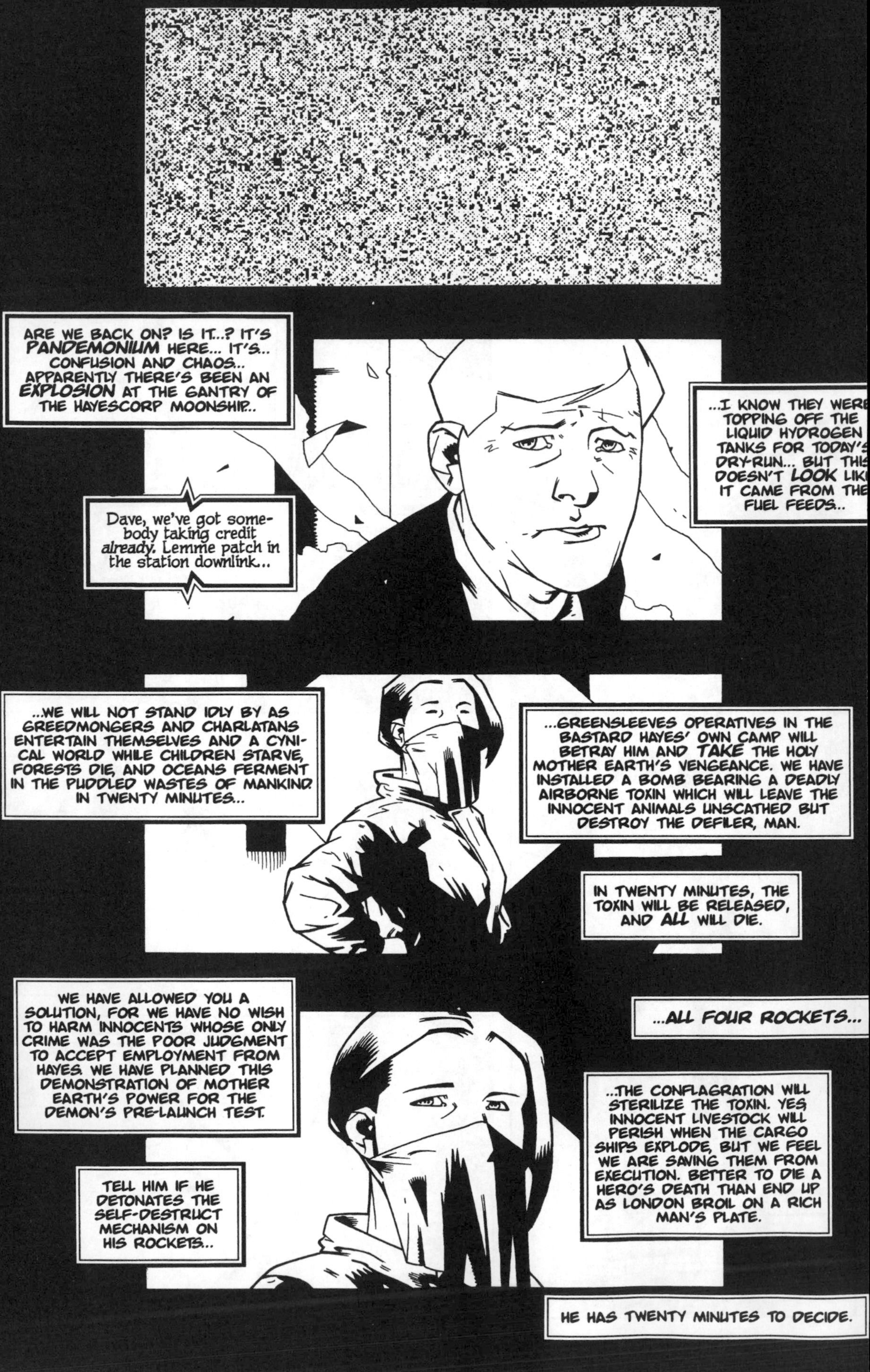

ARE WE BACK ON? IS IT...? IT'S PANDEMONIUM HERE... IT'S... CONFUSION AND CHAOS... APPARENTLY THERE'S BEEN AN EXPLOSION AT THE GANTRY OF THE HAYESCORP MOONSHIP...
...I KNOW THEY WERE TOPPING OFF THE LIQUID HYDROGEN TANKS FOR TODAY'S DRY-RUN... BUT THIS DOESN'T LOOK LIK IT CAME FROM THE FUEL FEEDS...
Dave, we've got somebody taking credit already. Lemme patch in the station downlink...
...WE WILL NOT STAND IDLY BY AS GREEDMONGERS AND CHARLATANS ENTERTAIN THEMSELVES AND A CYNICAL WORLD WHILE CHILDREN STARVE, FORESTS DIE, AND OCEANS FERMENT IN THE PUDDLED WASTES OF MANKIND IN TWENTY MINUTES...
...GREENSLEEVES OPERATIVES IN THE BASTARD HAYES' OWN CAMP WILL BETRAY HIM AND TAKE THE HOLY MOTHER EARTH'S VENGEANCE. WE HAVE INSTALLED A BOMB BEARING A DEADLY AIRBORNE TOXIN WHICH WILL LEAVE THE INNOCENT ANIMALS UNSCATHED BUT DESTROY THE DEFILER, MAN.
IN TWENTY MINUTES, THE TOXIN WILL BE RELEASED, AND ALL WILL DIE.
WE HAVE ALLOWED YOU A SOLUTION, FOR WE HAVE NO WISH TO HARM INNOCENTS WHOSE ONLY CRIME WAS THE POOR JUDGMENT TO ACCEPT EMPLOYMENT FROM HAYES. WE HAVE PLANNED THIS DEMONSTRATION OF MOTHER EARTH'S POWER FOR THE DEMON'S PRE-LAUNCH TEST.
TELL HIM IF HE DETONATES THE SELF-DESTRUCT MECHANISM ON HIS ROCKETS...
...ALL FOUR ROCKETS...
...THE CONFLAGRATION WILL STERILIZE THE TOXIN. YES, INNOCENT LIVESTOCK WILL PERISH WHEN THE CARGO SHIPS EXPLODE, BUT WE FEEL WE ARE SAVING THEM FROM EXECUTION. BETTER TO DIE A HERO'S DEATH THAN END UP AS LONDON BROIL ON A RICH MAN'S PLATE.
HE HAS TWENTY MINUTES TO DECIDE.

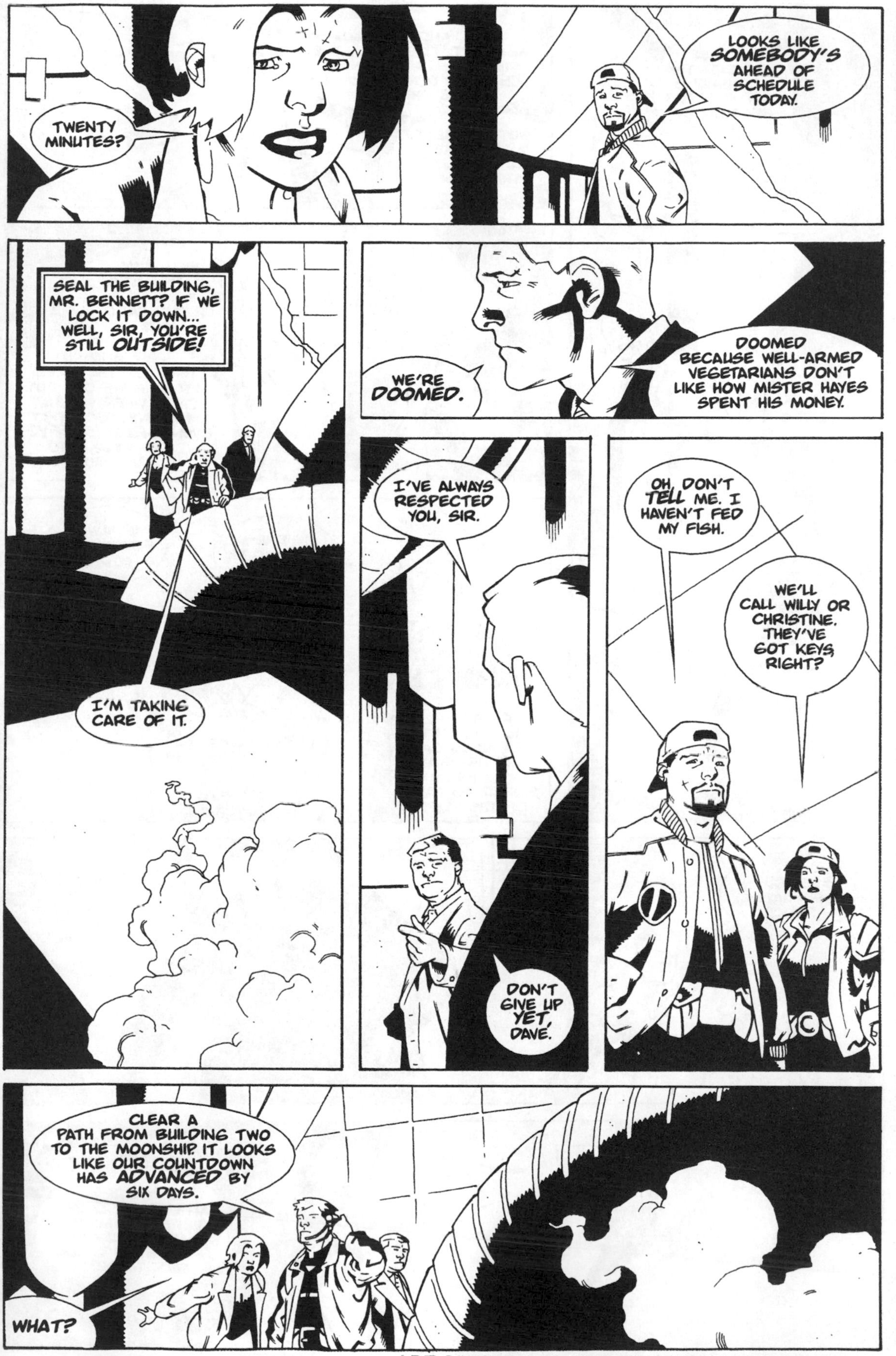
TWENTY MINUTES?
LOOKS LIKE SOMEBODY'S AHEAD OF SCHEDULE TODAY.
SEAL THE BUILDING, MR. BENNETT? IF WE LOCK IT DOWN... WELL, SIR, YOU'RE STILL OUTSIDE!
I'M TAKING CARE OF IT.
WE'RE DOOMED.
DOOMED BECAUSE WELL-ARMED VEGETARIANS DON'T LIKE HOW MISTER HAYES SPENT HIS MONEY.
I'VE ALWAYS RESPECTED YOU, SIR.
DON'T GIVE UP YET, DAVE.
OH, DON'T TELL ME. I HAVEN'T FED MY FISH.
WE'LL CALL WILLY OR CHRISTINE. THEY'VE GOT KEYS, RIGHT?
CLEAR A PATH FROM BUILDING TWO TO THE MOONSHIP. IT LOOKS LIKE OUR COUNTDOWN HAS ADVANCED BY SIX DAYS.
WHAT?

THINK, AND BE QUICK ABOUT IT, ELISABETH. THE TERRORISTS SAID WE'LL *DIE* IF WE DON'T BLOW UP THE SHIPS...

...BUT THE HEAT AND FLAME WILL STERILIZE THE TOXIN.

I AGREE, BENNETT. THE MOONSHIP IS FULLY STOCKED, BECAUSE OF TODAY'S TEST.

FUEL, SUPPLIES, EQUIPMENT, THE WORKS.

WHAT?

IT WAS A DRESS REHEARSAL. EVEN THE CARGO SHIPS WERE FULLY SUPPLIED.

WELL, I'M NOT PREPARED TO FOREGO ALL OF OUR HARD WORK.

...AND THINK OF THE GREAT PR SPIN WE CAN PUT ON IT WHEN WE SAVE THE LIVESTOCK THAT EVEN *GREENSLEEVES* WAS WILLING TO DESTROY.

WHERE'S THE STORY, DAVE?

WE ALWAYS FOLLOW THE STORY.

EVEN IF IT'S GOING STRAIGHT UP.

WE'RE GOING UP, TOO, AREN'T WE? HAYES SAID THE NEWSVAN WAS PROVISIONED AS PART OF THE TEST.

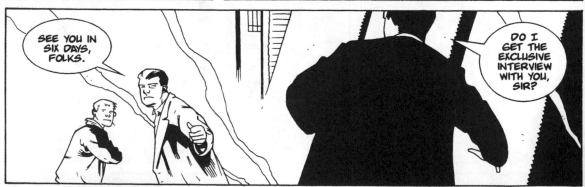

SEE YOU IN SIX DAYS, FOLKS.

DO I GET THE EXCLUSIVE INTERVIEW WITH YOU, SIR?

TELL YOU WHAT, DAVE...

...IF THERE'S ANYONE *ELSE* UP THERE, YOU MIGHT WANT TO TALK TO *THEM* BEFORE YOU TALK TO ME.

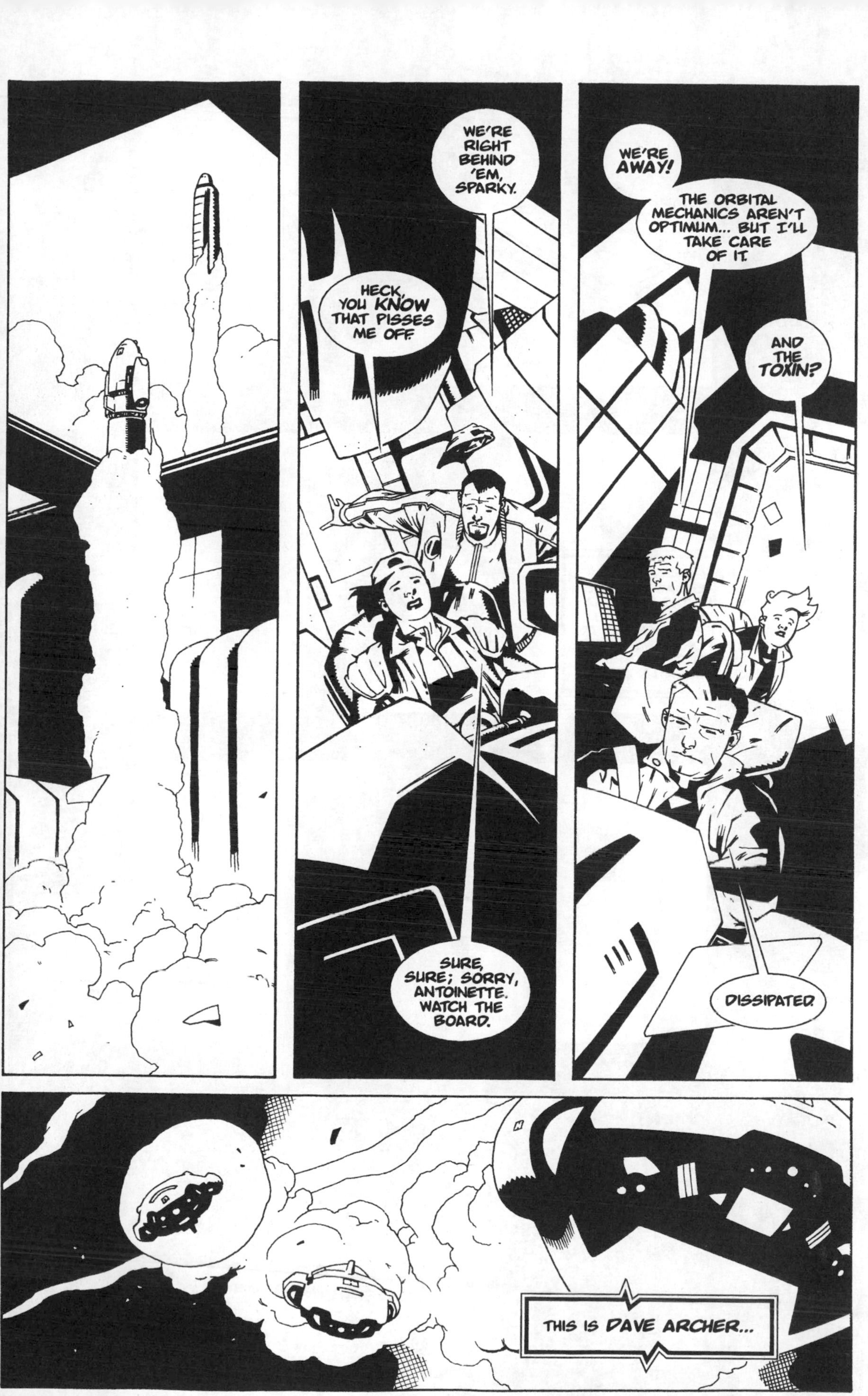
WE'RE RIGHT BEHIND 'EM, SPARKY.
HECK, YOU KNOW THAT PISSES ME OFF.
SURE, SURE; SORRY, ANTOINETTE. WATCH THE BOARD.
WE'RE AWAY!
THE ORBITAL MECHANICS AREN'T OPTIMUM... BUT I'LL TAKE CARE OF IT.
AND THE TOXIN?
DISSIPATED.
THIS IS DAVE ARCHER...

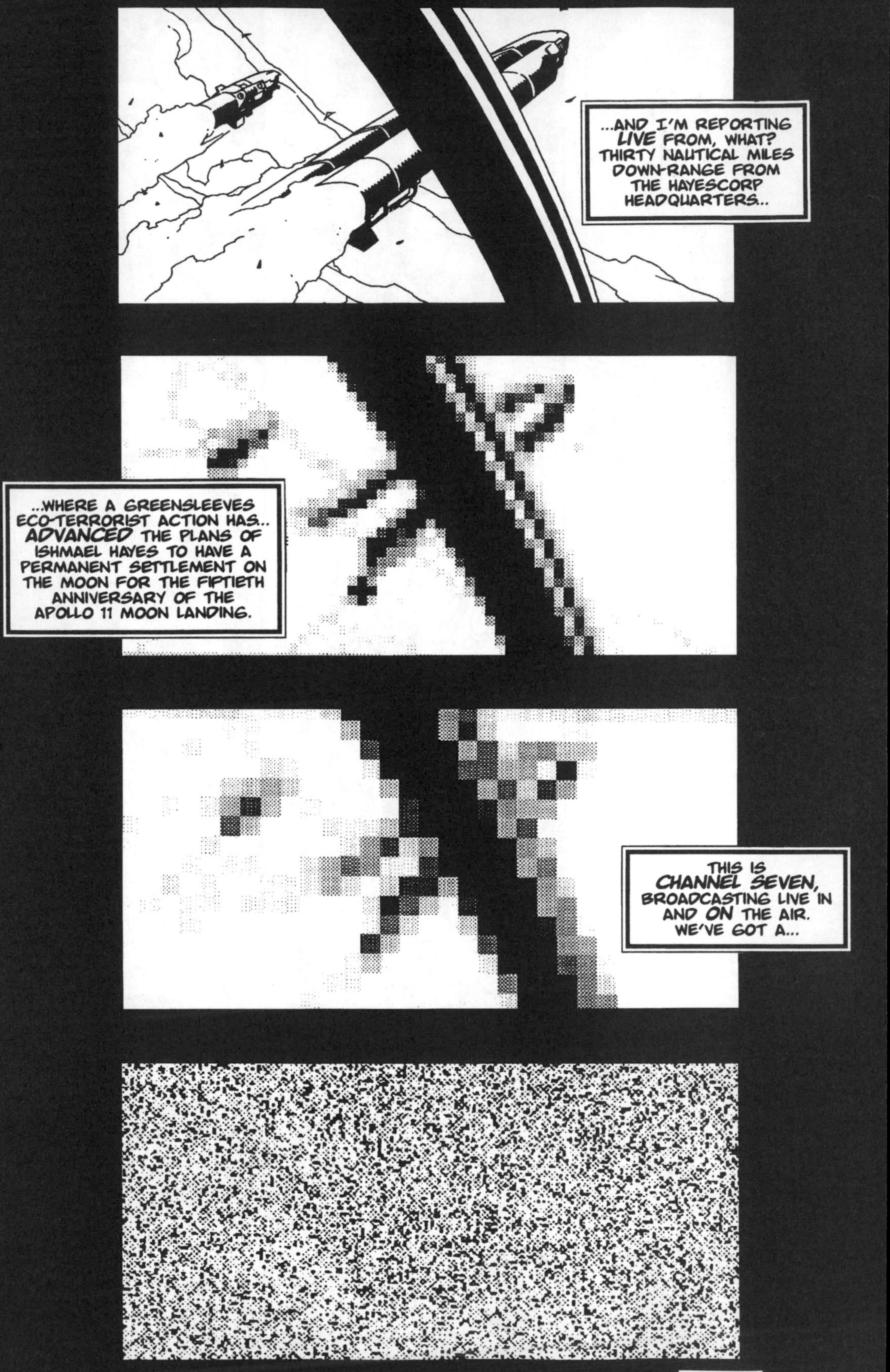
...AND I'M REPORTING LIVE FROM, WHAT? THIRTY NAUTICAL MILES DOWN-RANGE FROM THE HAYESCORP HEADQUARTERS...
...WHERE A GREENSLEEVES ECO-TERRORIST ACTION HAS... ADVANCED THE PLANS OF ISHMAEL HAYES TO HAVE A PERMANENT SETTLEMENT ON THE MOON FOR THE FIFTIETH ANNIVERSARY OF THE APOLLO 11 MOON LANDING.
THIS IS CHANNEL SEVEN, BROADCASTING LIVE IN AND ON THE AIR. WE'VE GOT A...
Rats.

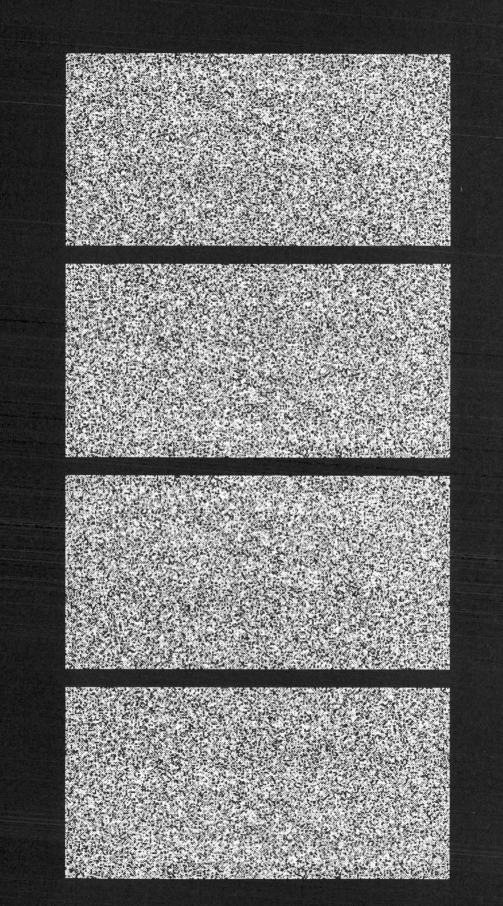

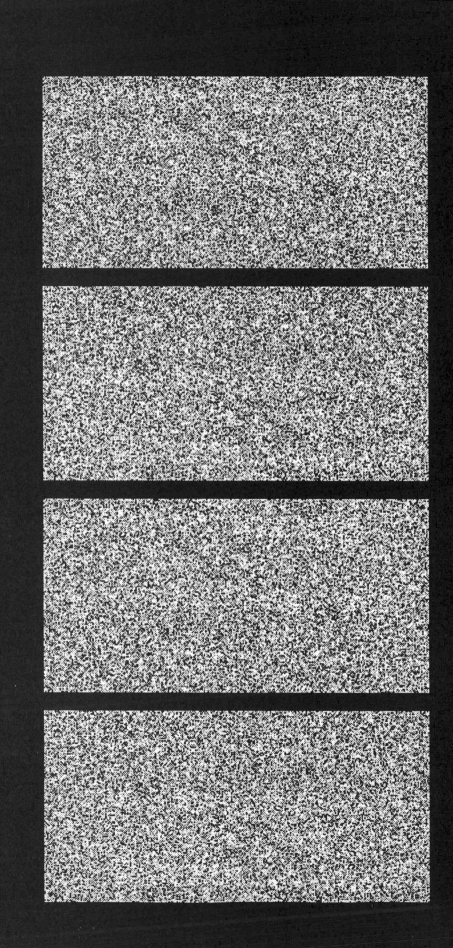

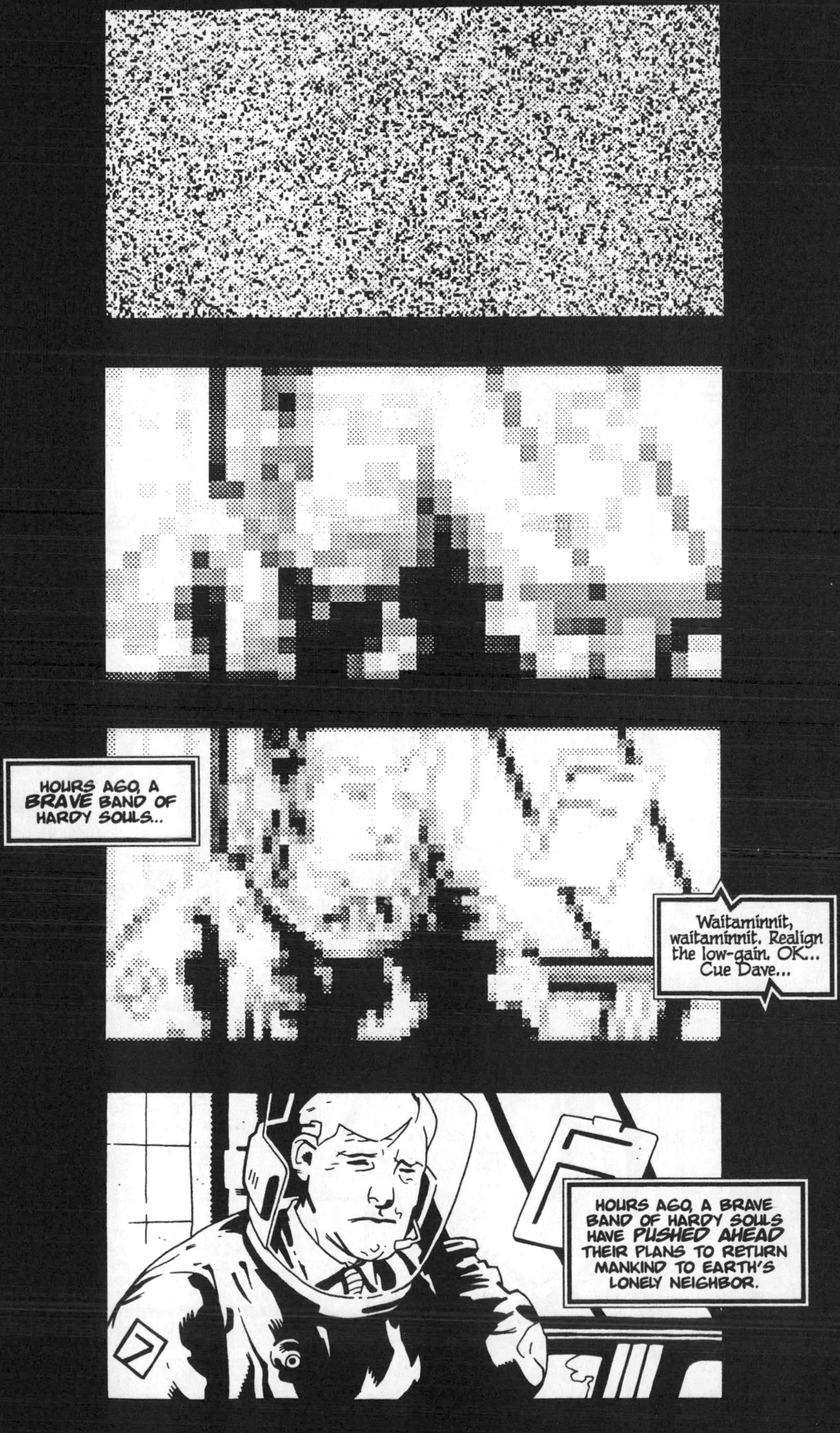
HOURS AGO, A BRAVE BAND OF HARDY SOULS...
Waitaminnit, waitaminnit. Realign the low-gain. OK... Cue Dave...
HOURS AGO, A BRAVE BAND OF HARDY SOULS HAVE PUSHED AHEAD THEIR PLANS TO RETURN MANKIND TO EARTH'S LONELY NEIGHBOR.

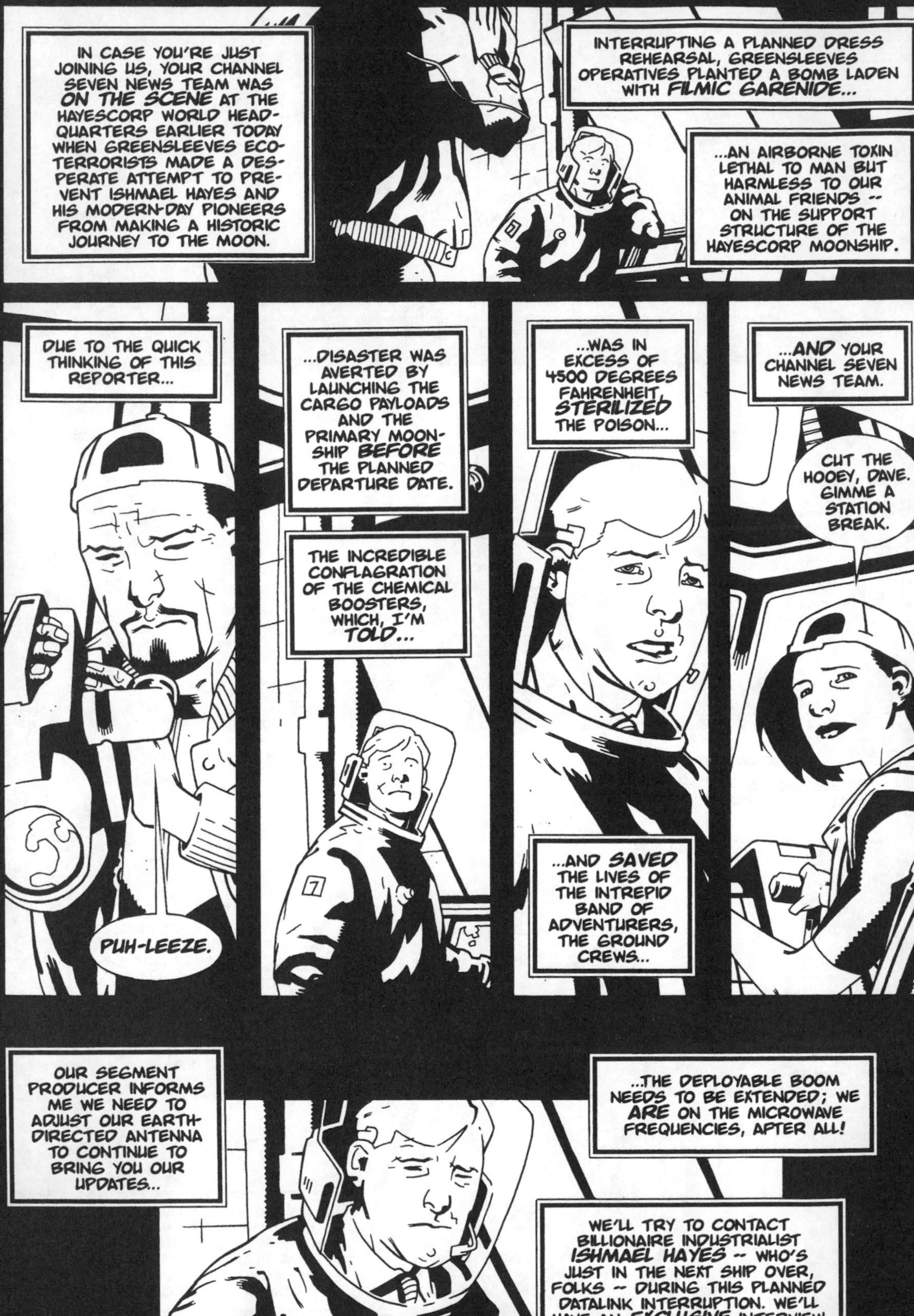
IN CASE YOU'RE JUST JOINING US, YOUR CHANNEL SEVEN NEWS TEAM WAS ON THE SCENE AT THE HAYESCORP WORLD HEADQUARTERS EARLIER TODAY WHEN GREENSLEEVES ECO-TERRORISTS MADE A DESPERATE ATTEMPT TO PREVENT ISHMAEL HAYES AND HIS MODERN-DAY PIONEERS FROM MAKING A HISTORIC JOURNEY TO THE MOON.
INTERRUPTING A PLANNED DRESS REHEARSAL, GREENSLEEVES OPERATIVES PLANTED A BOMB LADEN WITH FILMIC GARENIDE...
...AN AIRBORNE TOXIN LETHAL TO MAN BUT HARMLESS TO OUR ANIMAL FRIENDS -- ON THE SUPPORT STRUCTURE OF THE HAYESCORP MOONSHIP.
DUE TO THE QUICK THINKING OF THIS REPORTER...
PUH-LEEZE.
...DISASTER WAS AVERTED BY LAUNCHING THE CARGO PAYLOADS AND THE PRIMARY MOONSHIP BEFORE THE PLANNED DEPARTURE DATE.
THE INCREDIBLE CONFLAGRATION OF THE CHEMICAL BOOSTERS, WHICH, I'M TOLD...
...WAS IN EXCESS OF 4500 DEGREES FAHRENHEIT, STERILIZED THE POISON...
...AND SAVED THE LIVES OF THE INTREPID BAND OF ADVENTURERS, THE GROUND CREWS...
...AND YOUR CHANNEL SEVEN NEWS TEAM.
CUT THE HOOEY, DAVE. GIMME A STATION BREAK.
OUR SEGMENT PRODUCER INFORMS ME WE NEED TO ADJUST OUR EARTH-DIRECTED ANTENNA TO CONTINUE TO BRING YOU OUR UPDATES...
...THE DEPLOYABLE BOOM NEEDS TO BE EXTENDED; WE ARE ON THE MICROWAVE FREQUENCIES, AFTER ALL!
WE'LL TRY TO CONTACT BILLIONAIRE INDUSTRIALIST ISHMAEL HAYES -- WHO'S JUST IN THE NEXT SHIP OVER, FOLKS -- DURING THIS PLANNED DATALINK INTERRUPTION. WE'LL HAVE AN EXCLUSIVE INTERVIEW WITH THE MAN WHO HAS MADE HIS DREAM A REALITY...

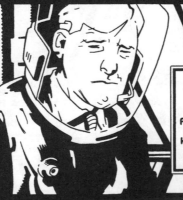

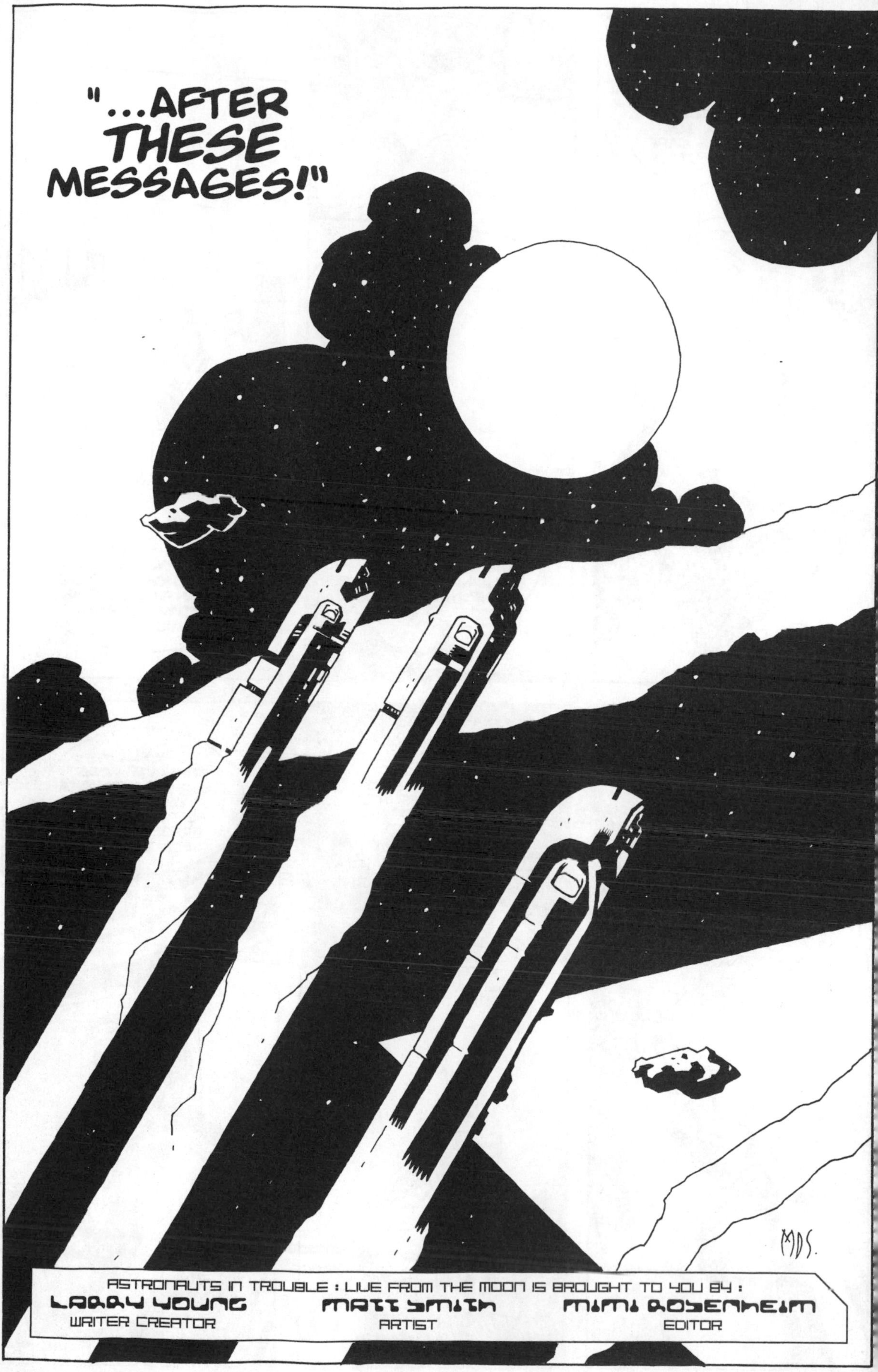
"...AFTER THESE MESSAGES!"
MDS.
ASTRONAUTS IN TROUBLE : LIVE FROM THE MOON IS BROUGHT TO YOU BY :
LARRY YOUNG
WRITER CREATOR
MATT SMITH
ARTIST
MIMI ROSENHEIM
EDITOR

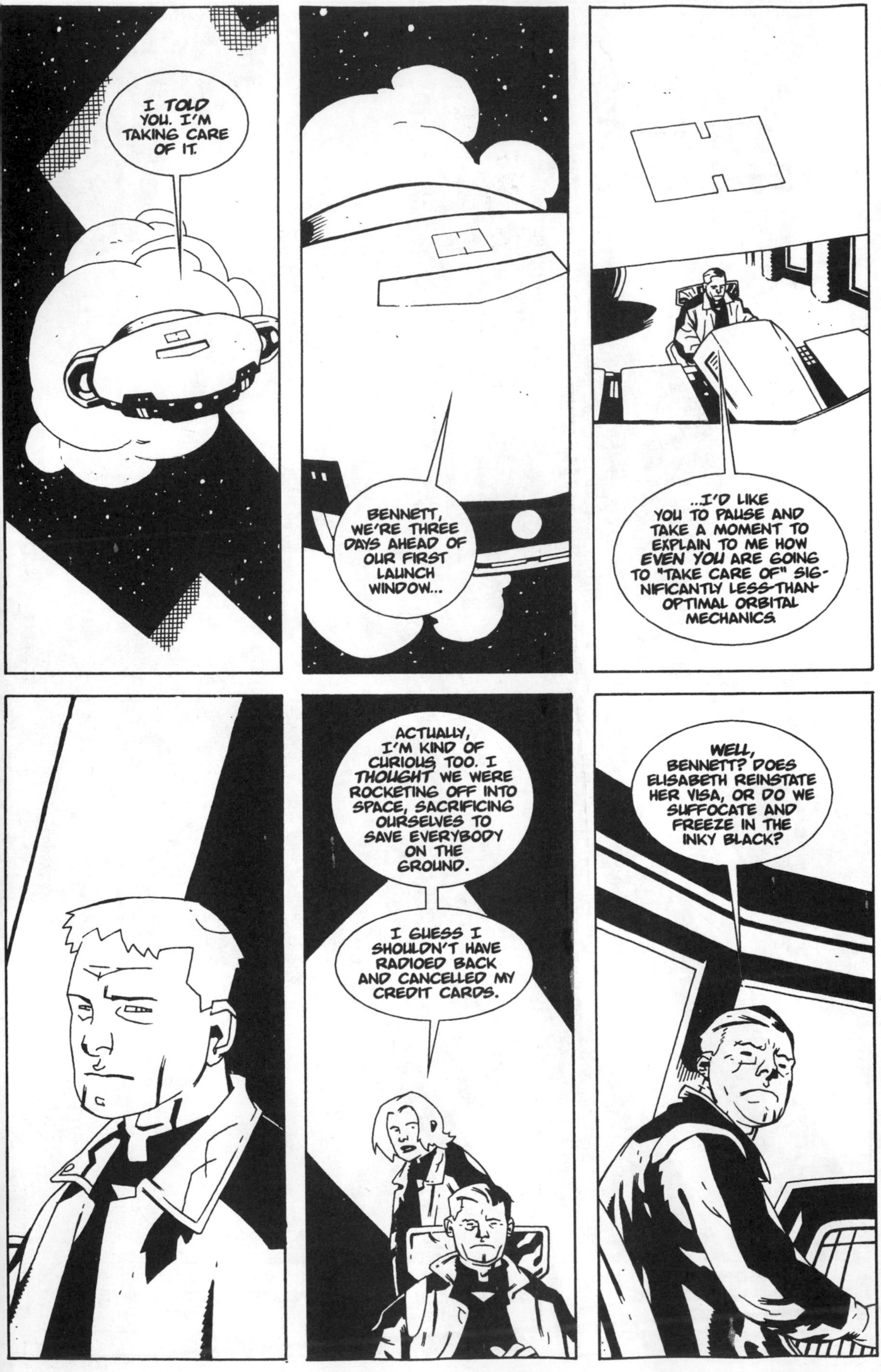
I TOLD YOU. I'M TAKING CARE OF IT.
BENNETT, WE'RE THREE DAYS AHEAD OF OUR FIRST LAUNCH WINDOW...
...I'D LIKE YOU TO PAUSE AND TAKE A MOMENT TO EXPLAIN TO ME HOW EVEN YOU ARE GOING TO "TAKE CARE OF" SIGNIFICANTLY LESS-THAN-OPTIMAL ORBITAL MECHANICS.
ACTUALLY, I'M KIND OF CURIOUS TOO. I THOUGHT WE WERE ROCKETING OFF INTO SPACE, SACRIFICING OURSELVES TO SAVE EVERYBODY ON THE GROUND.
I GUESS I SHOULDN'T HAVE RADIOED BACK AND CANCELLED MY CREDIT CARDS.
WELL, BENNETT? DOES ELISABETH REINSTATE HER VISA, OR DO WE SUFFOCATE AND FREEZE IN THE INKY BLACK?

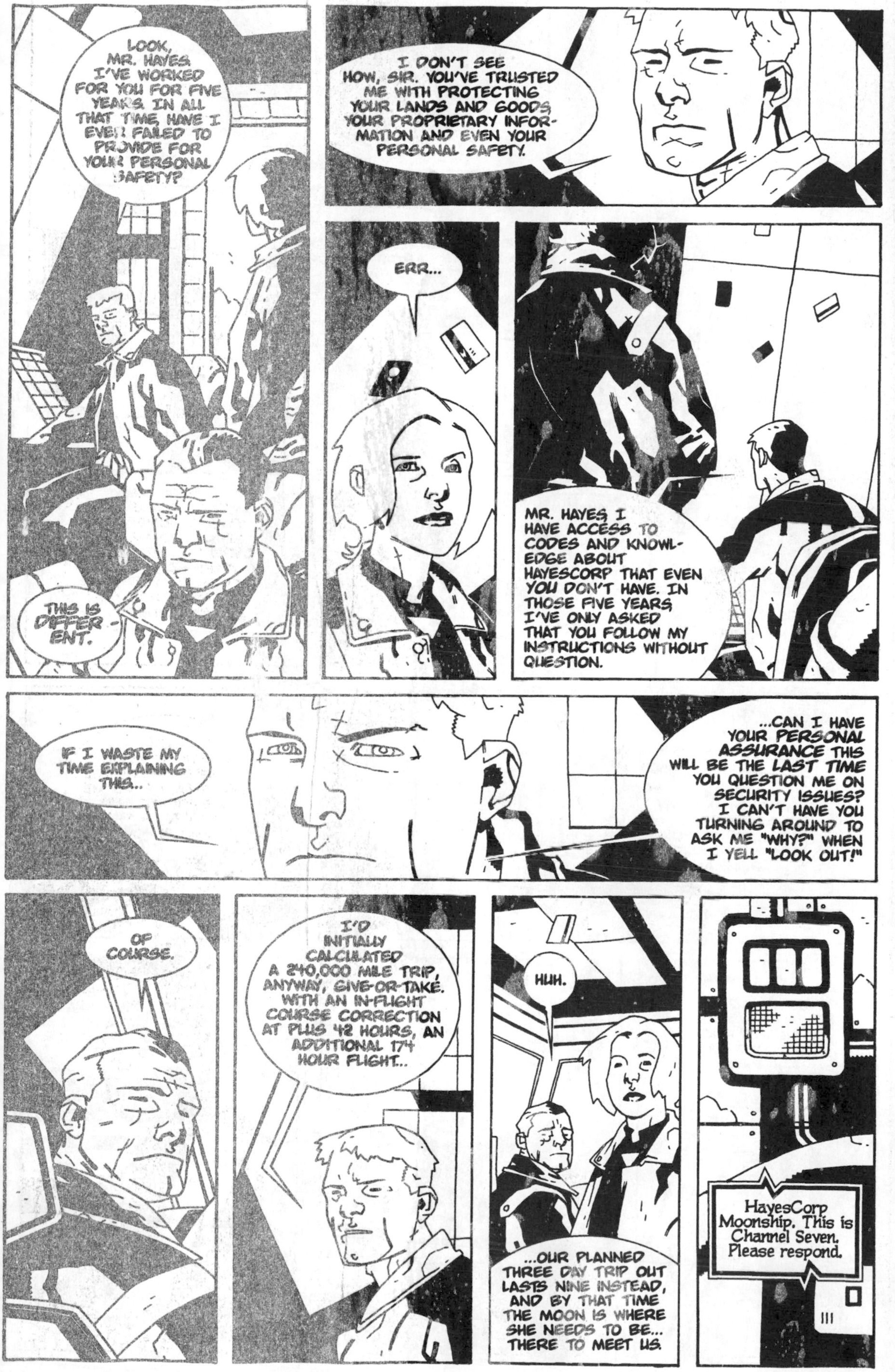
LOOK, MR. HAYES. I'VE WORKED FOR YOU FOR FIVE YEARS. IN ALL THAT TIME, HAVE I EVER FAILED TO PROVIDE FOR YOUR PERSONAL SAFETY?
THIS IS DIFFERENT.
I DON'T SEE HOW, SIR. YOU'VE TRUSTED ME WITH PROTECTING YOUR LANDS AND GOODS, YOUR PROPRIETARY INFORMATION AND EVEN YOUR PERSONAL SAFETY.
ERR...
MR. HAYES, I HAVE ACCESS TO CODES AND KNOWLEDGE ABOUT HAYESCORP THAT EVEN YOU DON'T HAVE. IN THOSE FIVE YEARS, I'VE ONLY ASKED THAT YOU FOLLOW MY INSTRUCTIONS WITHOUT QUESTION.
IF I WASTE MY TIME EXPLAINING THIS...
...CAN I HAVE YOUR PERSONAL ASSURANCE THIS WILL BE THE LAST TIME YOU QUESTION ME ON SECURITY ISSUES? I CAN'T HAVE YOU TURNING AROUND TO ASK ME "WHY?" WHEN I YELL "LOOK OUT!"
OF COURSE.
I'D INITIALLY CALCULATED A 240,000 MILE TRIP, ANYWAY, GIVE-OR-TAKE. WITH AN IN-FLIGHT COURSE CORRECTION AT PLUS 42 HOURS, AN ADDITIONAL 174 HOUR FLIGHT...
HUH.
...OUR PLANNED THREE DAY TRIP OUT LASTS NINE INSTEAD, AND BY THAT TIME THE MOON IS WHERE SHE NEEDS TO BE... THERE TO MEET US.
HayesCorp Moonship. This is Channel Seven. Please respond.

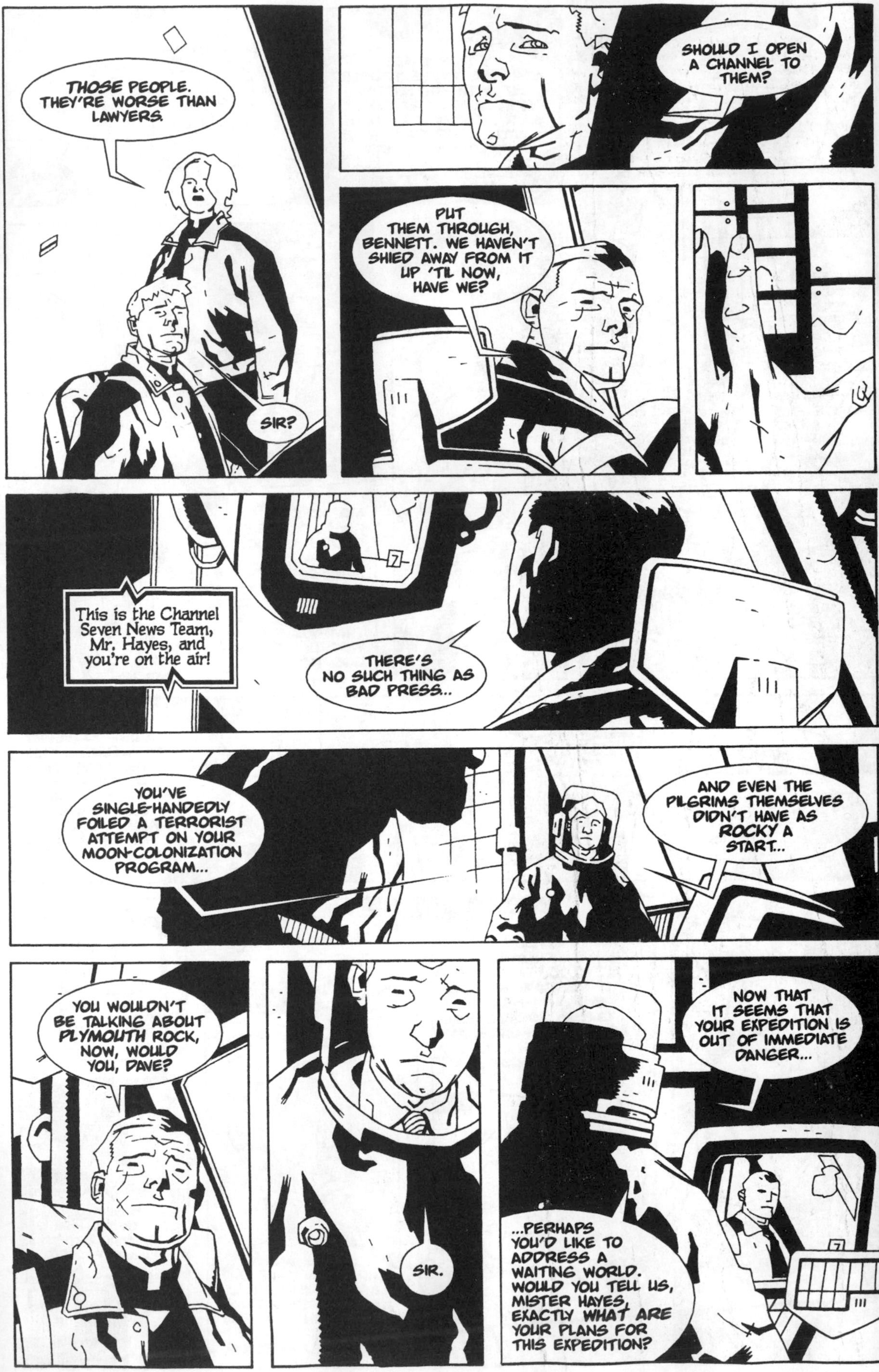
THOSE PEOPLE. THEY'RE WORSE THAN LAWYERS.
SIR?
SHOULD I OPEN A CHANNEL TO THEM?
PUT THEM THROUGH, BENNETT. WE HAVEN'T SHIED AWAY FROM IT UP 'TIL NOW, HAVE WE?
This is the Channel Seven News Team, Mr. Hayes, and you're on the air!
THERE'S NO SUCH THING AS BAD PRESS...
YOU'VE SINGLE-HANDEDLY FOILED A TERRORIST ATTEMPT ON YOUR MOON-COLONIZATION PROGRAM...
AND EVEN THE PILGRIMS THEMSELVES DIDN'T HAVE AS ROCKY A START...
YOU WOULDN'T BE TALKING ABOUT PLYMOUTH ROCK, NOW, WOULD YOU, DAVE?
SIR.
NOW THAT IT SEEMS THAT YOUR EXPEDITION IS OUT OF IMMEDIATE DANGER...
...PERHAPS YOU'D LIKE TO ADDRESS A WAITING WORLD. WOULD YOU TELL US, MISTER HAYES, EXACTLY WHAT ARE YOUR PLANS FOR THIS EXPEDITION?

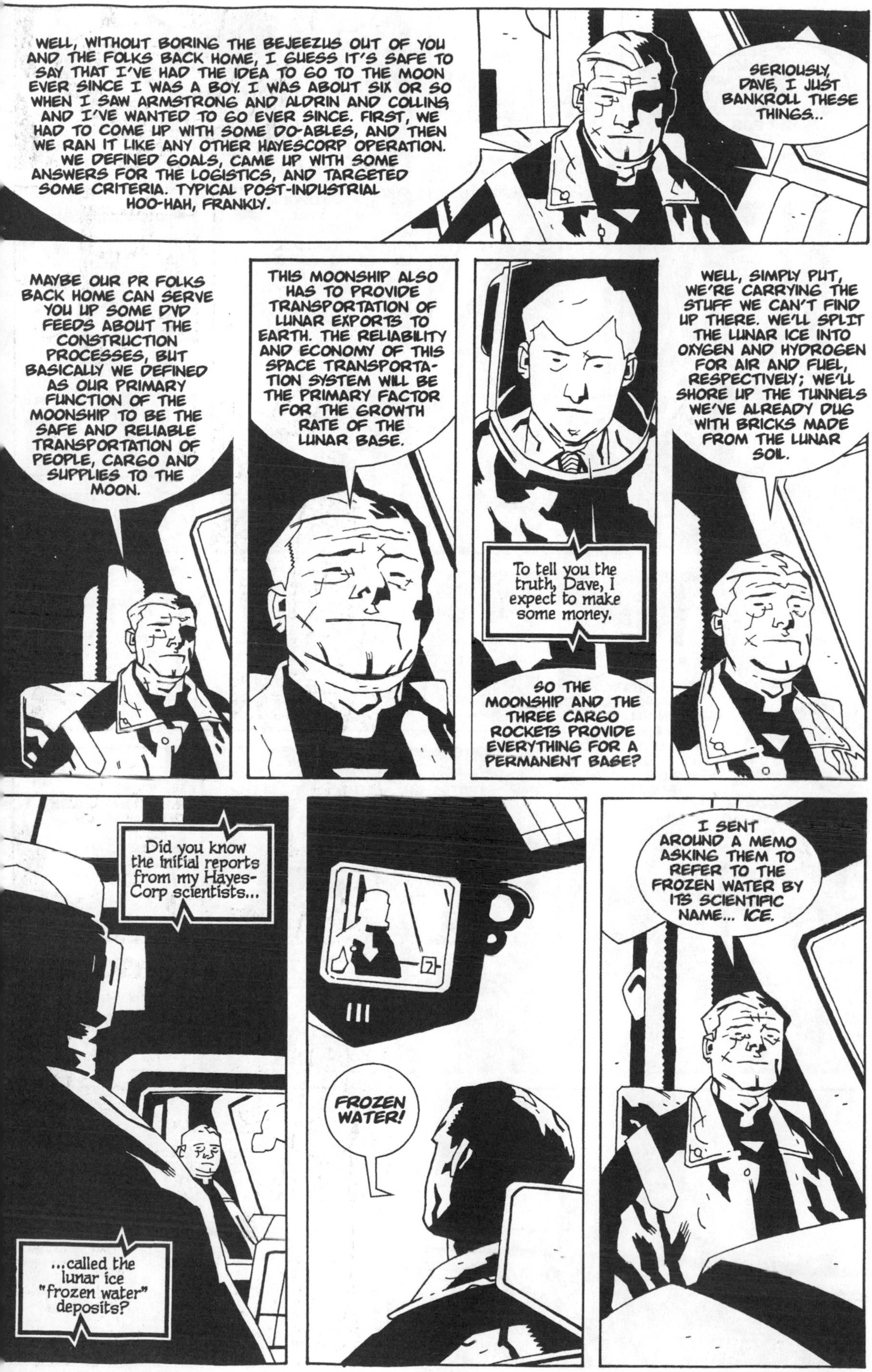
WELL, WITHOUT BORING THE BEJEEZUS OUT OF YOU AND THE FOLKS BACK HOME, I GUESS IT'S SAFE TO SAY THAT I'VE HAD THE IDEA TO GO TO THE MOON EVER SINCE I WAS A BOY. I WAS ABOUT SIX OR SO WHEN I SAW ARMSTRONG AND ALDRIN AND COLLINS, AND I'VE WANTED TO GO EVER SINCE. FIRST, WE HAD TO COME UP WITH SOME DO-ABLES, AND THEN WE RAN IT LIKE ANY OTHER HAYESCORP OPERATION. WE DEFINED GOALS, CAME UP WITH SOME ANSWERS FOR THE LOGISTICS, AND TARGETED SOME CRITERIA. TYPICAL POST-INDUSTRIAL HOO-HAH, FRANKLY.
SERIOUSLY, DAVE, I JUST BANKROLL THESE THINGS...
MAYBE OUR PR FOLKS BACK HOME CAN SERVE YOU UP SOME DVD FEEDS ABOUT THE CONSTRUCTION PROCESSES, BUT BASICALLY WE DEFINED AS OUR PRIMARY FUNCTION OF THE MOONSHIP TO BE THE SAFE AND RELIABLE TRANSPORTATION OF PEOPLE, CARGO AND SUPPLIES TO THE MOON.
THIS MOONSHIP ALSO HAS TO PROVIDE TRANSPORTATION OF LUNAR EXPORTS TO EARTH. THE RELIABILITY AND ECONOMY OF THIS SPACE TRANSPORTATION SYSTEM WILL BE THE PRIMARY FACTOR FOR THE GROWTH RATE OF THE LUNAR BASE.
To tell you the truth, Dave, I expect to make some money.
SO THE MOONSHIP AND THE THREE CARGO ROCKETS PROVIDE EVERYTHING FOR A PERMANENT BASE?
WELL, SIMPLY PUT, WE'RE CARRYING THE STUFF WE CAN'T FIND UP THERE. WE'LL SPLIT THE LUNAR ICE INTO OXYGEN AND HYDROGEN FOR AIR AND FUEL, RESPECTIVELY; WE'LL SHORE UP THE TUNNELS WE'VE ALREADY DUG WITH BRICKS MADE FROM THE LUNAR SOIL.
Did you know the initial reports from my Hayes-Corp scientists...
...called the lunar ice "frozen water" deposits?
FROZEN WATER!
I SENT AROUND A MEMO ASKING THEM TO REFER TO THE FROZEN WATER BY ITS SCIENTIFIC NAME... ICE.

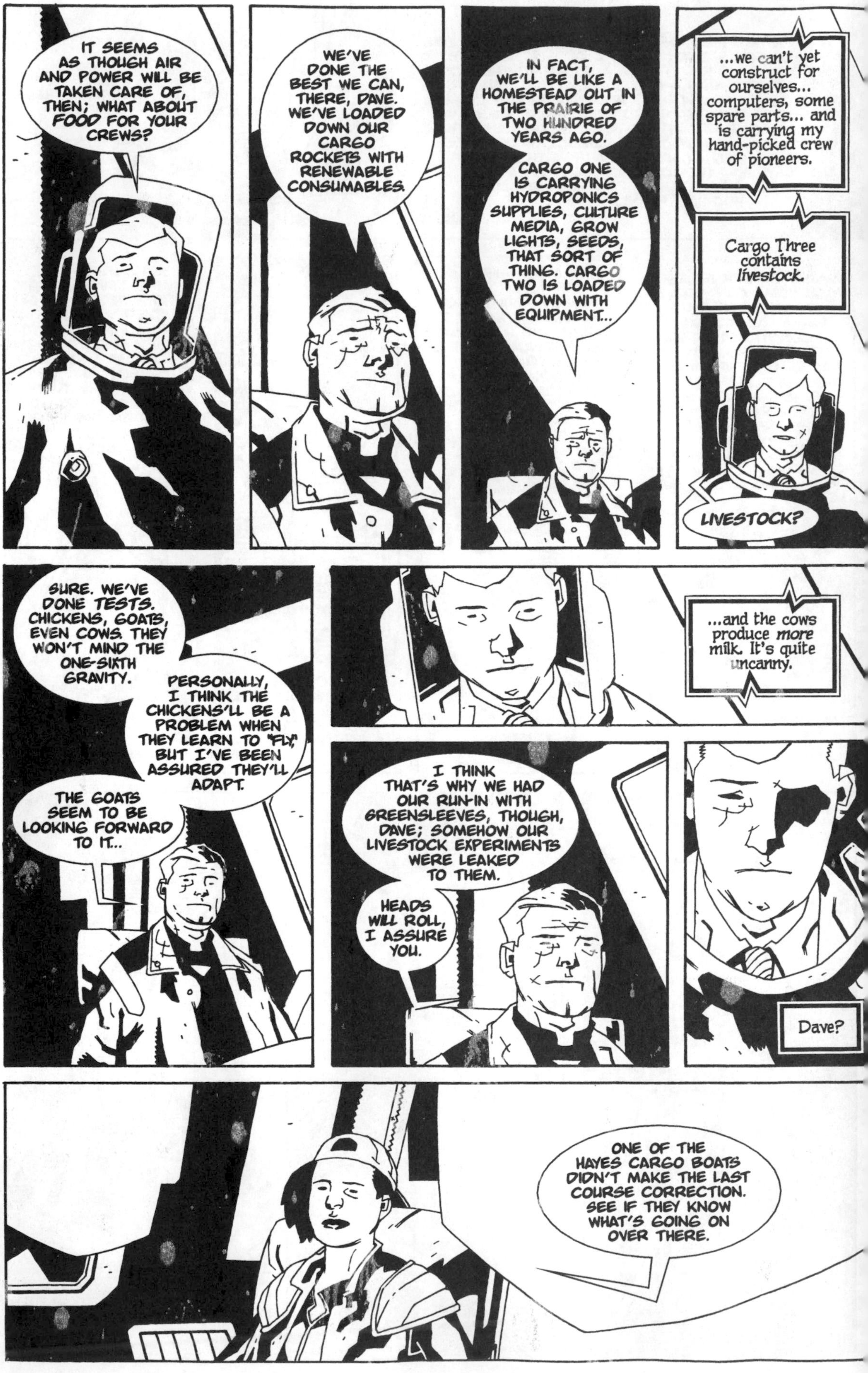
IT SEEMS AS THOUGH AIR AND POWER WILL BE TAKEN CARE OF, THEN; WHAT ABOUT FOOD FOR YOUR CREWS?
WE'VE DONE THE BEST WE CAN, THERE, DAVE. WE'VE LOADED DOWN OUR CARGO ROCKETS WITH RENEWABLE CONSUMABLES.
IN FACT, WE'LL BE LIKE A HOMESTEAD OUT IN THE PRAIRIE OF TWO HUNDRED YEARS AGO.
CARGO ONE IS CARRYING HYDROPONICS SUPPLIES, CULTURE MEDIA, GROW LIGHTS, SEEDS, THAT SORT OF THING. CARGO TWO IS LOADED DOWN WITH EQUIPMENT...
...we can't yet construct for ourselves... computers, some spare parts... and is carrying my hand-picked crew of pioneers.
Cargo Three contains livestock.
LIVESTOCK?
SURE. WE'VE DONE TESTS. CHICKENS, GOATS, EVEN COWS. THEY WON'T MIND THE ONE-SIXTH GRAVITY.
PERSONALLY, I THINK THE CHICKENS'LL BE A PROBLEM WHEN THEY LEARN TO "FLY," BUT I'VE BEEN ASSURED THEY'LL ADAPT.
THE GOATS SEEM TO BE LOOKING FORWARD TO IT...
...and the cows produce more milk. It's quite uncanny.
I THINK THAT'S WHY WE HAD OUR RUN-IN WITH GREENSLEEVES, THOUGH, DAVE; SOMEHOW OUR LIVESTOCK EXPERIMENTS WERE LEAKED TO THEM.
HEADS WILL ROLL, I ASSURE YOU.
Dave?
ONE OF THE HAYES CARGO BOATS DIDN'T MAKE THE LAST COURSE CORRECTION. SEE IF THEY KNOW WHAT'S GOING ON OVER THERE.

Mr. Hayes, my segment producer informs me that Cargo Three did not make the last course correction. Is this according to plan?

WELL?

THAT'LL WRAP UP THIS LATEST UPDATE FROM THE CHANNEL SEVEN NEWS TEAM, HIGH ABOVE...

YOU ALL JUST SIT TIGHT OVER THERE. WE'LL GET BACK TO YOU, DAVE.

SIR, I CAN'T RAISE CARGO THREE. SHE'S NOT ONLINE.

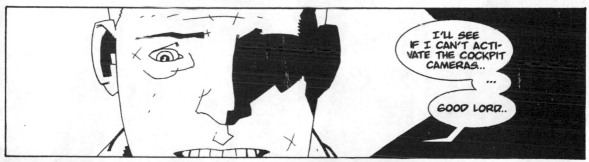

I'LL SEE IF I CAN'T ACTIVATE THE COCKPIT CAMERAS...

...

GOOD LORD...

CARGO 3 CAM ONE

MOO.

CARGO 3 CAM SIX

I HOPE THIS WON'T AFFECT MY DINNER.

WHAT DO YOU MEAN?

SHE'S WORRIED ABOUT THE UTENSILS ELOPING.

WHAT ARE YOU TALKING ABOUT?

THINK ABOUT IT, DAVE; WE MIGHT AS WELL WORRY ABOUT THE SPOONS AND THE FORKS RUNNING AWAY TOGETHER...

...NOW THAT WE'VE GOT COWS JUMPING OVER THE MOON.

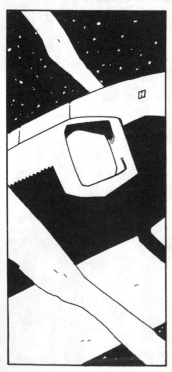

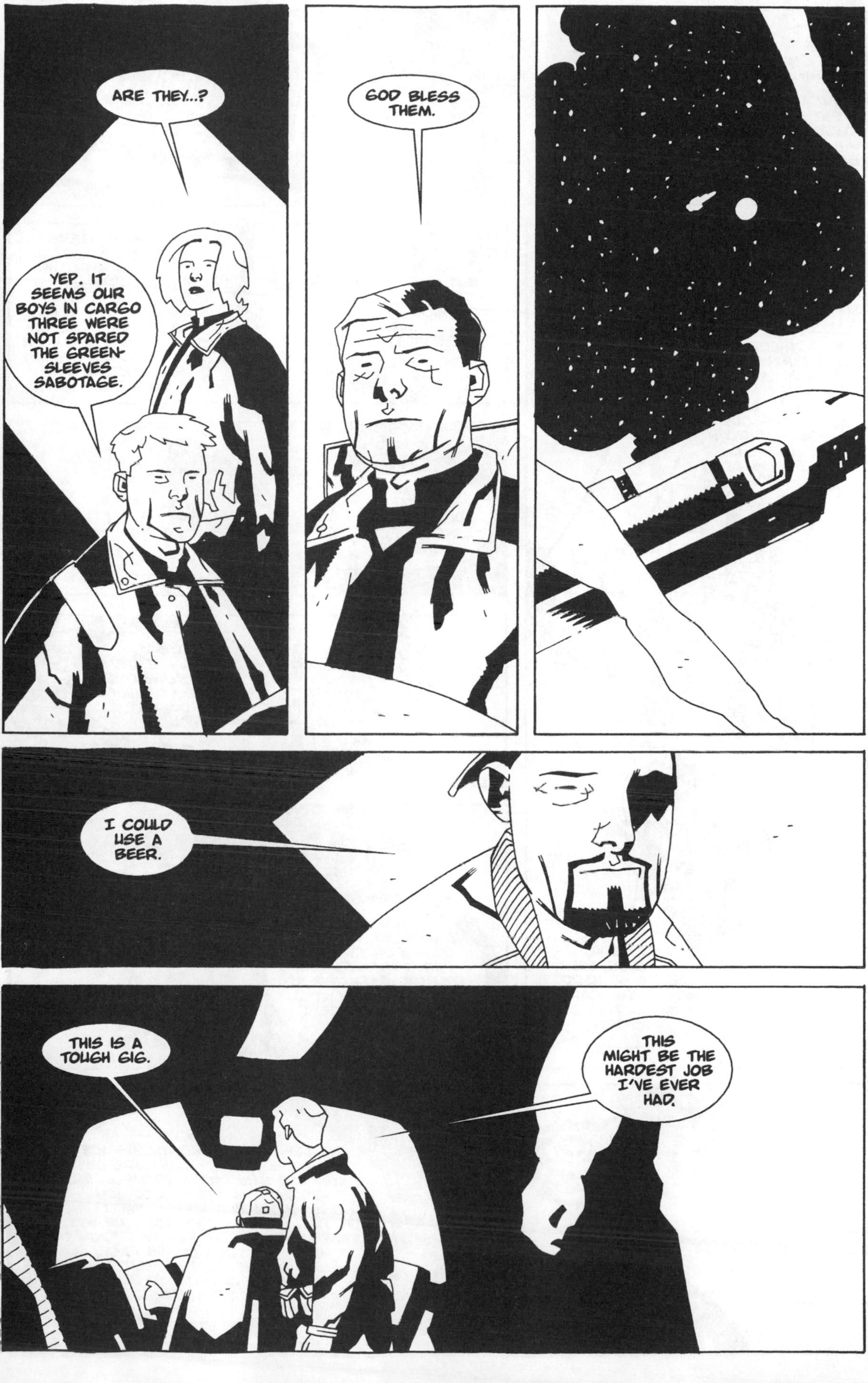
ARE THEY...?
YEP. IT SEEMS OUR BOYS IN CARGO THREE WERE NOT SPARED THE GREEN-SLEEVES SABOTAGE.
GOD BLESS THEM.
I COULD USE A BEER.
THIS IS A TOUGH GIG.
THIS MIGHT BE THE HARDEST JOB I'VE EVER HAD.

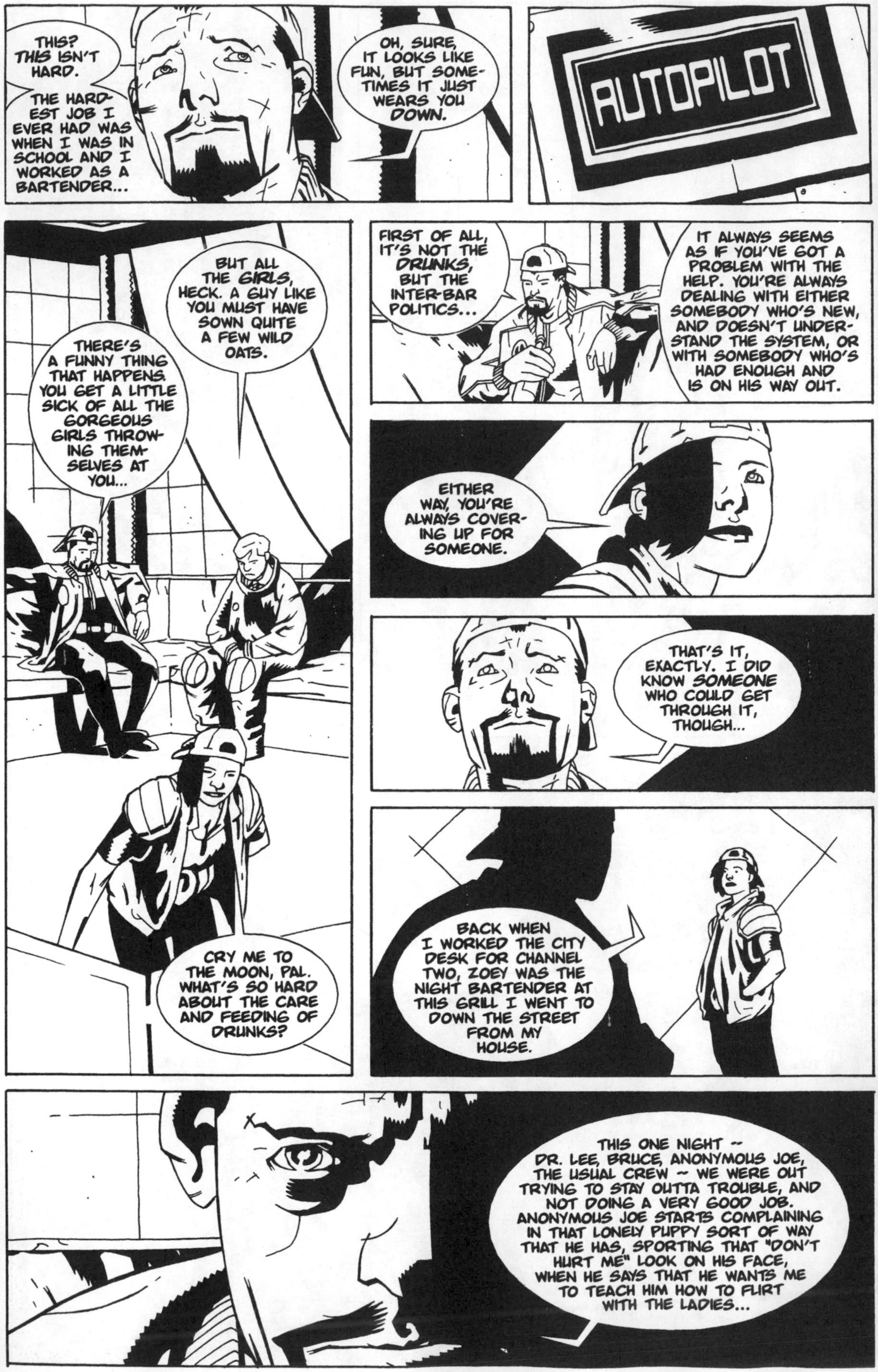
THIS? THIS ISN'T HARD.
THE HARDEST JOB I EVER HAD WAS WHEN I WAS IN SCHOOL AND I WORKED AS A BARTENDER...
OH, SURE, IT LOOKS LIKE FUN, BUT SOMETIMES IT JUST WEARS YOU DOWN.
AUTOPILOT
BUT ALL THE GIRLS, HECK. A GUY LIKE YOU MUST HAVE SOWN QUITE A FEW WILD OATS.
THERE'S A FUNNY THING THAT HAPPENS. YOU GET A LITTLE SICK OF ALL THE GORGEOUS GIRLS THROWING THEMSELVES AT YOU...
CRY ME TO THE MOON, PAL. WHAT'S SO HARD ABOUT THE CARE AND FEEDING OF DRUNKS?
FIRST OF ALL, IT'S NOT THE DRUNKS, BUT THE INTER-BAR POLITICS...
IT ALWAYS SEEMS AS IF YOU'VE GOT A PROBLEM WITH THE HELP. YOU'RE ALWAYS DEALING WITH EITHER SOMEBODY WHO'S NEW, AND DOESN'T UNDERSTAND THE SYSTEM, OR WITH SOMEBODY WHO'S HAD ENOUGH AND IS ON HIS WAY OUT.
EITHER WAY, YOU'RE ALWAYS COVERING UP FOR SOMEONE.
THAT'S IT, EXACTLY. I DID KNOW SOMEONE WHO COULD GET THROUGH IT, THOUGH...
BACK WHEN I WORKED THE CITY DESK FOR CHANNEL TWO, ZOEY WAS THE NIGHT BARTENDER AT THIS GRILL I WENT TO DOWN THE STREET FROM MY HOUSE.
THIS ONE NIGHT -- DR. LEE, BRUCE, ANONYMOUS JOE, THE USUAL CREW -- WE WERE OUT TRYING TO STAY OUTTA TROUBLE, AND NOT DOING A VERY GOOD JOB. ANONYMOUS JOE STARTS COMPLAINING IN THAT LONELY PUPPY SORT OF WAY THAT HE HAS, SPORTING THAT "DON'T HURT ME" LOOK ON HIS FACE, WHEN HE SAYS THAT HE WANTS ME TO TEACH HIM HOW TO FLIRT WITH THE LADIES...

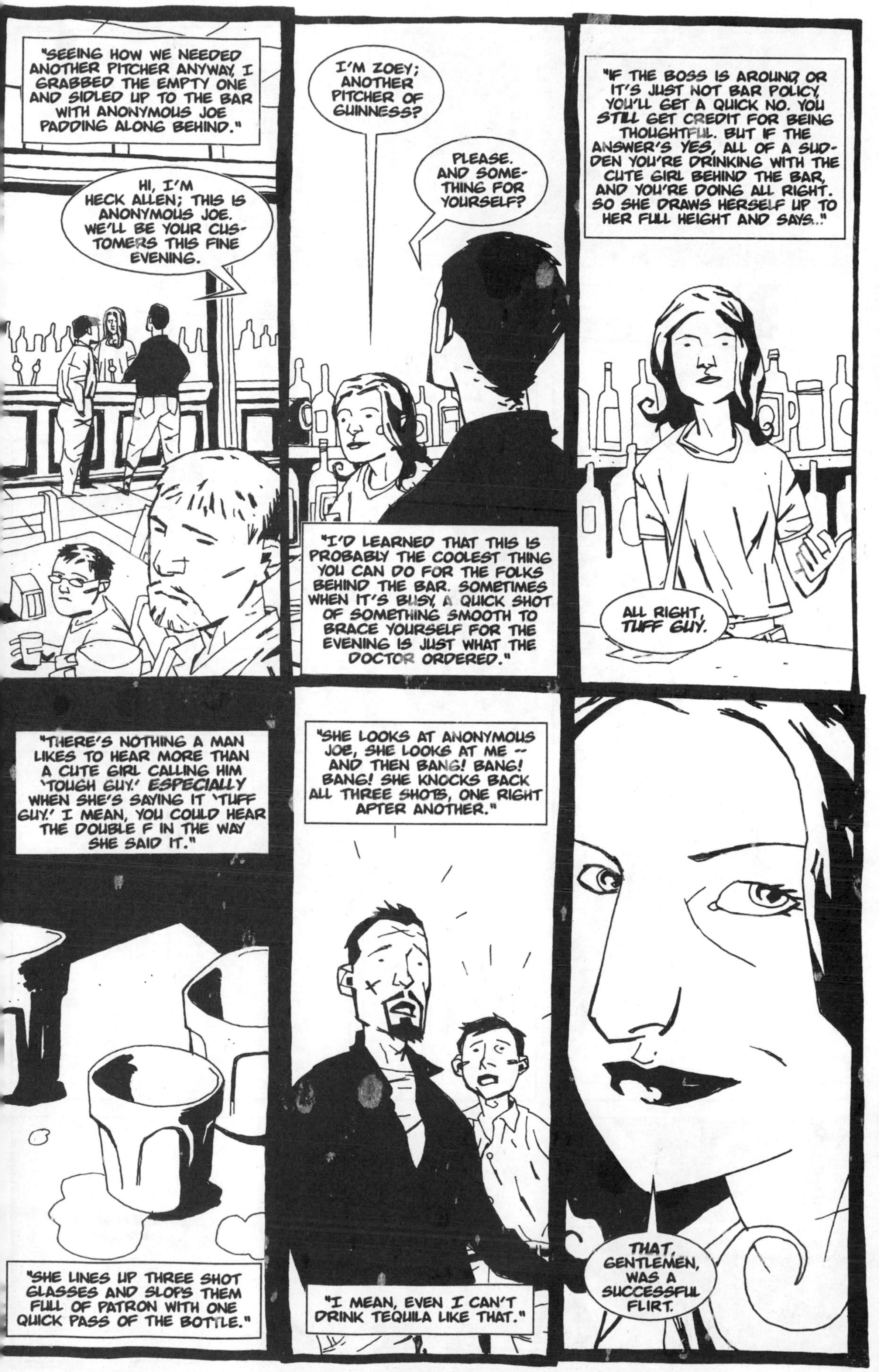
"SEEING HOW WE NEEDED ANOTHER PITCHER ANYWAY, I GRABBED THE EMPTY ONE AND SIDLED UP TO THE BAR WITH ANONYMOUS JOE PADDING ALONG BEHIND."
HI, I'M HECK ALLEN; THIS IS ANONYMOUS JOE. WE'LL BE YOUR CUSTOMERS THIS FINE EVENING.
I'M ZOEY; ANOTHER PITCHER OF GUINNESS?
PLEASE. AND SOMETHING FOR YOURSELF?
"I'D LEARNED THAT THIS IS PROBABLY THE COOLEST THING YOU CAN DO FOR THE FOLKS BEHIND THE BAR. SOMETIMES WHEN IT'S BUSY, A QUICK SHOT OF SOMETHING SMOOTH TO BRACE YOURSELF FOR THE EVENING IS JUST WHAT THE DOCTOR ORDERED."
"IF THE BOSS IS AROUND OR IT'S JUST NOT BAR POLICY, YOU'LL GET A QUICK NO. YOU STILL GET CREDIT FOR BEING THOUGHTFUL. BUT IF THE ANSWER'S YES, ALL OF A SUDDEN YOU'RE DRINKING WITH THE CUTE GIRL BEHIND THE BAR, AND YOU'RE DOING ALL RIGHT. SO SHE DRAWS HERSELF UP TO HER FULL HEIGHT AND SAYS..."
ALL RIGHT, TUFF GUY.
"THERE'S NOTHING A MAN LIKES TO HEAR MORE THAN A CUTE GIRL CALLING HIM 'TOUGH GUY.' ESPECIALLY WHEN SHE'S SAYING IT 'TUFF GUY.' I MEAN, YOU COULD HEAR THE DOUBLE F IN THE WAY SHE SAID IT."
"SHE LINES UP THREE SHOT GLASSES AND SLOPS THEM FULL OF PATRON WITH ONE QUICK PASS OF THE BOTTLE."
"SHE LOOKS AT ANONYMOUS JOE, SHE LOOKS AT ME -- AND THEN BANG! BANG! BANG! SHE KNOCKS BACK ALL THREE SHOTS, ONE RIGHT AFTER ANOTHER."
"I MEAN, EVEN I CAN'T DRINK TEQUILA LIKE THAT."
THAT, GENTLEMEN, WAS A SUCCESSFUL FLIRT.

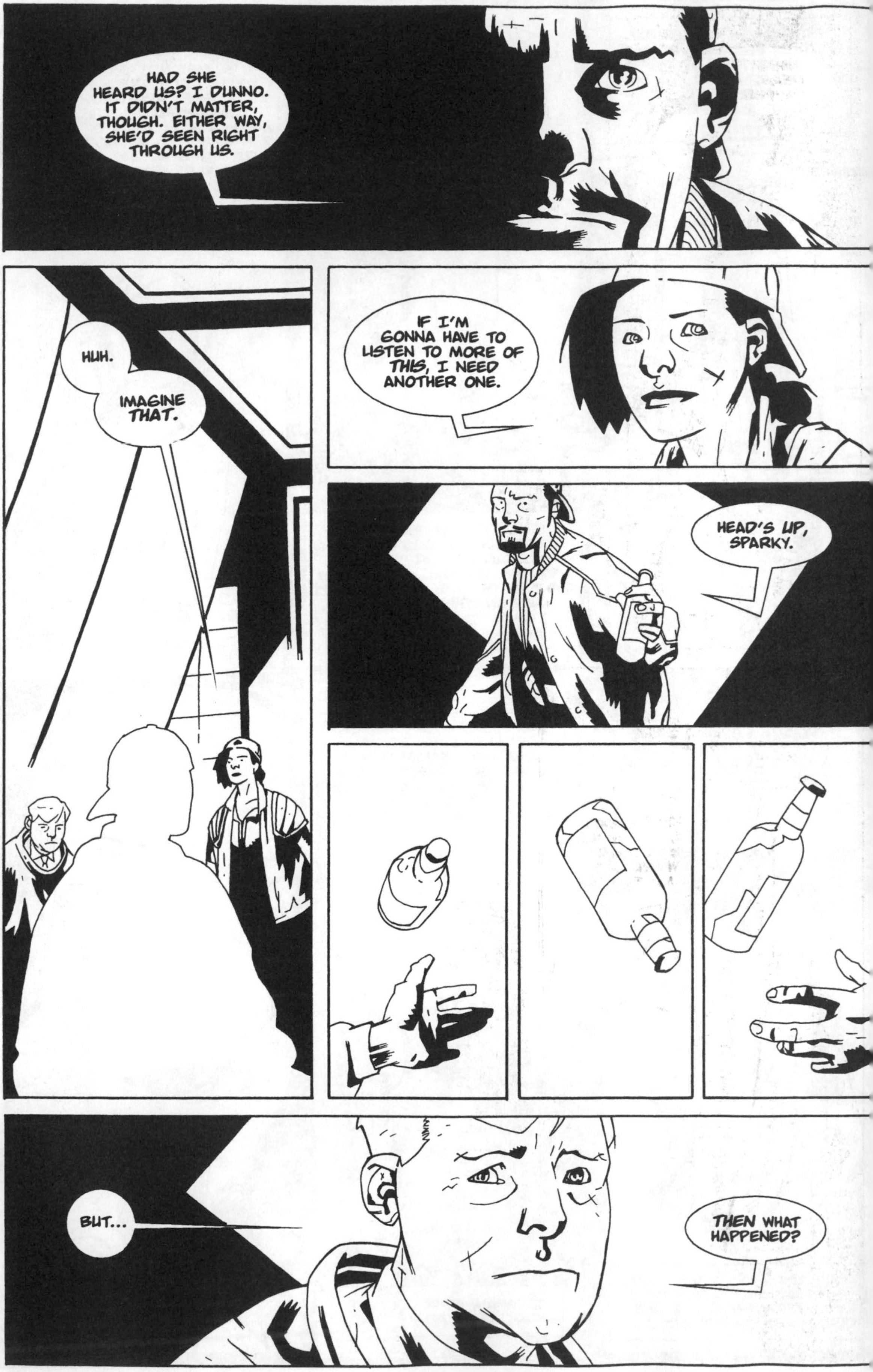
HAD SHE HEARD US? I DUNNO. IT DIDN'T MATTER, THOUGH. EITHER WAY, SHE'D SEEN RIGHT THROUGH US.
HUH.
IMAGINE THAT.
IF I'M GONNA HAVE TO LISTEN TO MORE OF THIS, I NEED ANOTHER ONE.
HEAD'S UP, SPARKY.
BUT...
THEN WHAT HAPPENED?

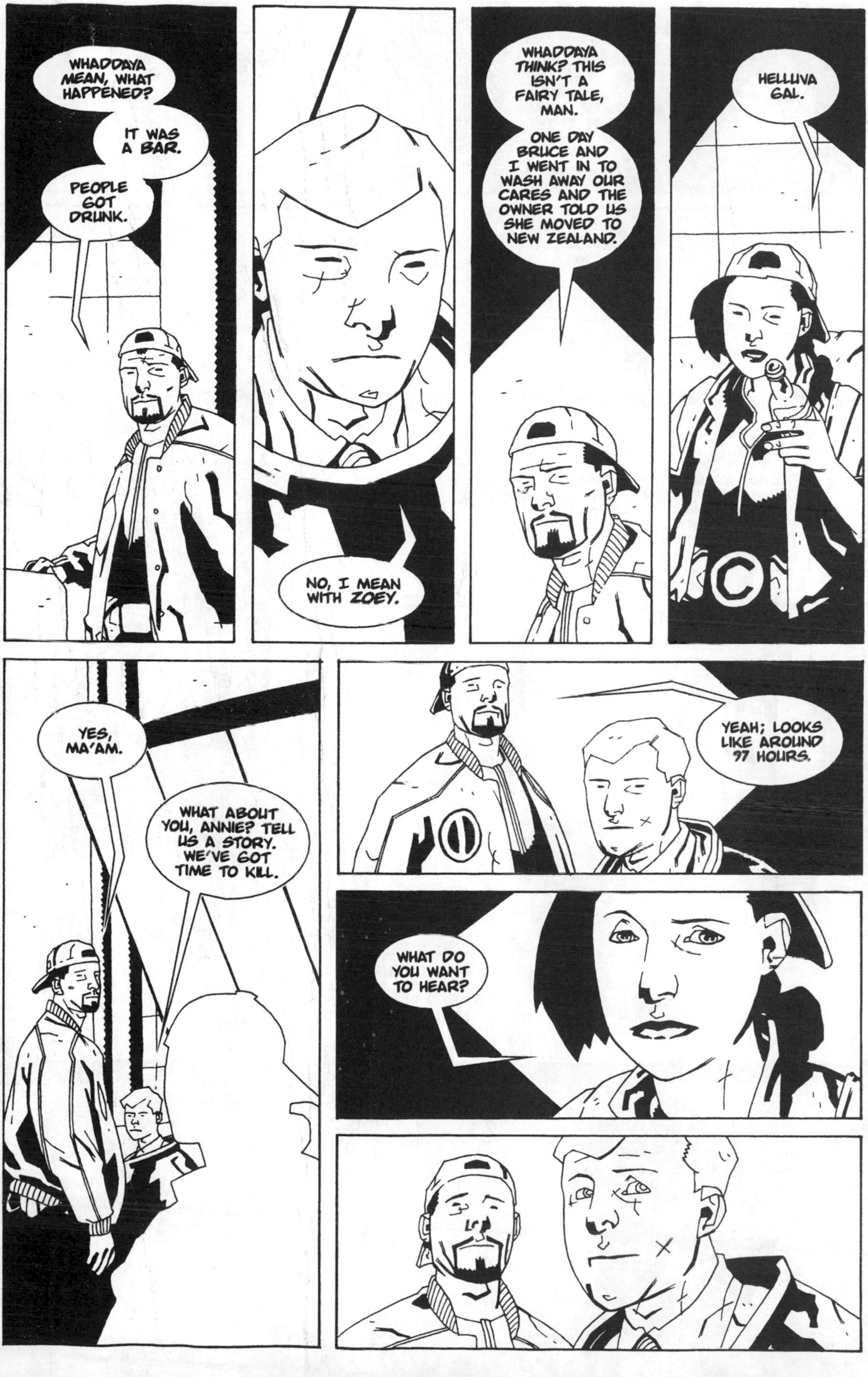
WHADDAYA MEAN, WHAT HAPPENED?
IT WAS A BAR.
PEOPLE GOT DRUNK.
NO, I MEAN WITH ZOEY.
WHADDAYA THINK? THIS ISN'T A FAIRY TALE, MAN.
ONE DAY BRUCE AND I WENT IN TO WASH AWAY OUR CARES AND THE OWNER TOLD US SHE MOVED TO NEW ZEALAND.
HELLUVA GAL.
YES, MA'AM.
WHAT ABOUT YOU, ANNIE? TELL US A STORY. WE'VE GOT TIME TO KILL.
YEAH; LOOKS LIKE AROUND 97 HOURS.
WHAT DO YOU WANT TO HEAR?

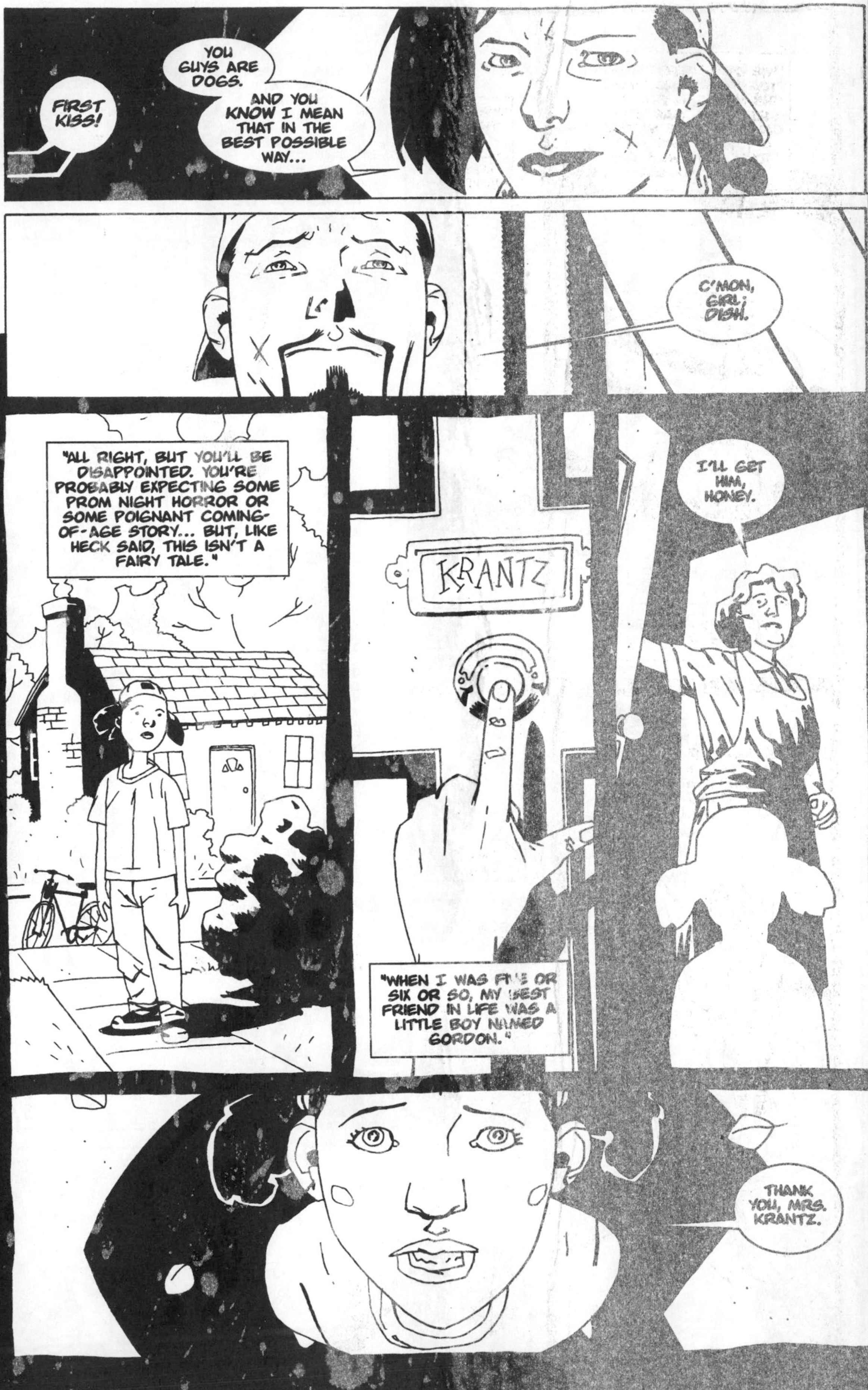
FIRST KISS!
YOU GUYS ARE DOGS.
AND YOU KNOW I MEAN THAT IN THE BEST POSSIBLE WAY...
C'MON, GIRL, DISH.
"ALL RIGHT, BUT YOU'LL BE DISAPPOINTED. YOU'RE PROBABLY EXPECTING SOME PROM NIGHT HORROR OR SOME POIGNANT COMING-OF-AGE STORY... BUT, LIKE HECK SAID, THIS ISN'T A FAIRY TALE."
KRANTZ
"WHEN I WAS FIVE OR SIX OR SO, MY BEST FRIEND IN LIFE WAS A LITTLE BOY NAMED GORDON."
I'LL GET HIM, HONEY.
THANK YOU, MRS. KRANTZ.

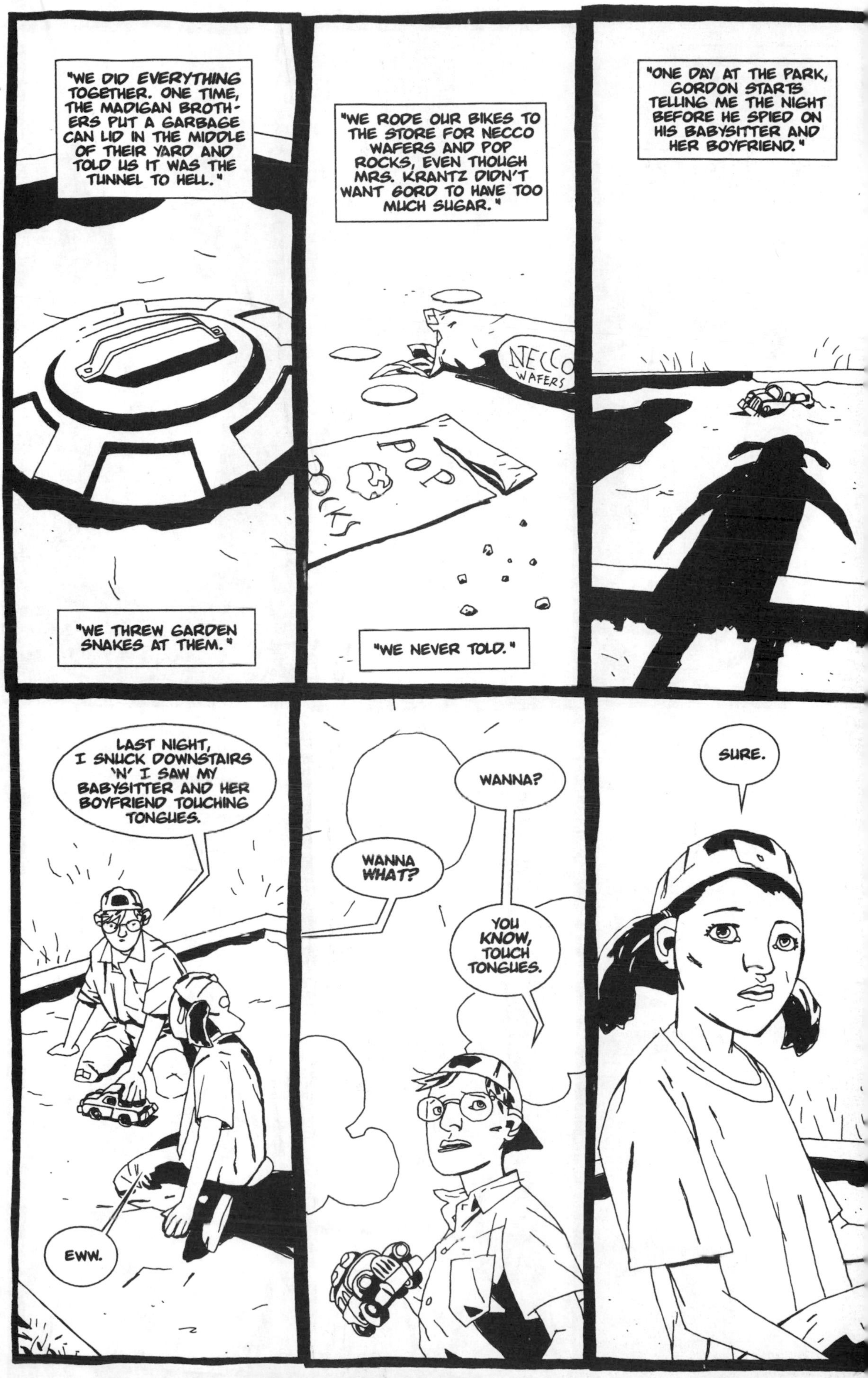
"WE DID EVERYTHING TOGETHER. ONE TIME, THE MADIGAN BROTH-ERS PUT A GARBAGE CAN LID IN THE MIDDLE OF THEIR YARD AND TOLD US IT WAS THE TUNNEL TO HELL."
"WE THREW GARDEN SNAKES AT THEM."
"WE RODE OUR BIKES TO THE STORE FOR NECCO WAFERS AND POP ROCKS, EVEN THOUGH MRS. KRANTZ DIDN'T WANT GORD TO HAVE TOO MUCH SUGAR."
NECCO WAFERS
POP ROCKS
"WE NEVER TOLD."
"ONE DAY AT THE PARK, GORDON STARTS TELLING ME THE NIGHT BEFORE HE SPIED ON HIS BABYSITTER AND HER BOYFRIEND."
LAST NIGHT, I SNUCK DOWNSTAIRS 'N' I SAW MY BABYSITTER AND HER BOYFRIEND TOUCHING TONGUES.
EWW.
WANNA?
WANNA WHAT?
YOU KNOW, TOUCH TONGUES.
SURE.

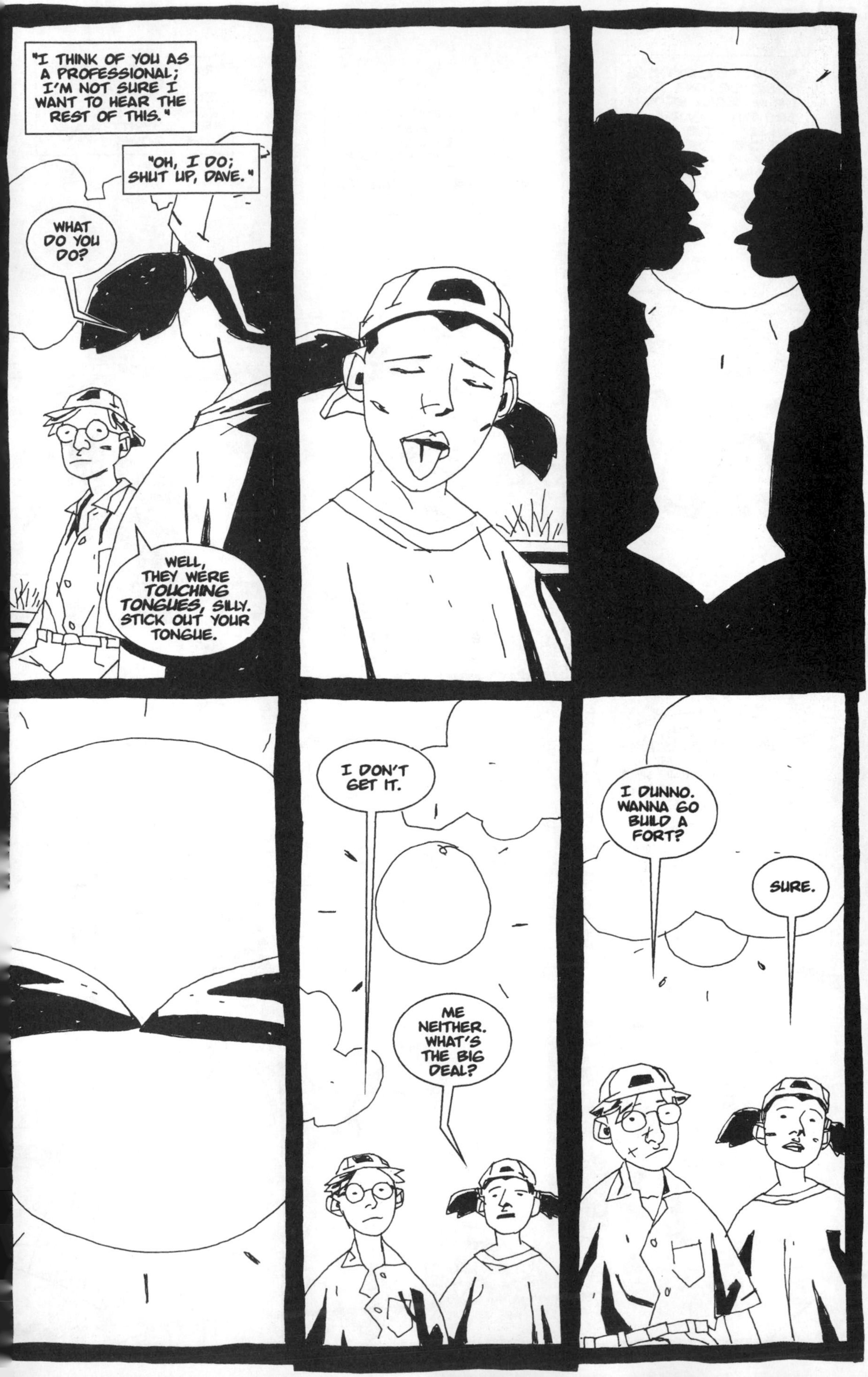
"I THINK OF YOU AS A PROFESSIONAL; I'M NOT SURE I WANT TO HEAR THE REST OF THIS."
"OH, I DO; SHUT UP, DAVE."
WHAT DO YOU DO?
WELL, THEY WERE TOUCHING TONGUES, SILLY. STICK OUT YOUR TONGUE.
I DON'T GET IT.
ME NEITHER. WHAT'S THE BIG DEAL?
I DUNNO. WANNA GO BUILD A FORT?
SURE.

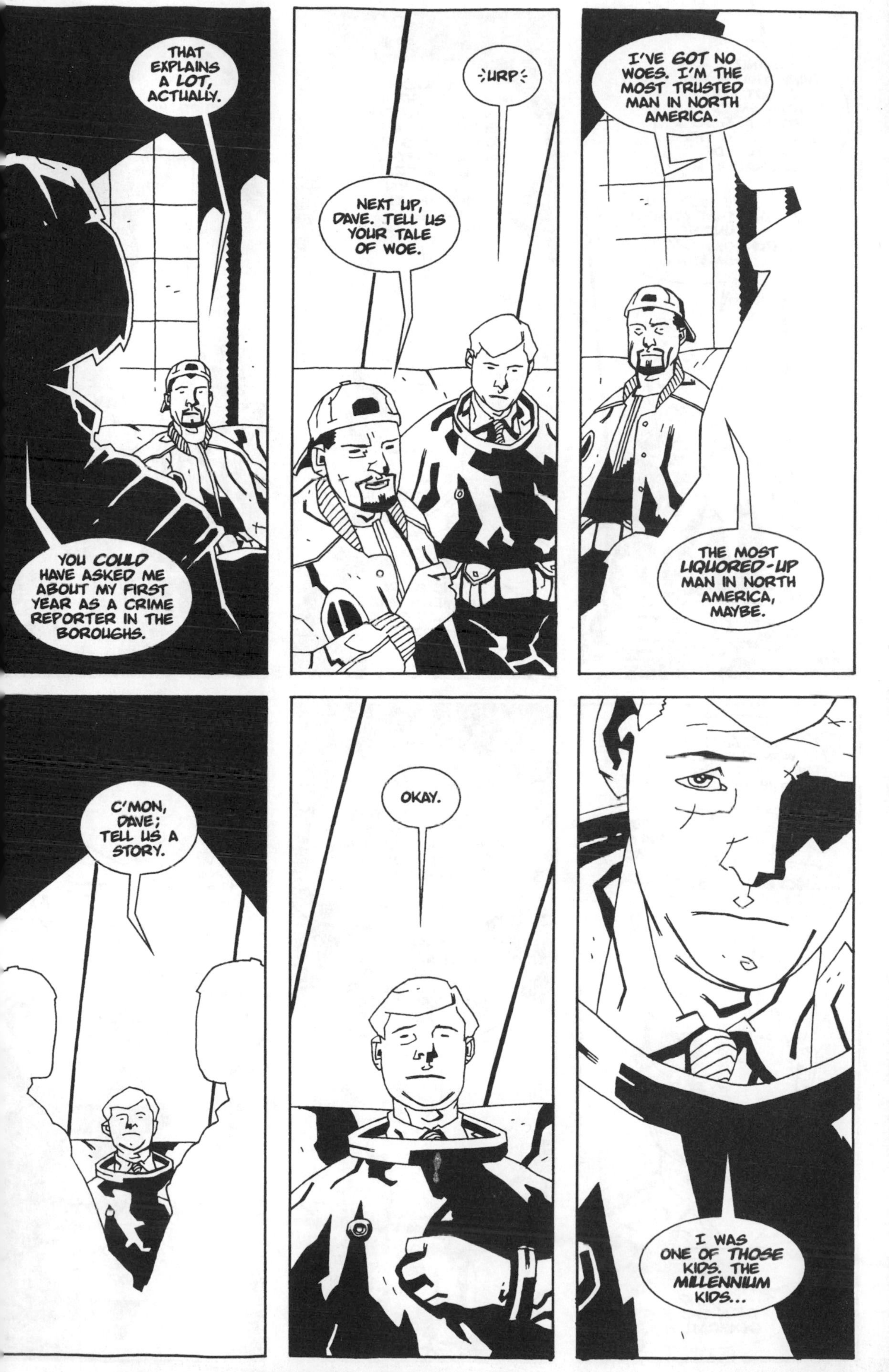
THAT EXPLAINS A LOT, ACTUALLY.
YOU COULD HAVE ASKED ME ABOUT MY FIRST YEAR AS A CRIME REPORTER IN THE BOROUGHS.
NEXT UP, DAVE. TELL US YOUR TALE OF WOE.
URP
I'VE GOT NO WOES. I'M THE MOST TRUSTED MAN IN NORTH AMERICA.
THE MOST LIQUORED-UP MAN IN NORTH AMERICA, MAYBE.
C'MON, DAVE; TELL US A STORY.
OKAY.
I WAS ONE OF THOSE KIDS. THE MILLENNIUM KIDS...

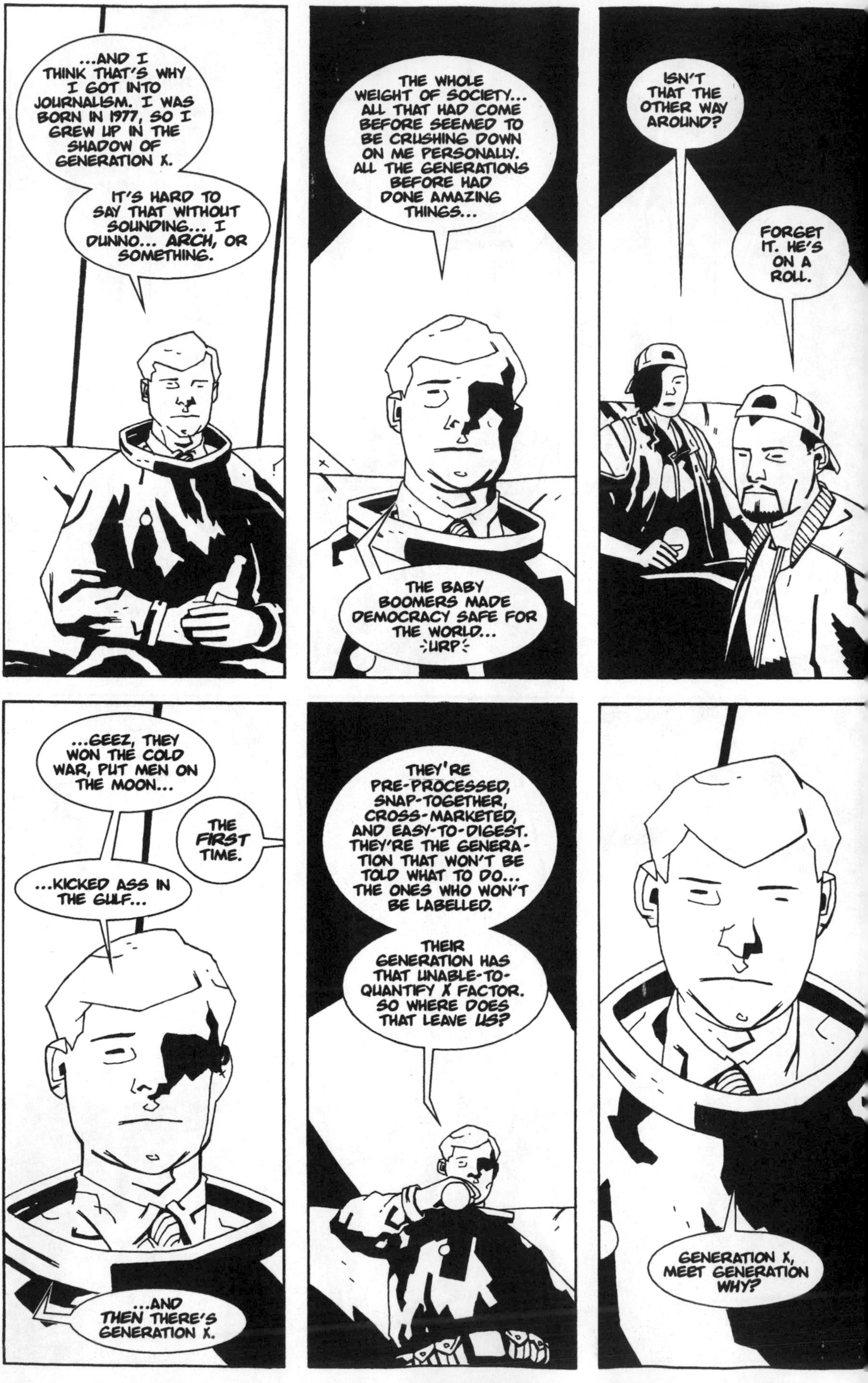
...AND I THINK THAT'S WHY I GOT INTO JOURNALISM. I WAS BORN IN 1977, SO I GREW UP IN THE SHADOW OF GENERATION X.
IT'S HARD TO SAY THAT WITHOUT SOUNDING... I DUNNO... ARCH, OR SOMETHING.
THE WHOLE WEIGHT OF SOCIETY... ALL THAT HAD COME BEFORE SEEMED TO BE CRUSHING DOWN ON ME PERSONALLY. ALL THE GENERATIONS BEFORE HAD DONE AMAZING THINGS...
THE BABY BOOMERS MADE DEMOCRACY SAFE FOR THE WORLD... URP
ISN'T THAT THE OTHER WAY AROUND?
FORGET IT. HE'S ON A ROLL.
...GEEZ, THEY WON THE COLD WAR, PUT MEN ON THE MOON...
THE FIRST TIME.
...KICKED ASS IN THE GULF...
...AND THEN THERE'S GENERATION X.
THEY'RE PRE-PROCESSED, SNAP-TOGETHER, CROSS-MARKETED, AND EASY-TO-DIGEST. THEY'RE THE GENERATION THAT WON'T BE TOLD WHAT TO DO... THE ONES WHO WON'T BE LABELLED.
THEIR GENERATION HAS THAT UNABLE-TO-QUANTIFY X FACTOR. SO WHERE DOES THAT LEAVE US?
GENERATION X, MEET GENERATION WHY?

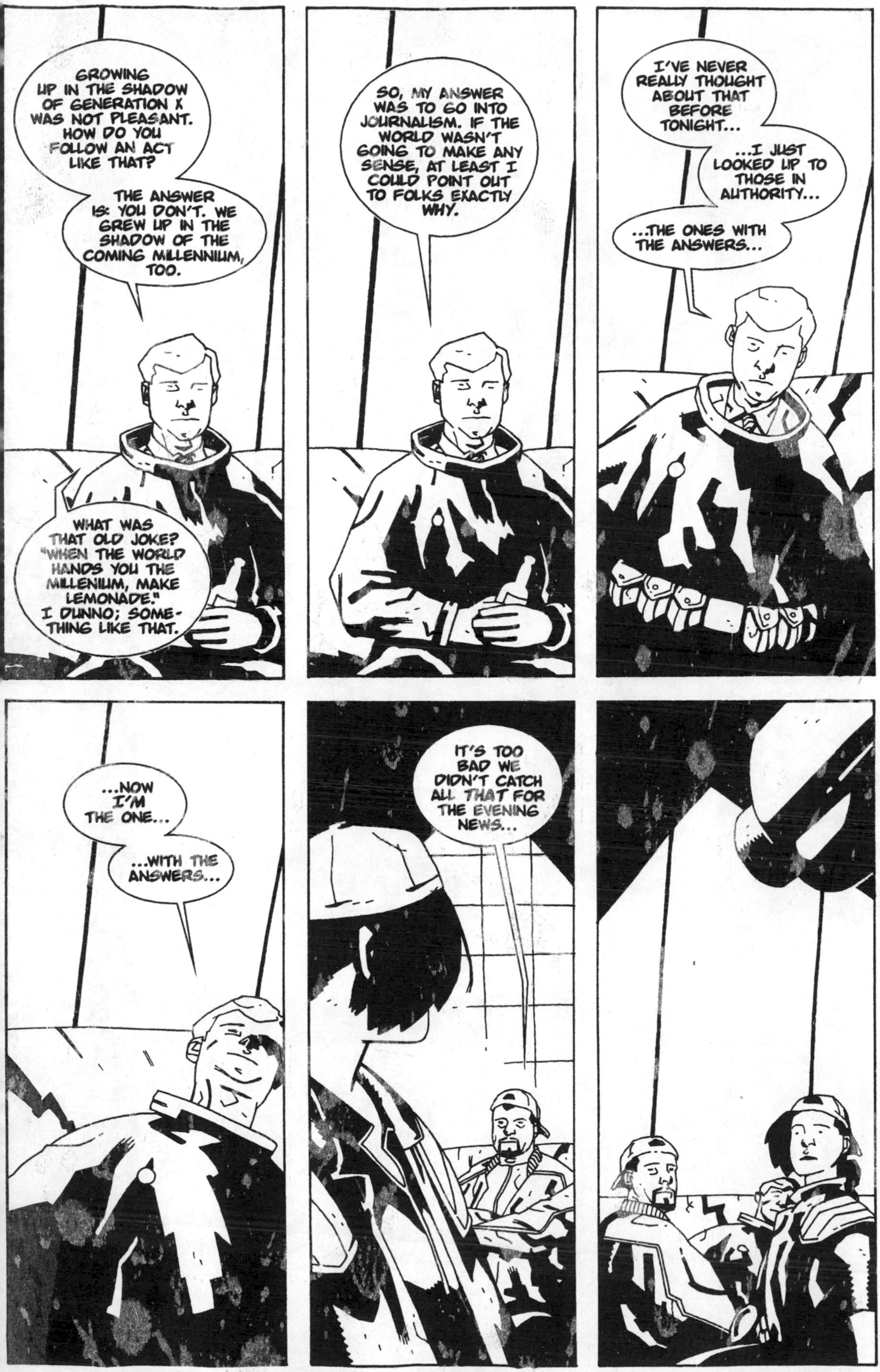

GROWING UP IN THE SHADOW OF GENERATION X WAS NOT PLEASANT. HOW DO YOU FOLLOW AN ACT LIKE THAT?
THE ANSWER IS: YOU DON'T. WE GREW UP IN THE SHADOW OF THE COMING MILLENNIUM, TOO.
WHAT WAS THAT OLD JOKE? "WHEN THE WORLD HANDS YOU THE MILLENIUM, MAKE LEMONADE." I DUNNO; SOMETHING LIKE THAT.
SO, MY ANSWER WAS TO GO INTO JOURNALISM. IF THE WORLD WASN'T GOING TO MAKE ANY SENSE, AT LEAST I COULD POINT OUT TO FOLKS EXACTLY WHY.
I'VE NEVER REALLY THOUGHT ABOUT THAT BEFORE TONIGHT...
...I JUST LOOKED UP TO THOSE IN AUTHORITY...
...THE ONES WITH THE ANSWERS...
...NOW I'M THE ONE...
...WITH THE ANSWERS...
IT'S TOO BAD WE DIDN'T CATCH ALL *THAT* FOR THE EVENING NEWS...

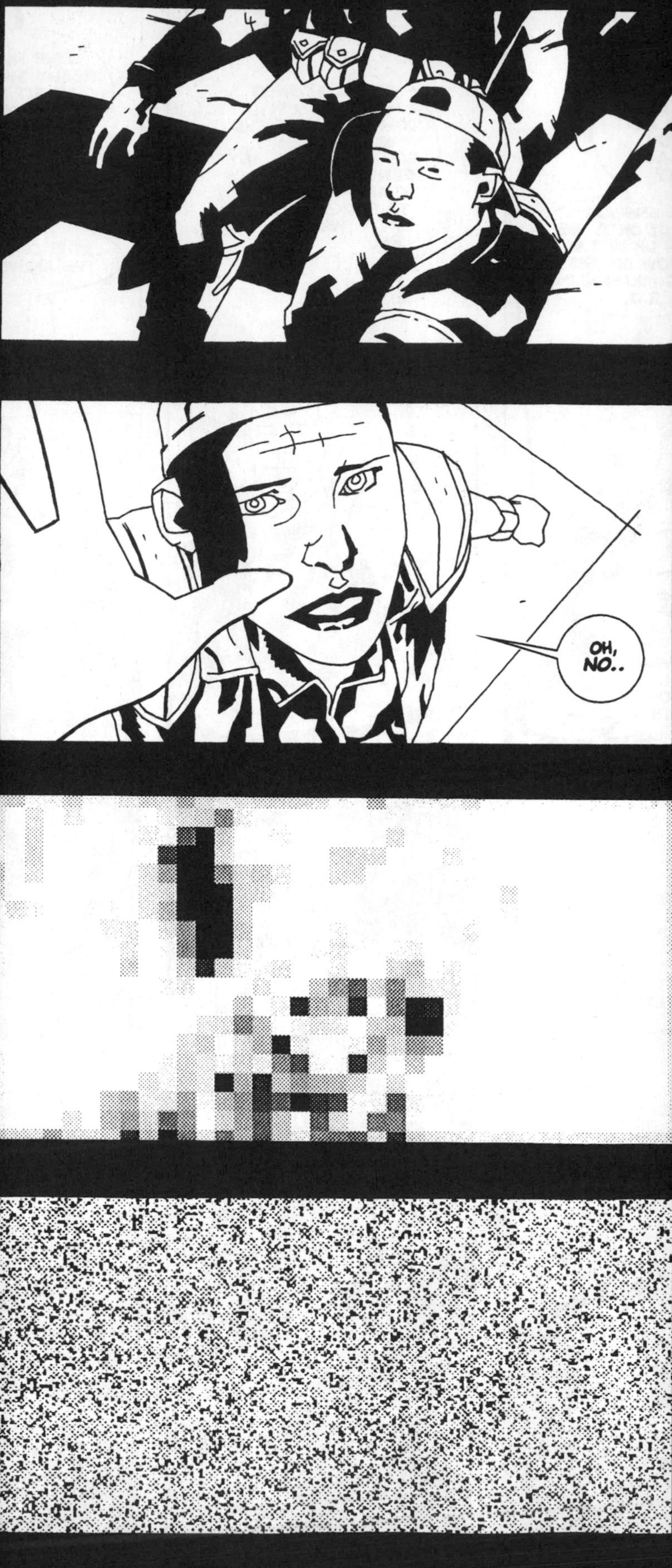
OH, NO..

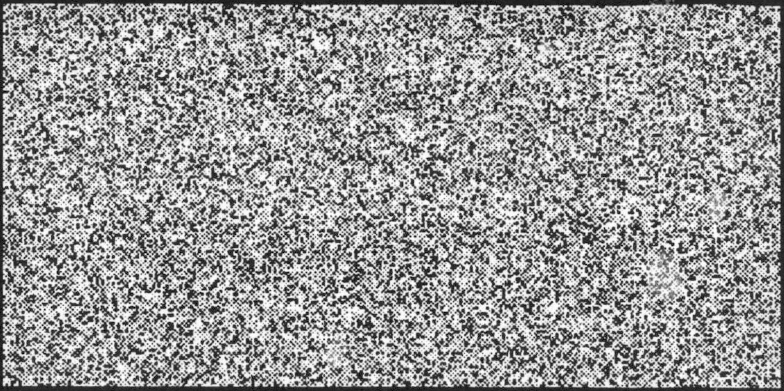

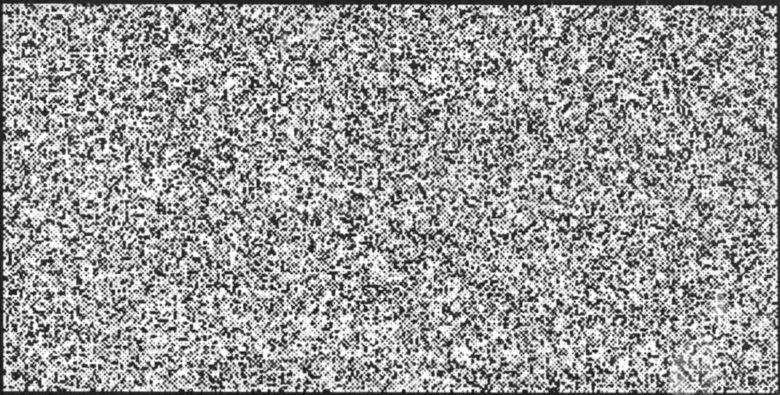

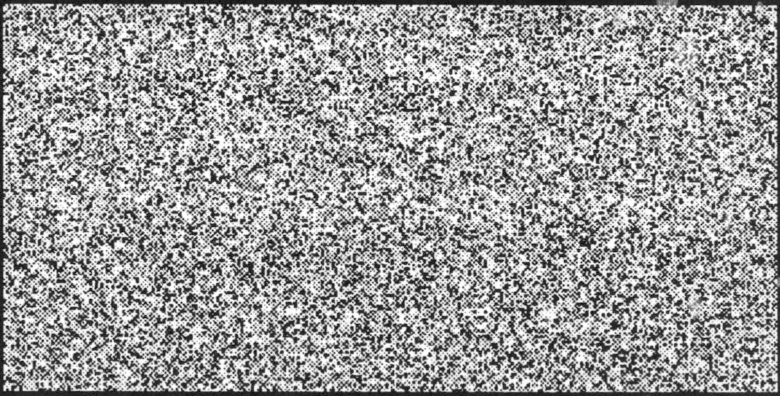

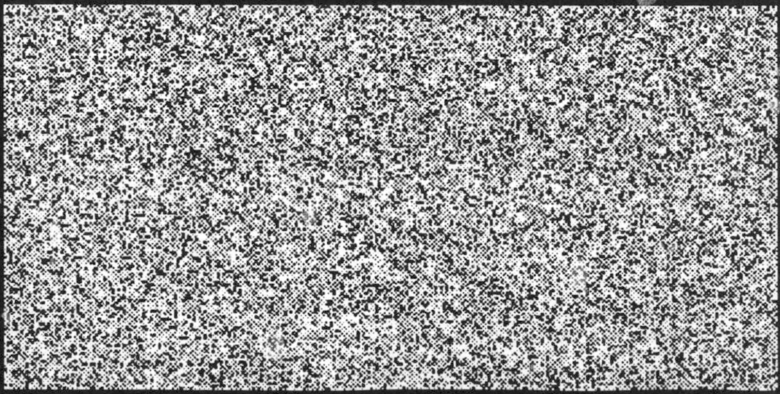

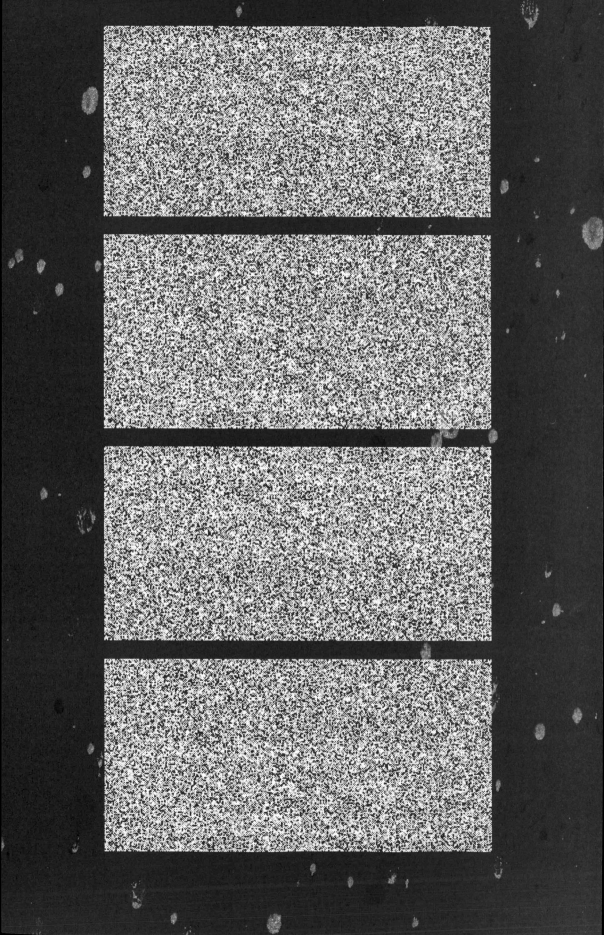

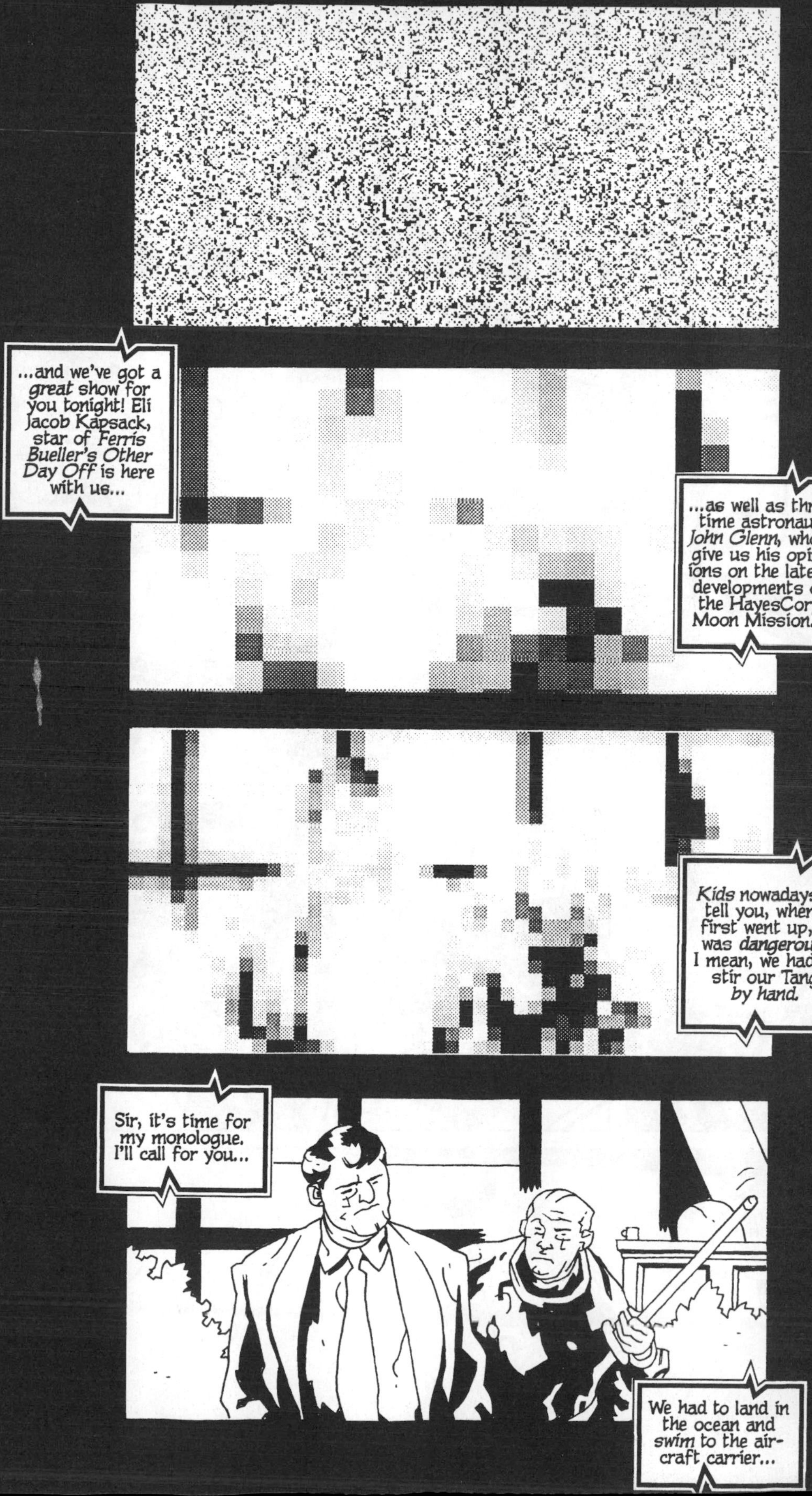
...and we've got a *great* show for you tonight! Eli Jacob Kapsack, star of *Ferris Bueller's Other Day Off* is here with us...
...as well as three time astronaut *John Glenn*, who'll give us his opinions on the latest developments of the HayesCorp Moon Mission...
Kids nowadays. I tell you, when *I* first went up, it was *dangerous.* I mean, we had to stir our Tang *by hand.*
Sir, it's time for my monologue. I'll call for you...
We had to land in the ocean and *swim* to the aircraft carrier...

TURN IT OFF, YOU TWO.

BUT, ANNIE, JOHN GLENN IS ON LENO TO TALK ABOUT US.

GET OFF THE TELEVISION, DAVE. WE NEED THE ANTENNA TO CONTACT HAYES.

BETWEEN ALL THE BLASTING-OUT-AHEAD-OF-SCHEDULE...

...THE IN-FLIGHT COURSE CORRECTIONS AND DAVE'S INCESSANT SNORING...

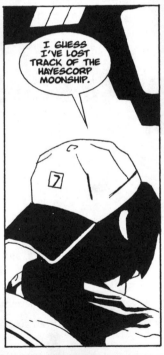

I GUESS I'VE LOST TRACK OF THE HAYESCORP MOONSHIP.

C'MON, C'MON, PAY UP.

DOUBLE OR NOTHING?

I DON'T THINK SO.

YOU GUYS JUST DON'T GET IT, DO YOU...?

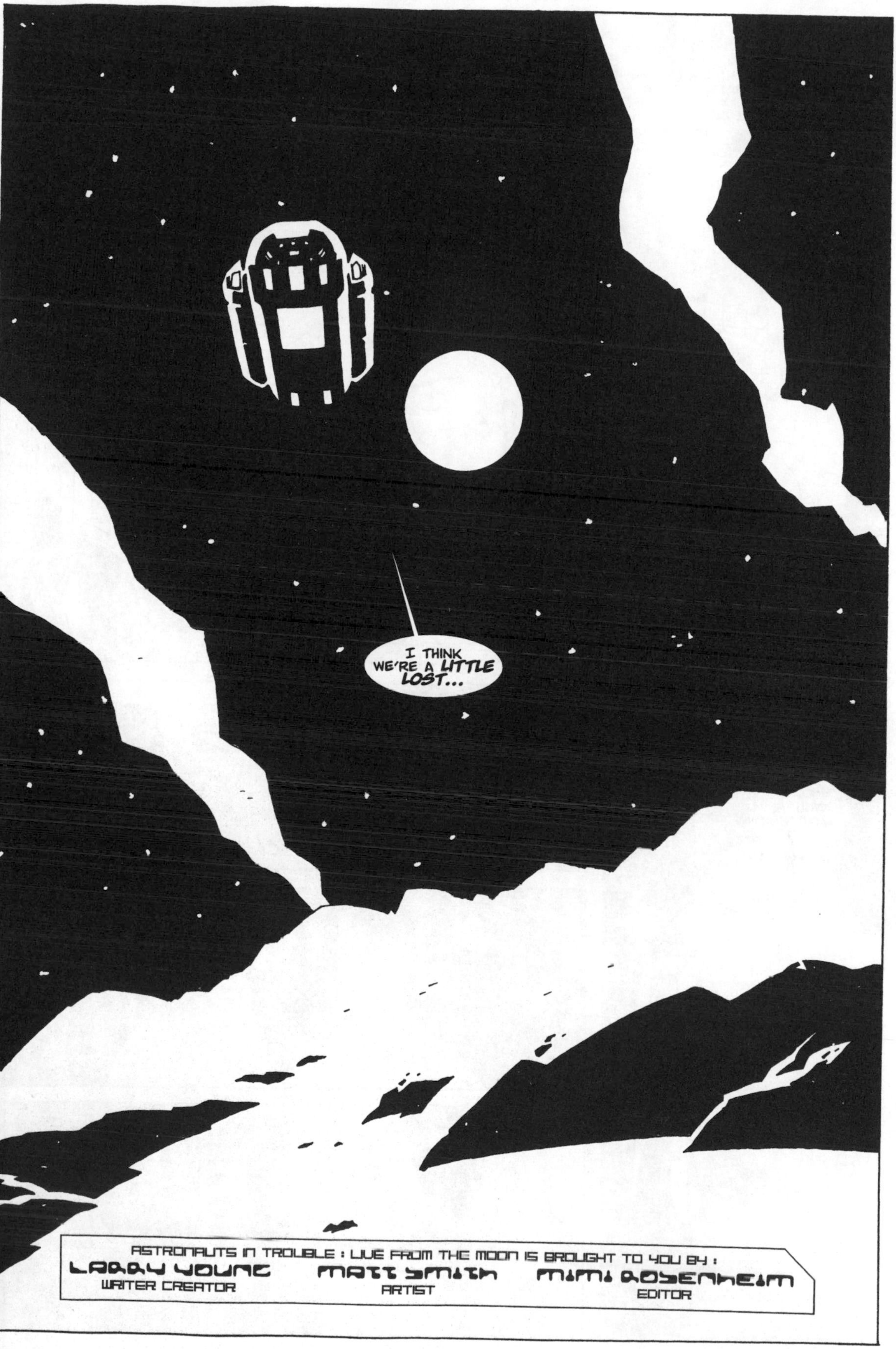
I THINK WE'RE A LITTLE LOST...
ASTRONAUTS IN TROUBLE : LIVE FROM THE MOON IS BROUGHT TO YOU BY :
LARRY YOUNG
WRITER CREATOR
MATT SMITH
ARTIST
MIMI ROSENHEIM
EDITOR

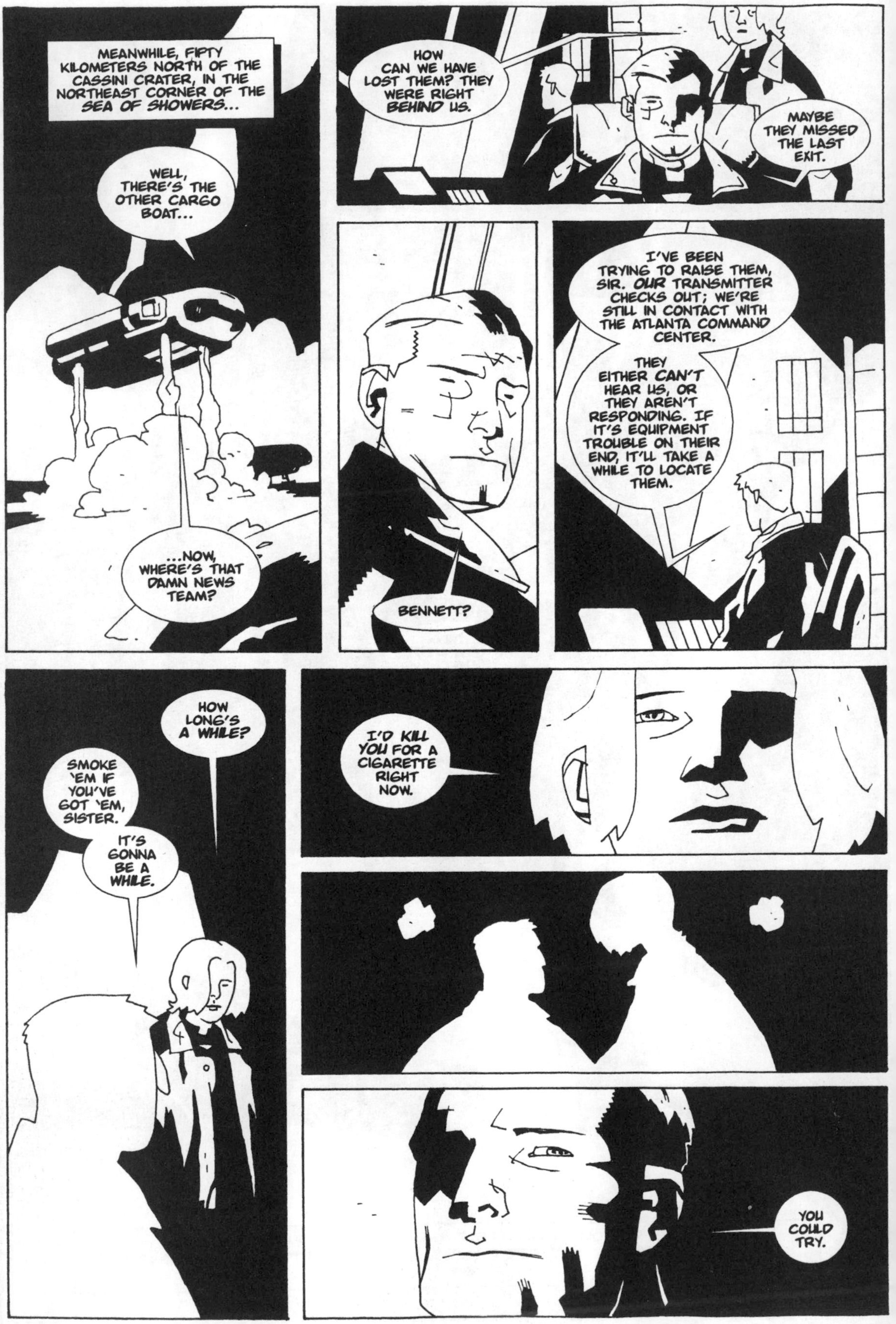
MEANWHILE, FIFTY KILOMETERS NORTH OF THE CASSINI CRATER, IN THE NORTHEAST CORNER OF THE SEA OF SHOWERS...
WELL, THERE'S THE OTHER CARGO BOAT...
...NOW, WHERE'S THAT DAMN NEWS TEAM?
HOW CAN WE HAVE LOST THEM? THEY WERE RIGHT BEHIND US.
MAYBE THEY MISSED THE LAST EXIT.
BENNETT?
I'VE BEEN TRYING TO RAISE THEM, SIR. OUR TRANSMITTER CHECKS OUT; WE'RE STILL IN CONTACT WITH THE ATLANTA COMMAND CENTER.
THEY EITHER CAN'T HEAR US, OR THEY AREN'T RESPONDING. IF IT'S EQUIPMENT TROUBLE ON THEIR END, IT'LL TAKE A WHILE TO LOCATE THEM.
HOW LONG'S A WHILE?
SMOKE 'EM IF YOU'VE GOT 'EM, SISTER.
IT'S GONNA BE A WHILE.
I'D KILL YOU FOR A CIGARETTE RIGHT NOW.
YOU COULD TRY.

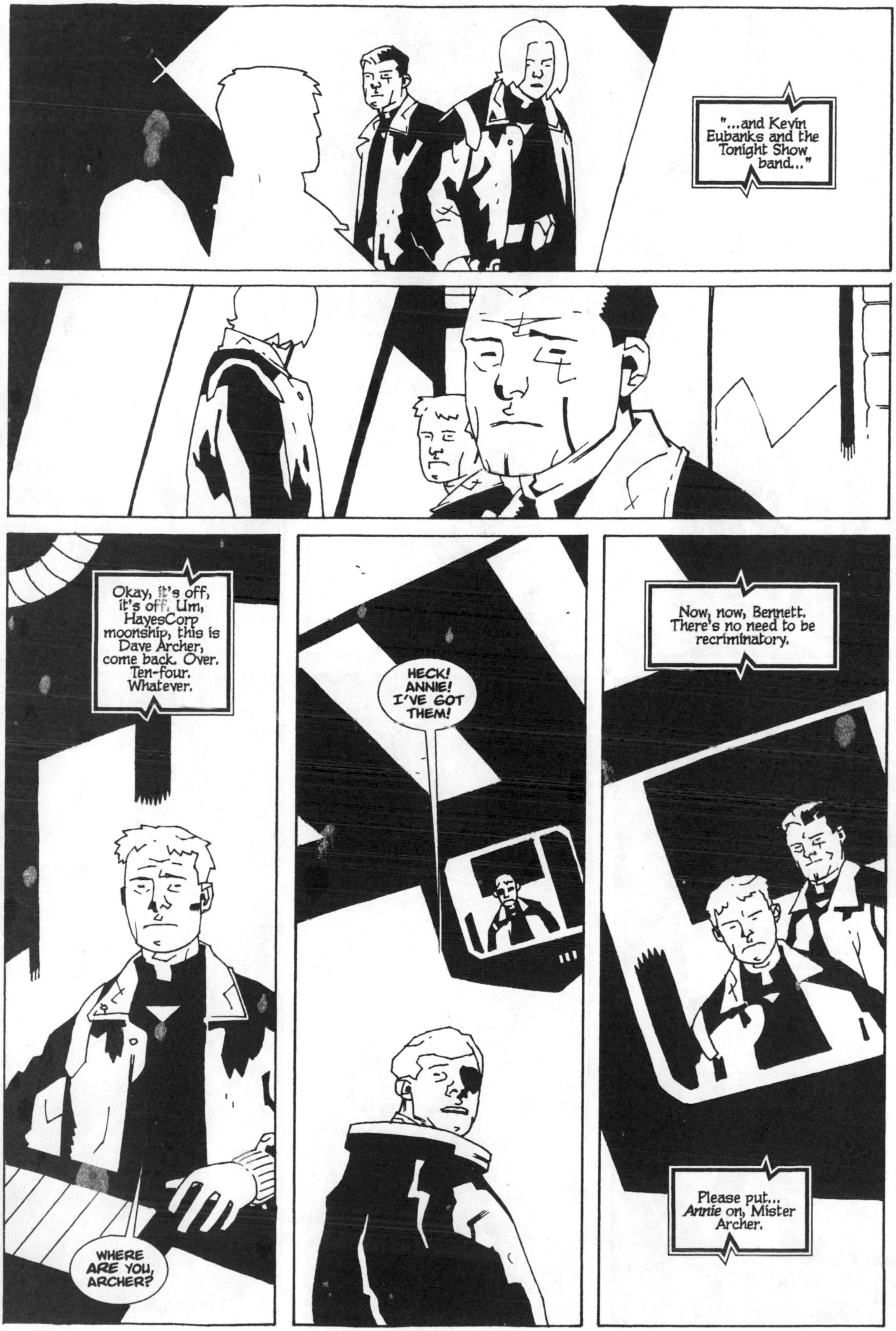

"...and Kevin Eubanks and the Tonight Show band..."
Okay, it's off, it's off. Um, HayesCorp moonship, this is Dave Archer, come back. Over. Ten-four. Whatever.
WHERE ARE YOU, ARCHER?
HECK! ANNIE! I'VE GOT THEM!
Now, now, Bennett. There's no need to be recriminatory.
Please put... *Annie* on, Mister Archer.

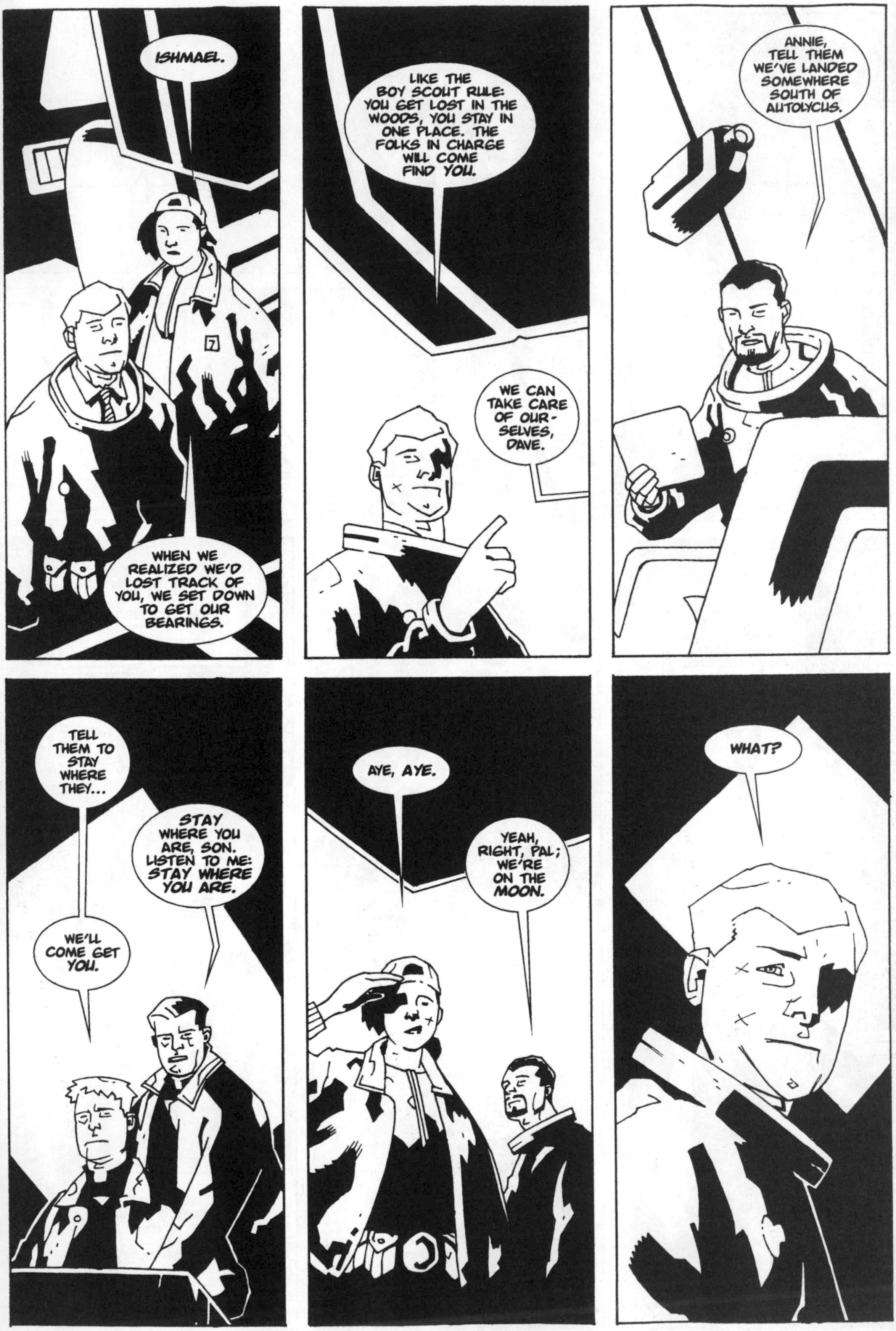
ISHMAEL.
WHEN WE REALIZED WE'D LOST TRACK OF YOU, WE SET DOWN TO GET OUR BEARINGS.
LIKE THE BOY SCOUT RULE: YOU GET LOST IN THE WOODS, YOU STAY IN ONE PLACE. THE FOLKS IN CHARGE WILL COME FIND YOU.
WE CAN TAKE CARE OF OUR-SELVES, DAVE.
ANNIE, TELL THEM WE'VE LANDED SOMEWHERE SOUTH OF AUTOLYCUS.
TELL THEM TO STAY WHERE THEY...
STAY WHERE YOU ARE, SON. LISTEN TO ME: STAY WHERE YOU ARE.
WE'LL COME GET YOU.
AYE, AYE.
YEAH, RIGHT, PAL; WE'RE ON THE MOON.
WHAT?

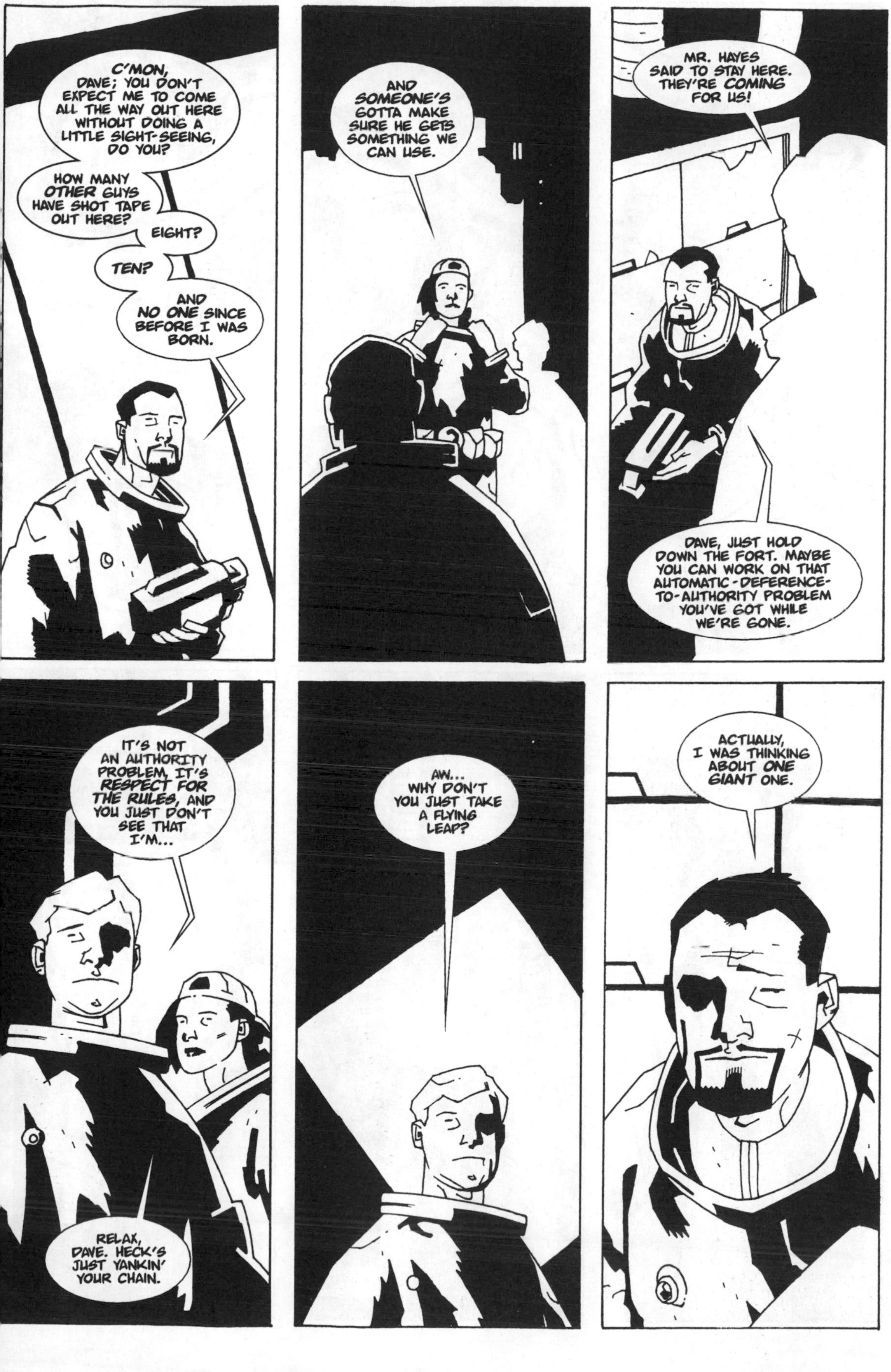
C'MON, DAVE; YOU DON'T EXPECT ME TO COME ALL THE WAY OUT HERE WITHOUT DOING A LITTLE SIGHT-SEEING, DO YOU?
HOW MANY OTHER GUYS HAVE SHOT TAPE OUT HERE?
EIGHT?
TEN?
AND NO ONE SINCE BEFORE I WAS BORN.
AND SOMEONE'S GOTTA MAKE SURE HE GETS SOMETHING WE CAN USE.
MR. HAYES SAID TO STAY HERE. THEY'RE COMING FOR US!
DAVE, JUST HOLD DOWN THE FORT. MAYBE YOU CAN WORK ON THAT AUTOMATIC-DEFERENCE-TO-AUTHORITY PROBLEM YOU'VE GOT WHILE WE'RE GONE.
IT'S NOT AN AUTHORITY PROBLEM, IT'S RESPECT FOR THE RULES, AND YOU JUST DON'T SEE THAT I'M...
RELAX, DAVE. HECK'S JUST YANKIN' YOUR CHAIN.
AW... WHY DON'T YOU JUST TAKE A FLYING LEAP?
ACTUALLY, I WAS THINKING ABOUT ONE GIANT ONE.

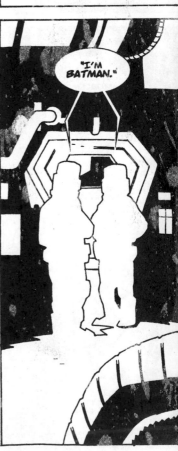

"I'M BATMAN."

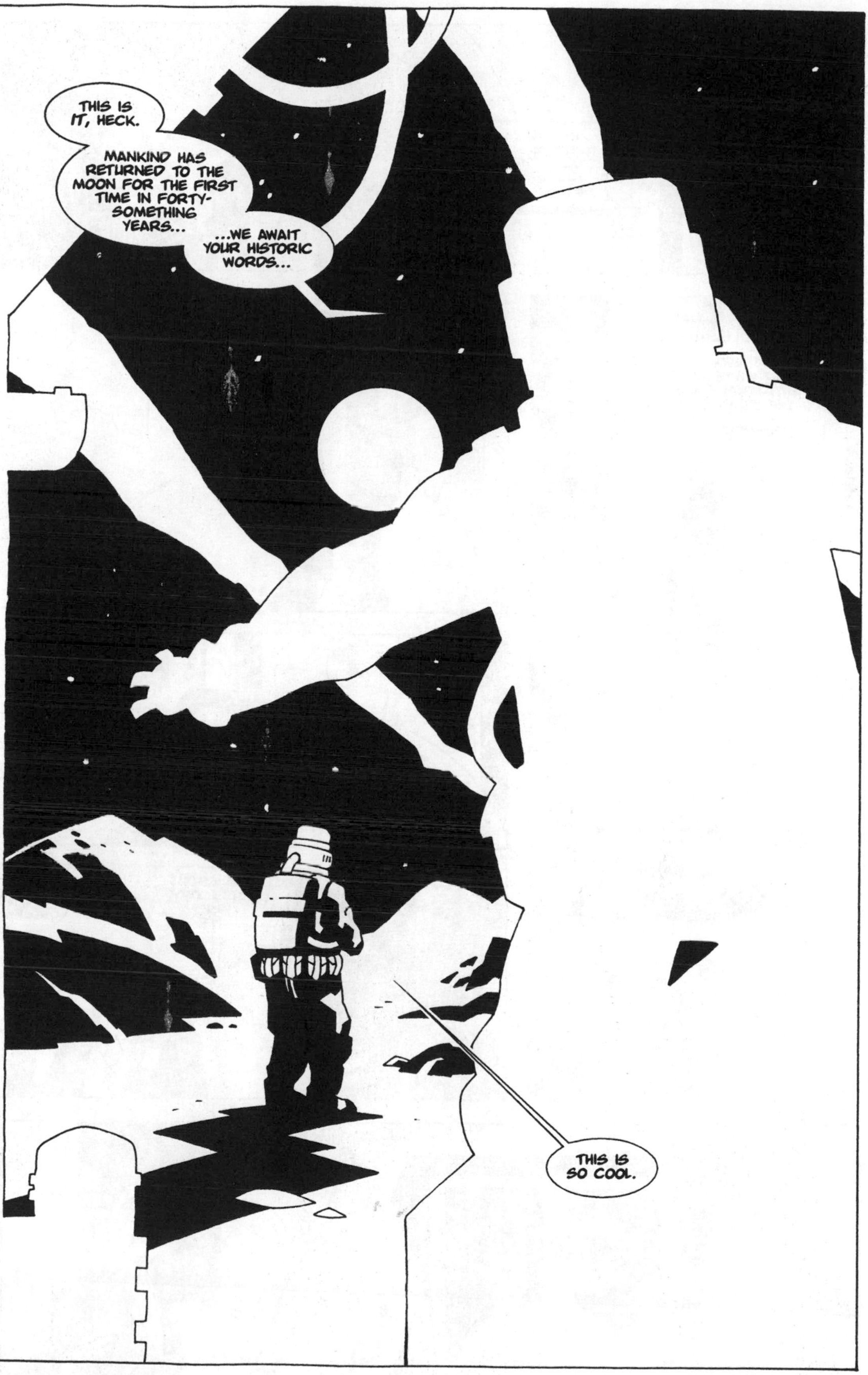
THIS IS IT, HECK.
MANKIND HAS RETURNED TO THE MOON FOR THE FIRST TIME IN FORTY-SOMETHING YEARS...
...WE AWAIT YOUR HISTORIC WORDS...
THIS IS SO COOL.

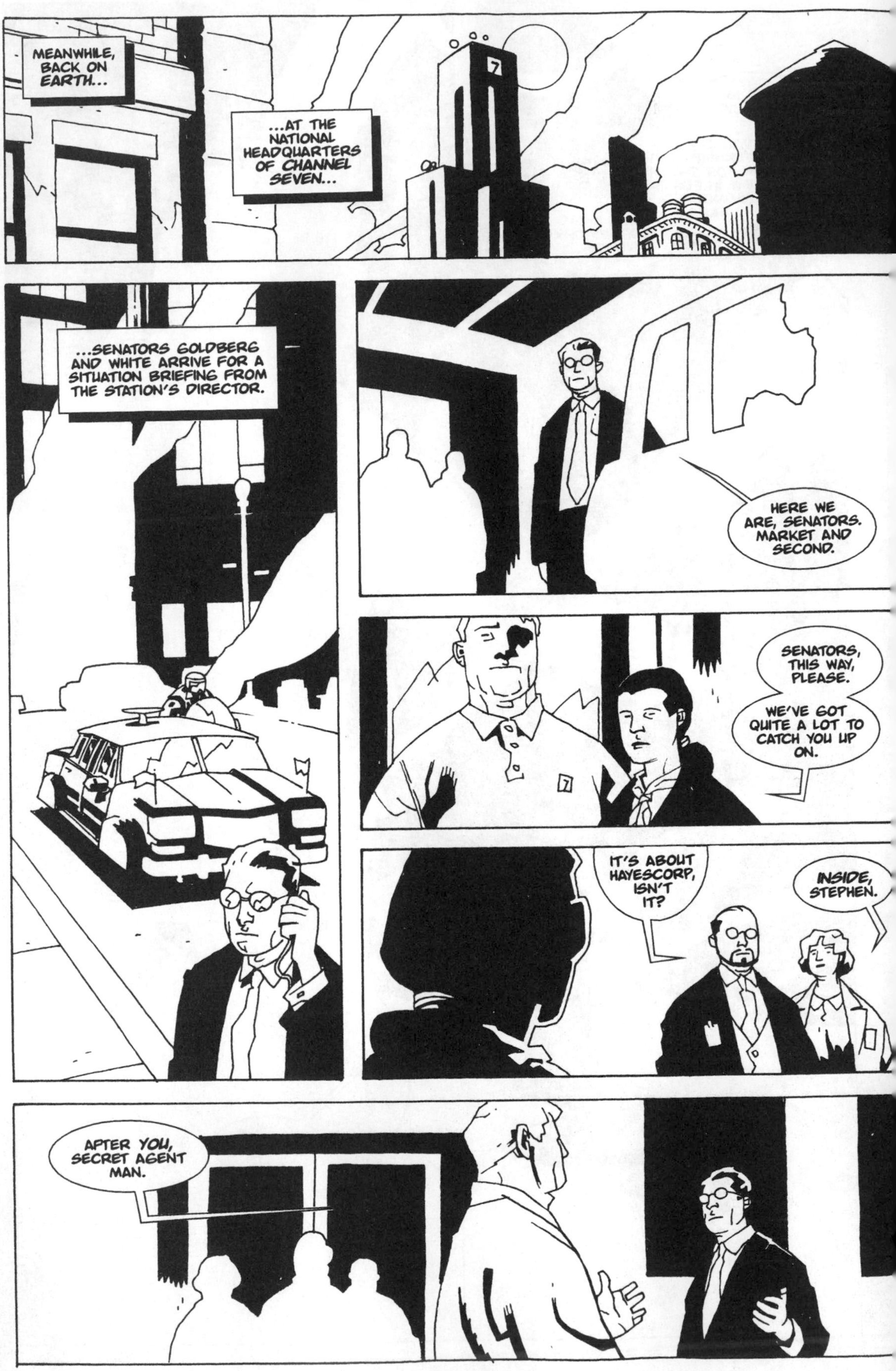
MEANWHILE, BACK ON EARTH...
...AT THE NATIONAL HEADQUARTERS OF CHANNEL SEVEN...
7
...SENATORS GOLDBERG AND WHITE ARRIVE FOR A SITUATION BRIEFING FROM THE STATION'S DIRECTOR.
HERE WE ARE, SENATORS. MARKET AND SECOND.
SENATORS, THIS WAY, PLEASE.
WE'VE GOT QUITE A LOT TO CATCH YOU UP ON.
IT'S ABOUT HAYESCORP, ISN'T IT?
INSIDE, STEPHEN.
AFTER YOU, SECRET AGENT MAN.

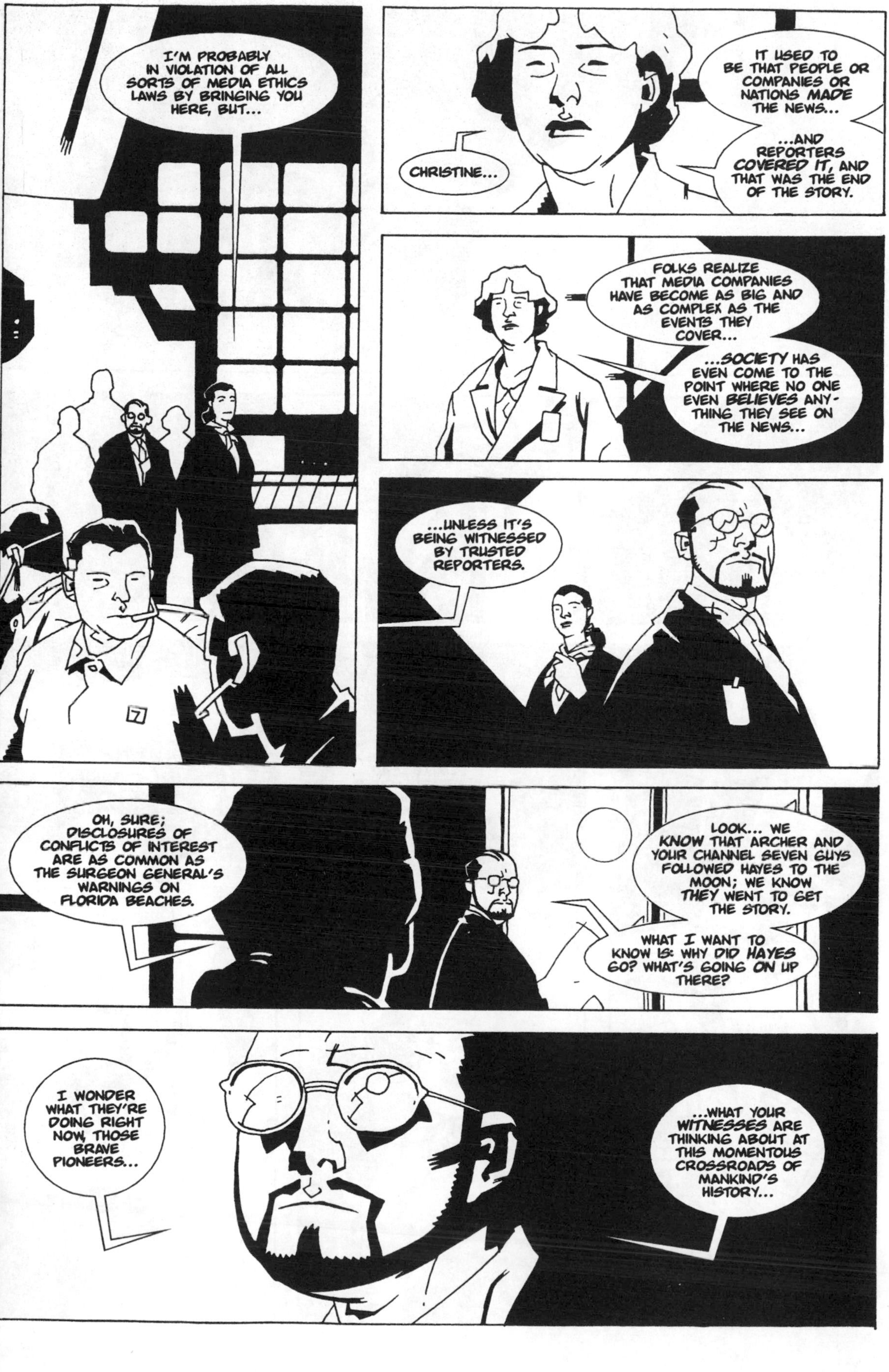
I'M PROBABLY IN VIOLATION OF ALL SORTS OF MEDIA ETHICS LAWS BY BRINGING YOU HERE, BUT...
CHRISTINE...
IT USED TO BE THAT PEOPLE OR COMPANIES OR NATIONS MADE THE NEWS...
...AND REPORTERS COVERED IT, AND THAT WAS THE END OF THE STORY.
FOLKS REALIZE THAT MEDIA COMPANIES HAVE BECOME AS BIG AND AS COMPLEX AS THE EVENTS THEY COVER...
...SOCIETY HAS EVEN COME TO THE POINT WHERE NO ONE EVEN BELIEVES ANY-THING THEY SEE ON THE NEWS...
...UNLESS IT'S BEING WITNESSED BY TRUSTED REPORTERS.
OH, SURE; DISCLOSURES OF CONFLICTS OF INTEREST ARE AS COMMON AS THE SURGEON GENERAL'S WARNINGS ON FLORIDA BEACHES.
LOOK... WE KNOW THAT ARCHER AND YOUR CHANNEL SEVEN GUYS FOLLOWED HAYES TO THE MOON; WE KNOW THEY WENT TO GET THE STORY.
WHAT I WANT TO KNOW IS: WHY DID HAYES GO? WHAT'S GOING ON UP THERE?
I WONDER WHAT THEY'RE DOING RIGHT NOW, THOSE BRAVE PIONEERS...
...WHAT YOUR WITNESSES ARE THINKING ABOUT AT THIS MOMENTOUS CROSSROADS OF MANKIND'S HISTORY...

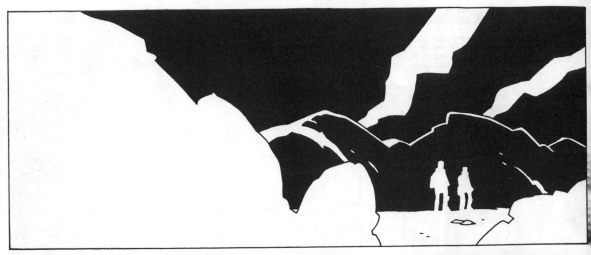

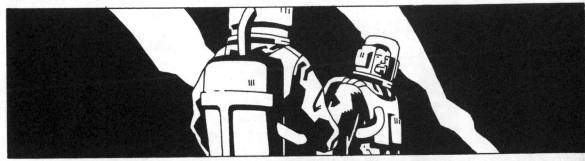

THE THING I HATE MOST ABOUT LOW-BUDGET BARBARIAN MOVIES...

...IS THAT THE FEMALE LEAD INVARIABLY LOOKS LIKE A CALIFORNIA WAITRESS...

...IN A LEATHER BIKINI.

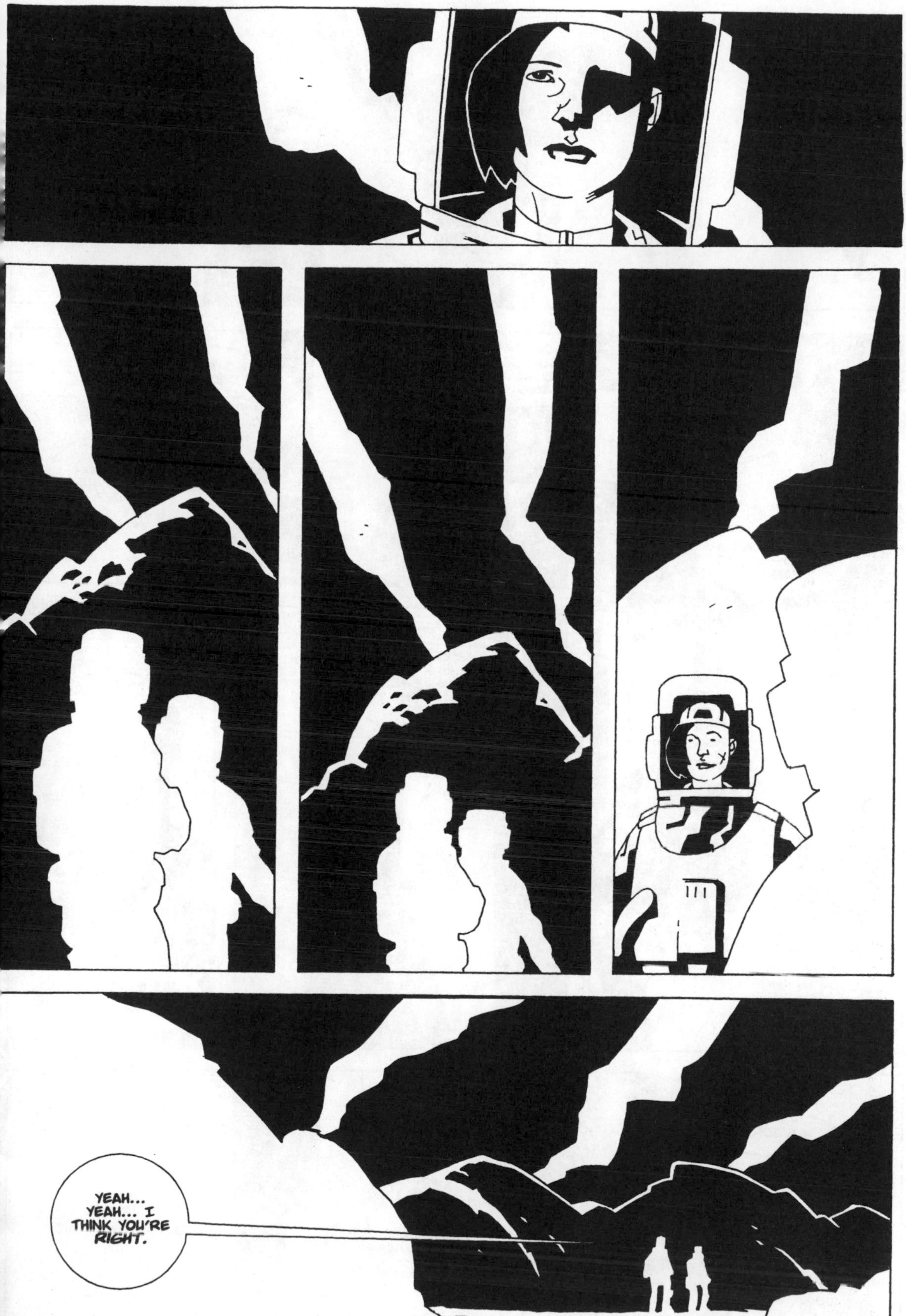
YEAH... YEAH... I THINK YOU'RE RIGHT.

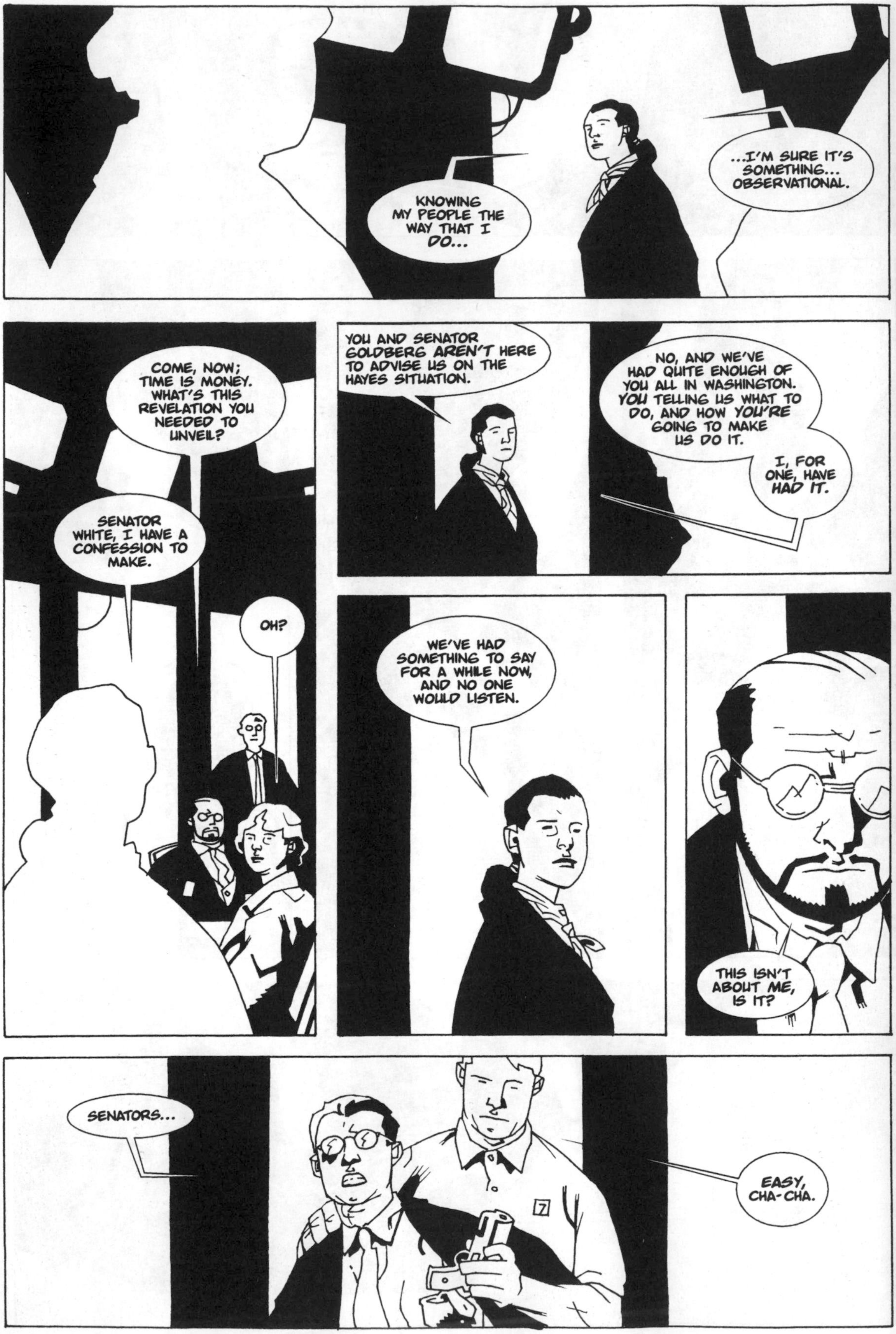
KNOWING MY PEOPLE THE WAY THAT I DO...
...I'M SURE IT'S SOMETHING... OBSERVATIONAL.
COME, NOW; TIME IS MONEY. WHAT'S THIS REVELATION YOU NEEDED TO UNVEIL?
SENATOR WHITE, I HAVE A CONFESSION TO MAKE.
OH?
YOU AND SENATOR GOLDBERG AREN'T HERE TO ADVISE US ON THE HAYES SITUATION.
NO, AND WE'VE HAD QUITE ENOUGH OF YOU ALL IN WASHINGTON. YOU TELLING US WHAT TO DO, AND HOW YOU'RE GOING TO MAKE US DO IT.
I, FOR ONE, HAVE HAD IT.
WE'VE HAD SOMETHING TO SAY FOR A WHILE NOW, AND NO ONE WOULD LISTEN.
THIS ISN'T ABOUT ME, IS IT?
SENATORS...
EASY, CHA-CHA.

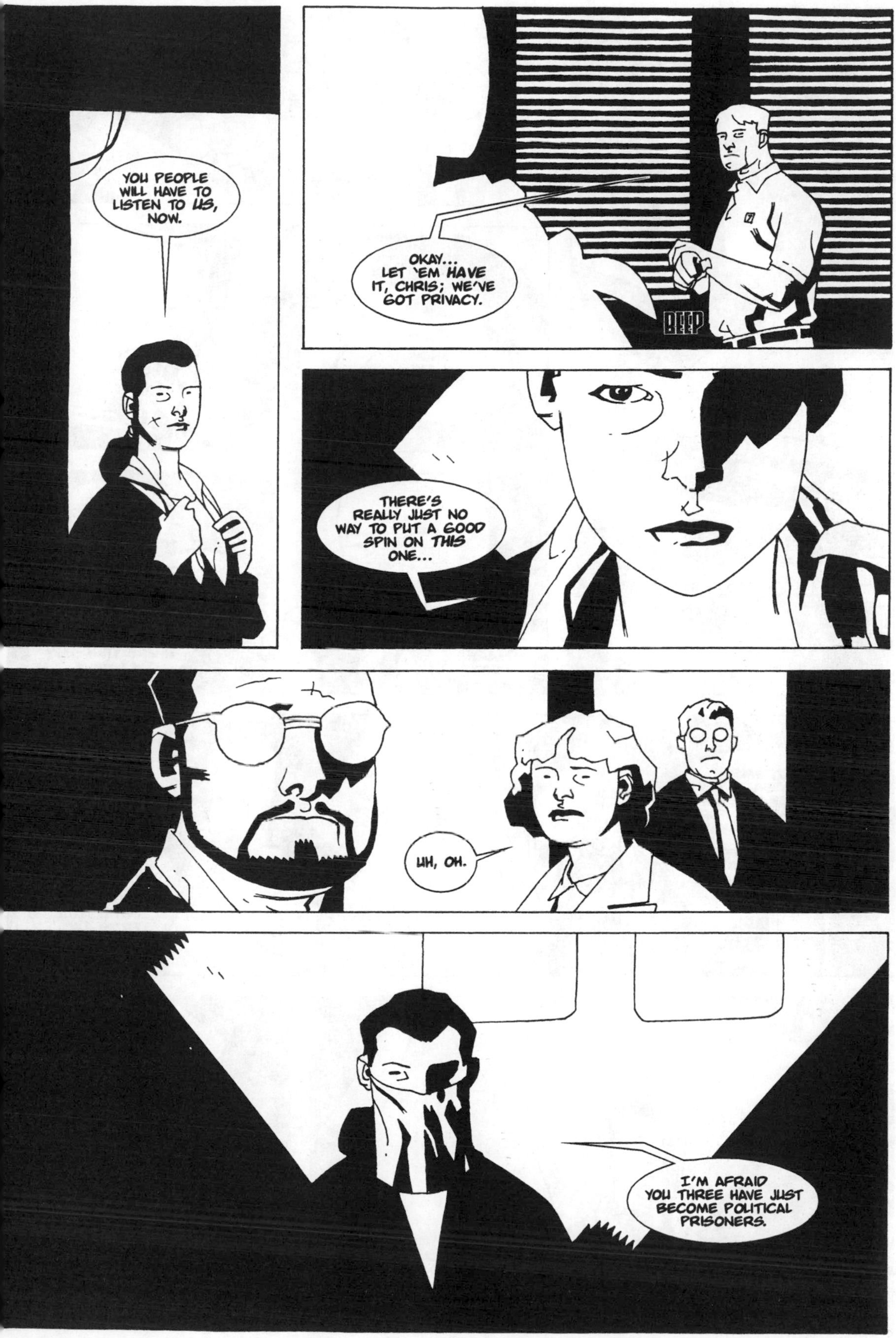
YOU PEOPLE WILL HAVE TO LISTEN TO US, NOW.
OKAY... LET 'EM HAVE IT, CHRIS; WE'VE GOT PRIVACY.
BEEP
THERE'S REALLY JUST NO WAY TO PUT A GOOD SPIN ON THIS ONE...
UH, OH.
I'M AFRAID YOU THREE HAVE JUST BECOME POLITICAL PRISONERS.

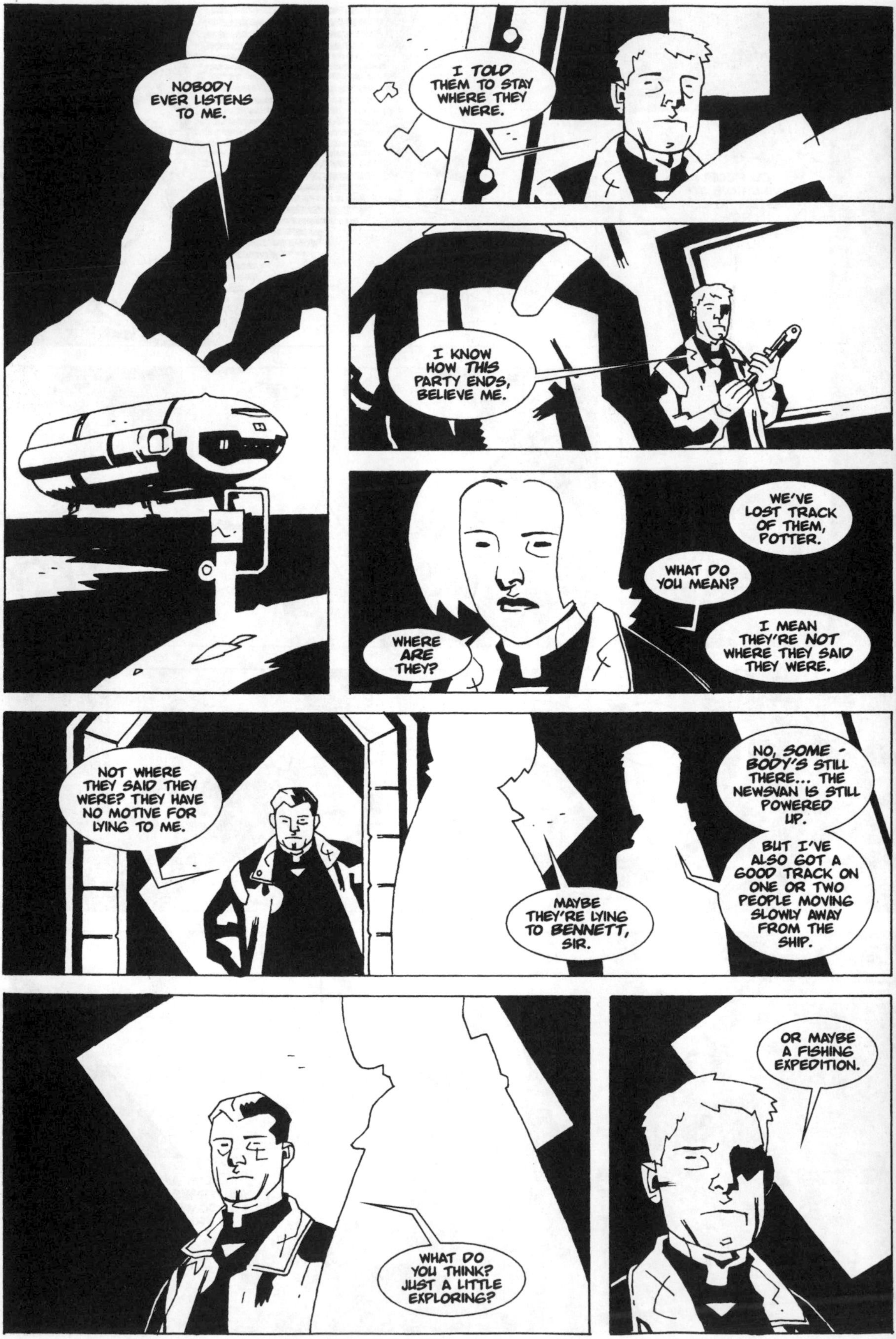
NOBODY EVER LISTENS TO ME.
I TOLD THEM TO STAY WHERE THEY WERE.
I KNOW HOW THIS PARTY ENDS, BELIEVE ME.
WE'VE LOST TRACK OF THEM, POTTER.
WHAT DO YOU MEAN?
I MEAN THEY'RE NOT WHERE THEY SAID THEY WERE.
WHERE ARE THEY?
NOT WHERE THEY SAID THEY WERE? THEY HAVE NO MOTIVE FOR LYING TO ME.
MAYBE THEY'RE LYING TO BENNETT, SIR.
NO, SOME-BODY'S STILL THERE... THE NEWSVAN IS STILL POWERED UP.
BUT I'VE ALSO GOT A GOOD TRACK ON ONE OR TWO PEOPLE MOVING SLOWLY AWAY FROM THE SHIP.
WHAT DO YOU THINK? JUST A LITTLE EXPLORING?
OR MAYBE A FISHING EXPEDITION.

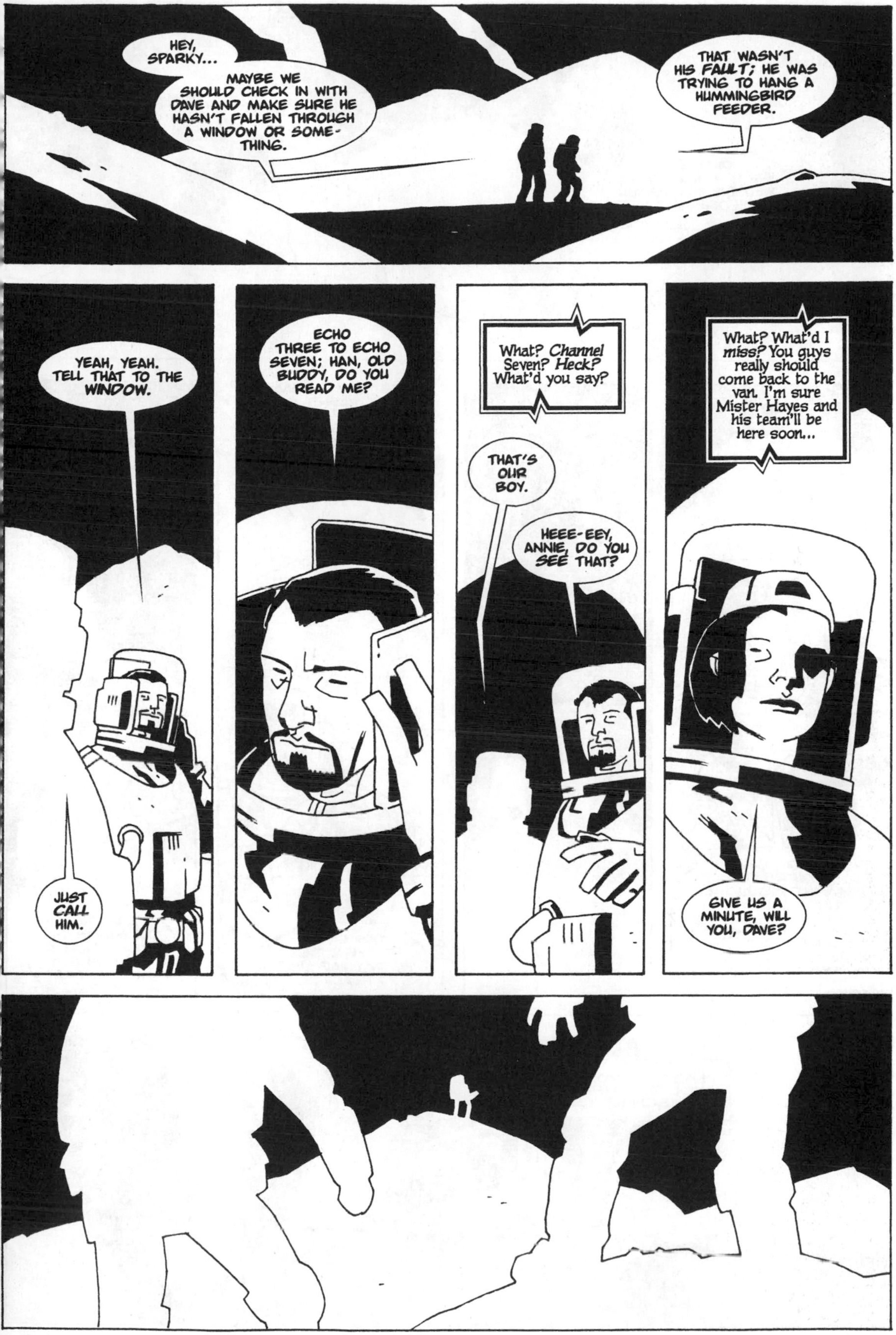

HEY, SPARKY...
MAYBE WE SHOULD CHECK IN WITH DAVE AND MAKE SURE HE HASN'T FALLEN THROUGH A WINDOW OR SOME-THING.
THAT WASN'T HIS FAULT; HE WAS TRYING TO HANG A HUMMINGBIRD FEEDER.
YEAH, YEAH. TELL THAT TO THE WINDOW.
JUST CALL HIM.
ECHO THREE TO ECHO SEVEN; HAN, OLD BUDDY, DO YOU READ ME?
What? Channel Seven? Heck? What'd you say?
THAT'S OUR BOY.
HEEE-EEY, ANNIE, DO YOU SEE THAT?
What? What'd I miss? You guys really should come back to the van. I'm sure Mister Hayes and his team'll be here soon...
GIVE US A MINUTE, WILL YOU, DAVE?

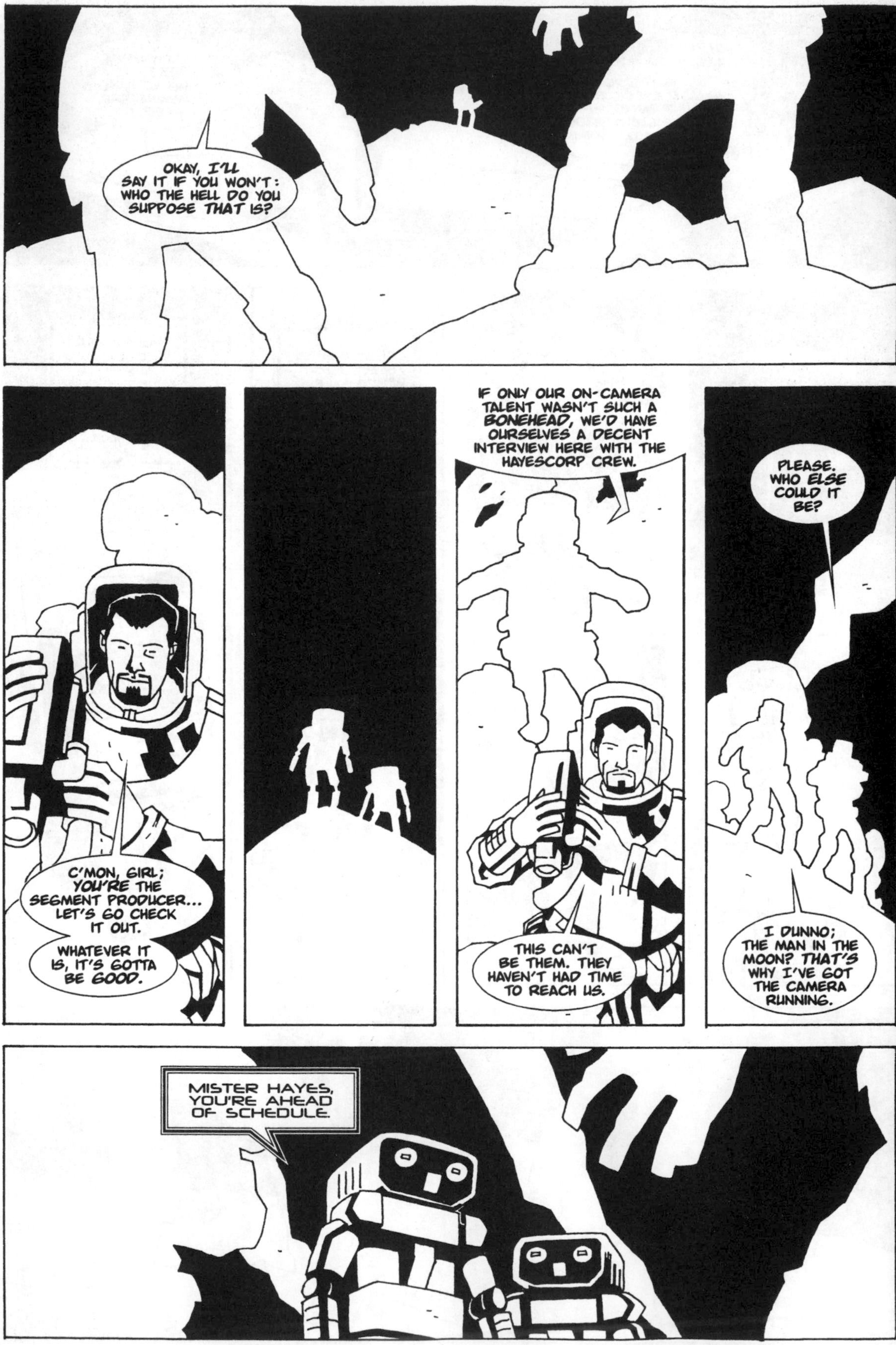
OKAY, I'LL SAY IT IF YOU WON'T: WHO THE HELL DO YOU SUPPOSE THAT IS?
C'MON, GIRL; YOU'RE THE SEGMENT PRODUCER... LET'S GO CHECK IT OUT.
WHATEVER IT IS, IT'S GOTTA BE GOOD.
IF ONLY OUR ON-CAMERA TALENT WASN'T SUCH A BONEHEAD, WE'D HAVE OURSELVES A DECENT INTERVIEW HERE WITH THE HAYESCORP CREW.
THIS CAN'T BE THEM. THEY HAVEN'T HAD TIME TO REACH US.
PLEASE. WHO ELSE COULD IT BE?
I DUNNO; THE MAN IN THE MOON? THAT'S WHY I'VE GOT THE CAMERA RUNNING.
MISTER HAYES, YOU'RE AHEAD OF SCHEDULE.

SEE? I TOLD YOU THIS'D BE GOOD.

WE HAVEN'T CLEARED LEVEL NINE YET, AND LEVEL EIGHT IS STILL UNPRESSURIZED.

IT'S MISTAKING US FOR THE HAYESCORP TEAM.

WHAT HAYESCORP TEAM? THIS WAS ALL A MISTAKE, REMEMBER?

THERE ISN'T SUPPOSED TO BE ANYONE HERE FOR ANOTHER THREE DAYS, MUCH LESS AN ENTIRE SQUAD OF EXCAVATORS.

I MEAN, THESE THINGS HAVE ONLY RUDIMENTARY PROGRAMMING.

IF LEVEL 9 ISN'T READY, AND LEVEL 8 ISN'T PRESSURIZED... HOW'S LEVEL ONE DOING?

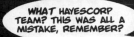

SPARKY...

WE'VE... ADVANCED THE SCHEDULE. TAKE US TO LEVEL ONE.

LEVEL ONE IS FULLY OPERATIONAL.

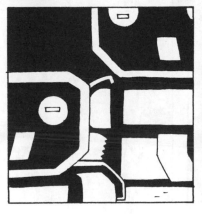

SURE.

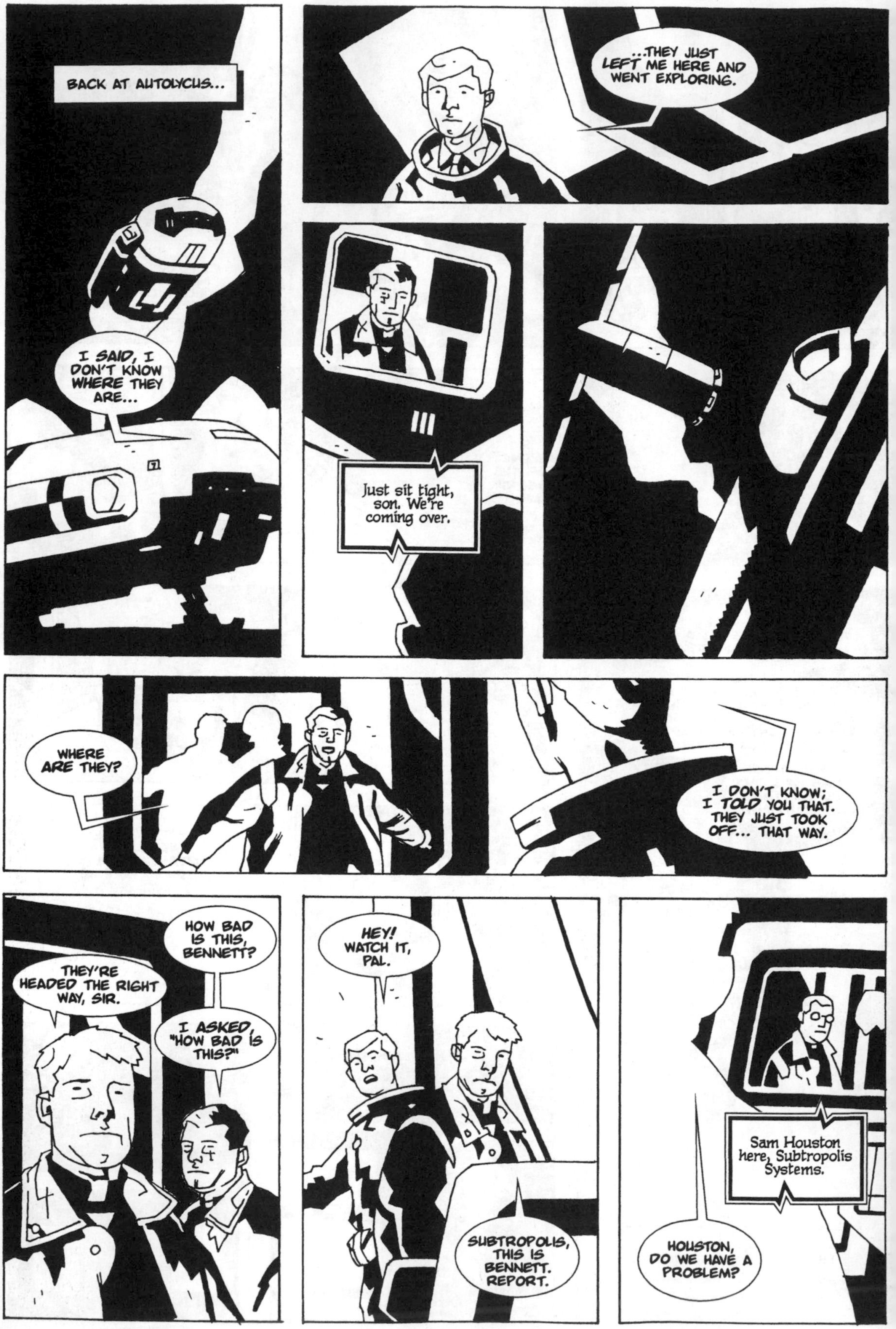
BACK AT AUTOLYCUS...
...THEY JUST LEFT ME HERE AND WENT EXPLORING.
I SAID, I DON'T KNOW WHERE THEY ARE...
Just sit tight, son. We're coming over.
WHERE ARE THEY?
I DON'T KNOW; I TOLD YOU THAT. THEY JUST TOOK OFF... THAT WAY.
HOW BAD IS THIS, BENNETT?
THEY'RE HEADED THE RIGHT WAY, SIR.
I ASKED, "HOW BAD IS THIS?"
HEY! WATCH IT, PAL.
SUBTROPOLIS, THIS IS BENNETT. REPORT.
Sam Houston here, Subtropolis Systems.
HOUSTON, DO WE HAVE A PROBLEM?

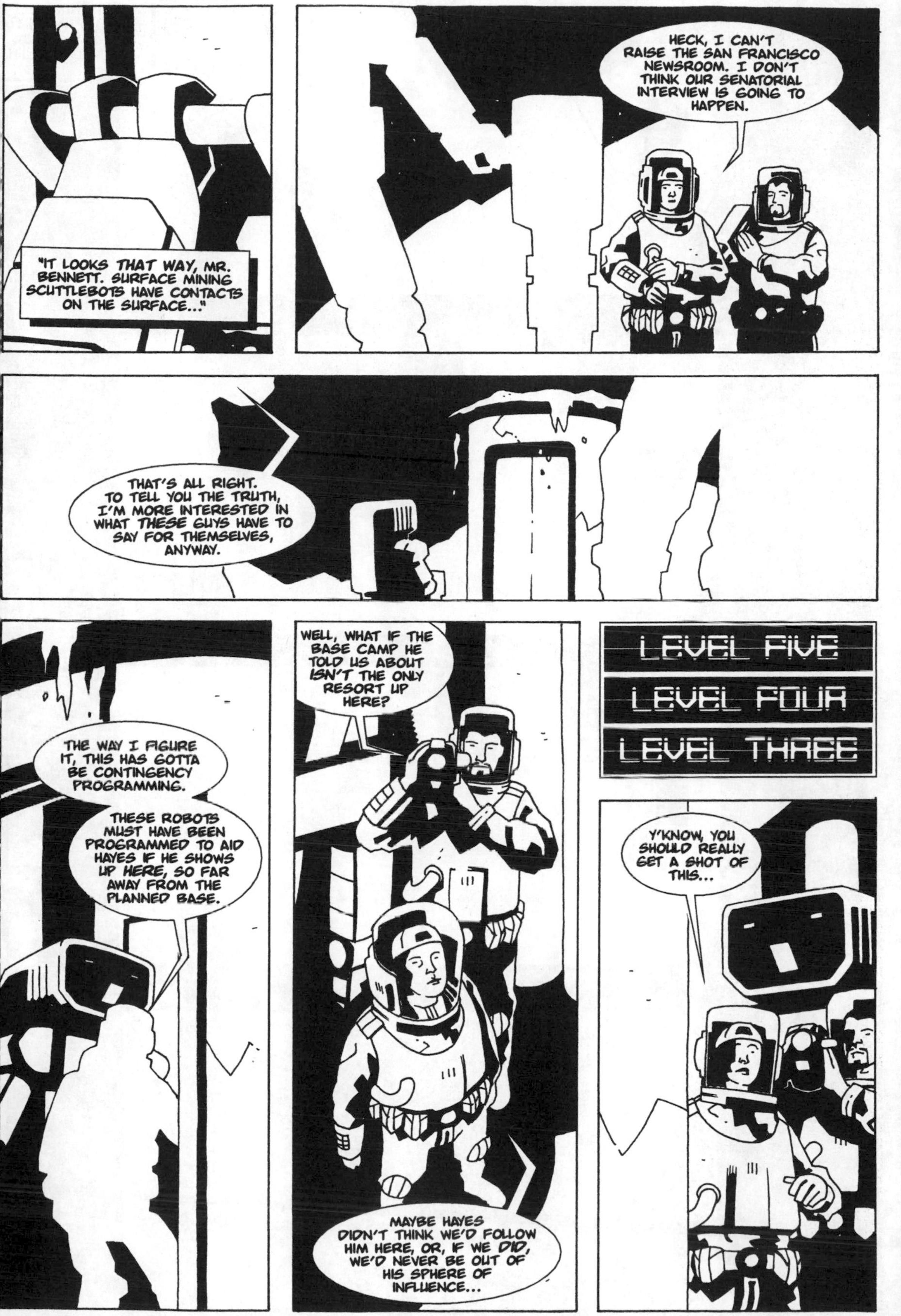
"IT LOOKS THAT WAY, MR. BENNETT. SURFACE MINING SCUTTLEBOTS HAVE CONTACTS ON THE SURFACE..."
HECK, I CAN'T RAISE THE SAN FRANCISCO NEWSROOM. I DON'T THINK OUR SENATORIAL INTERVIEW IS GOING TO HAPPEN.
THAT'S ALL RIGHT. TO TELL YOU THE TRUTH, I'M MORE INTERESTED IN WHAT THESE GUYS HAVE TO SAY FOR THEMSELVES, ANYWAY.
THE WAY I FIGURE IT, THIS HAS GOTTA BE CONTINGENCY PROGRAMMING.
THESE ROBOTS MUST HAVE BEEN PROGRAMMED TO AID HAYES IF HE SHOWS UP HERE, SO FAR AWAY FROM THE PLANNED BASE.
WELL, WHAT IF THE BASE CAMP HE TOLD US ABOUT ISN'T THE ONLY RESORT UP HERE?
MAYBE HAYES DIDN'T THINK WE'D FOLLOW HIM HERE, OR, IF WE DID, WE'D NEVER BE OUT OF HIS SPHERE OF INFLUENCE...
LEVEL FIVE
LEVEL FOUR
LEVEL THREE
Y'KNOW, YOU SHOULD REALLY GET A SHOT OF THIS...

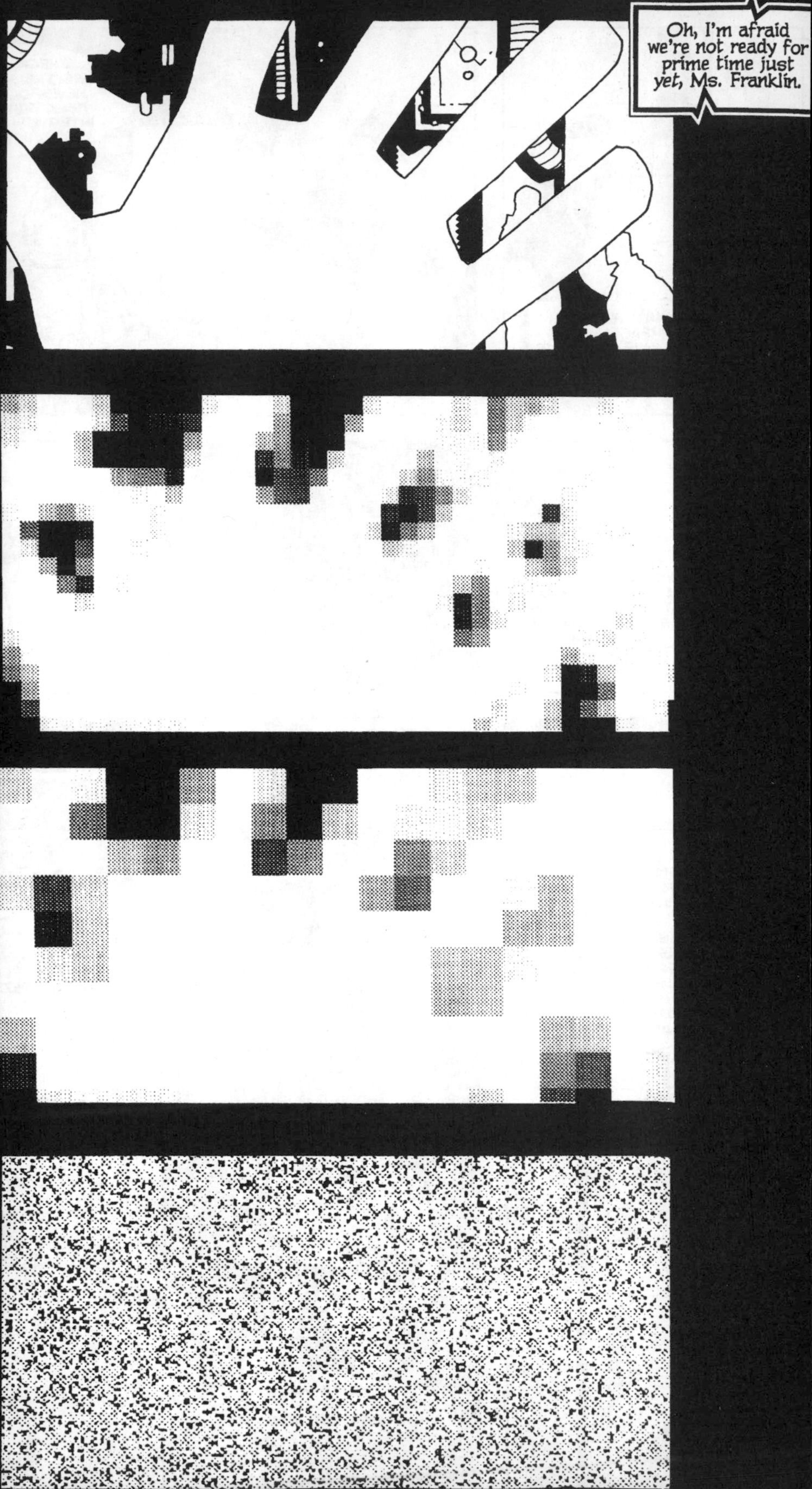
Oh, I'm afraid we're not ready for prime time just yet, Ms. Franklin.

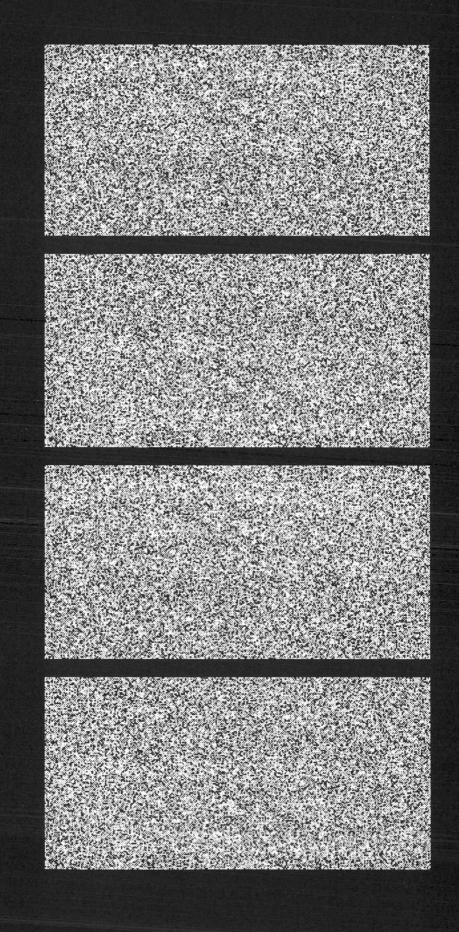

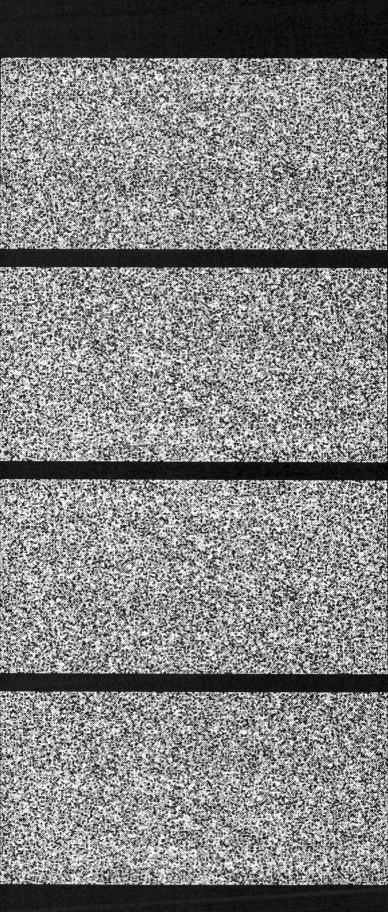

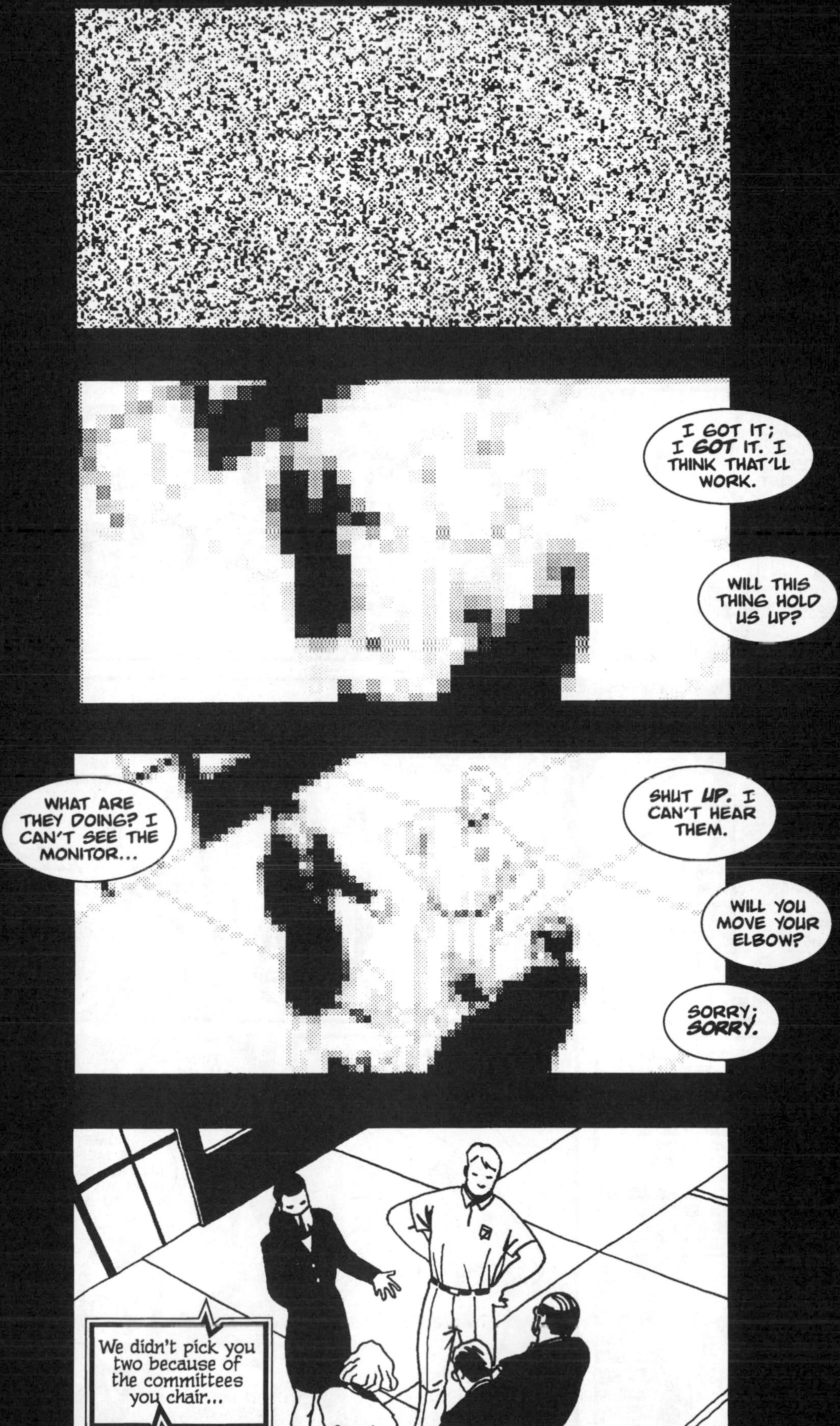
I GOT IT; I GOT IT. I THINK THAT'LL WORK.
WILL THIS THING HOLD US UP?
WHAT ARE THEY DOING? I CAN'T SEE THE MONITOR...
SHUT UP. I CAN'T HEAR THEM.
WILL YOU MOVE YOUR ELBOW?
SORRY; SORRY.
We didn't pick you two because of the committees you chair...

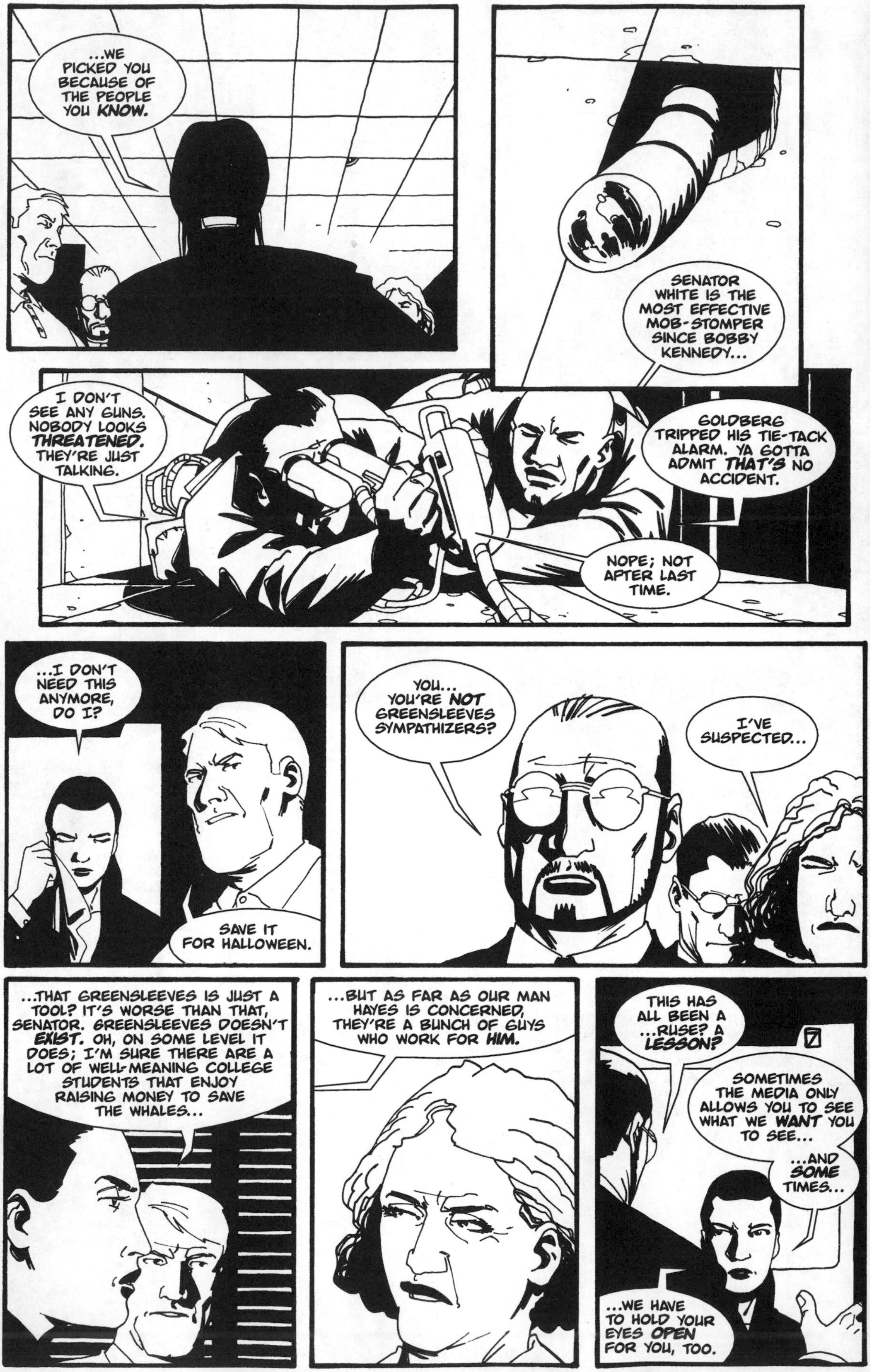
...WE PICKED YOU BECAUSE OF THE PEOPLE YOU KNOW.
SENATOR WHITE IS THE MOST EFFECTIVE MOB-STOMPER SINCE BOBBY KENNEDY...
I DON'T SEE ANY GUNS. NOBODY LOOKS THREATENED. THEY'RE JUST TALKING.
GOLDBERG TRIPPED HIS TIE-TACK ALARM. YA GOTTA ADMIT THAT'S NO ACCIDENT.
NOPE; NOT AFTER LAST TIME.
...I DON'T NEED THIS ANYMORE, DO I?
SAVE IT FOR HALLOWEEN.
YOU... YOU'RE NOT GREENSLEEVES SYMPATHIZERS?
I'VE SUSPECTED...
...THAT GREENSLEEVES IS JUST A TOOL? IT'S WORSE THAN THAT, SENATOR. GREENSLEEVES DOESN'T EXIST. OH, ON SOME LEVEL IT DOES; I'M SURE THERE ARE A LOT OF WELL-MEANING COLLEGE STUDENTS THAT ENJOY RAISING MONEY TO SAVE THE WHALES...
...BUT AS FAR AS OUR MAN HAYES IS CONCERNED, THEY'RE A BUNCH OF GUYS WHO WORK FOR HIM.
THIS HAS ALL BEEN A ...RUSE? A LESSON?
SOMETIMES THE MEDIA ONLY ALLOWS YOU TO SEE WHAT WE WANT YOU TO SEE...
...AND SOME TIMES...
...WE HAVE TO HOLD YOUR EYES OPEN FOR YOU, TOO.

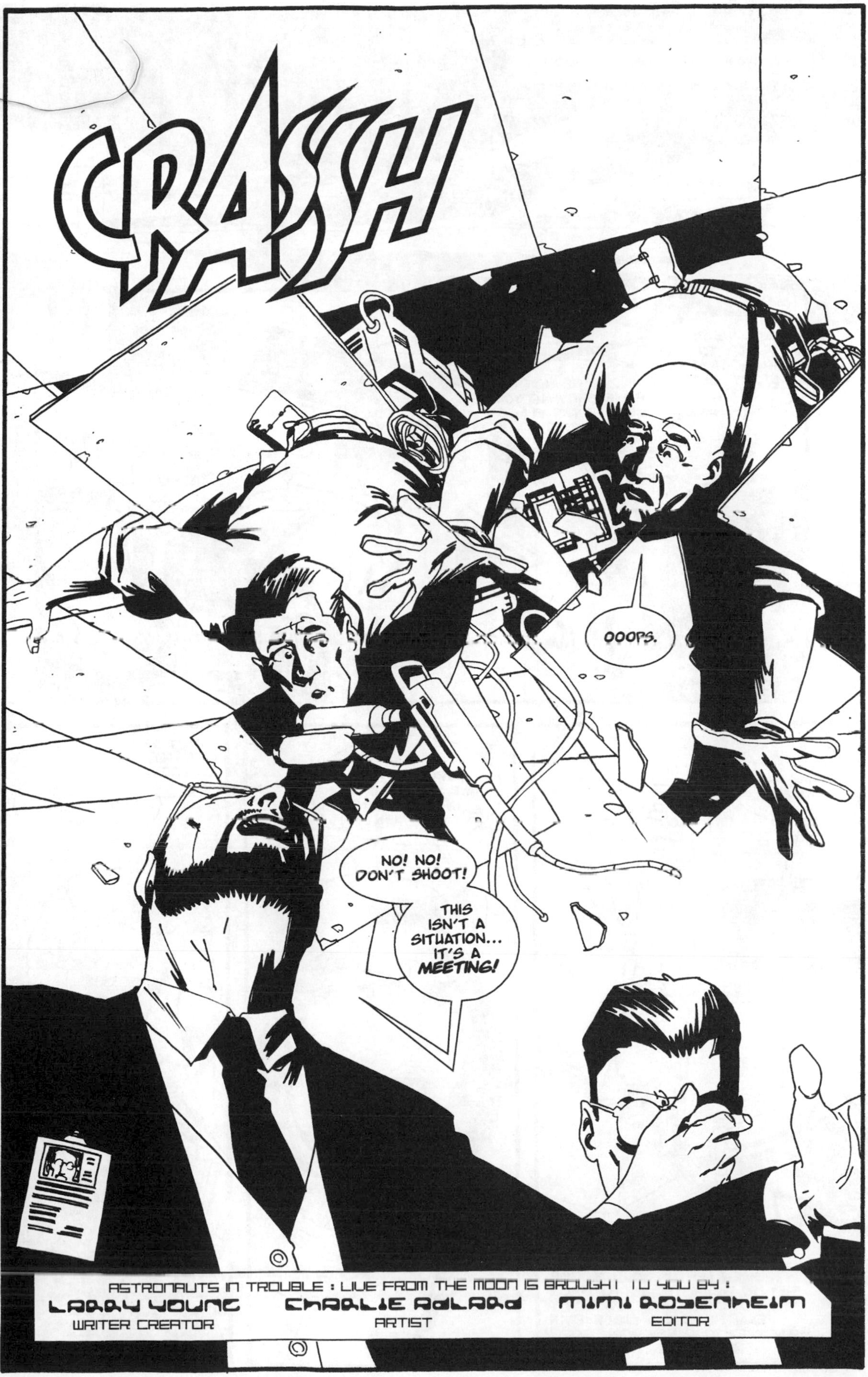
CRASH
OOOPS.
NO! NO! DON'T SHOOT!
THIS ISN'T A SITUATION... IT'S A MEETING!
ASTRONAUTS IN TROUBLE : LIVE FROM THE MOON IS BROUGHT TO YOU BY :
LARRY YOUNG
WRITER CREATOR
CHARLIE ADLARD
ARTIST
MIMI ROSENHEIM
EDITOR

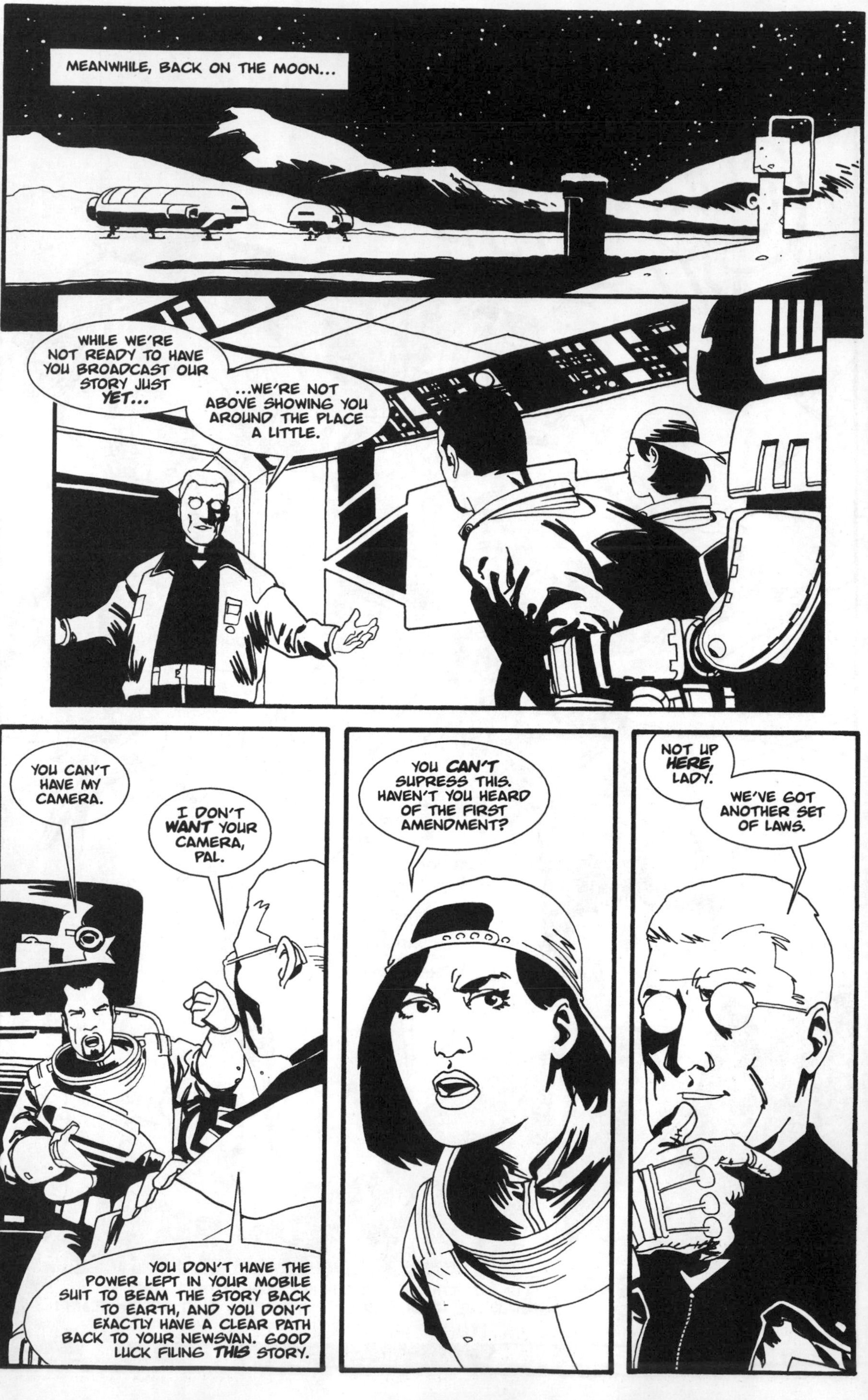
MEANWHILE, BACK ON THE MOON...
WHILE WE'RE NOT READY TO HAVE YOU BROADCAST OUR STORY JUST YET...
...WE'RE NOT ABOVE SHOWING YOU AROUND THE PLACE A LITTLE.
YOU CAN'T HAVE MY CAMERA.
I DON'T WANT YOUR CAMERA, PAL.
YOU DON'T HAVE THE POWER LEFT IN YOUR MOBILE SUIT TO BEAM THE STORY BACK TO EARTH, AND YOU DON'T EXACTLY HAVE A CLEAR PATH BACK TO YOUR NEWSVAN. GOOD LUCK FILING THIS STORY.
YOU CAN'T SUPRESS THIS. HAVEN'T YOU HEARD OF THE FIRST AMENDMENT?
NOT UP HERE, LADY.
WE'VE GOT ANOTHER SET OF LAWS.

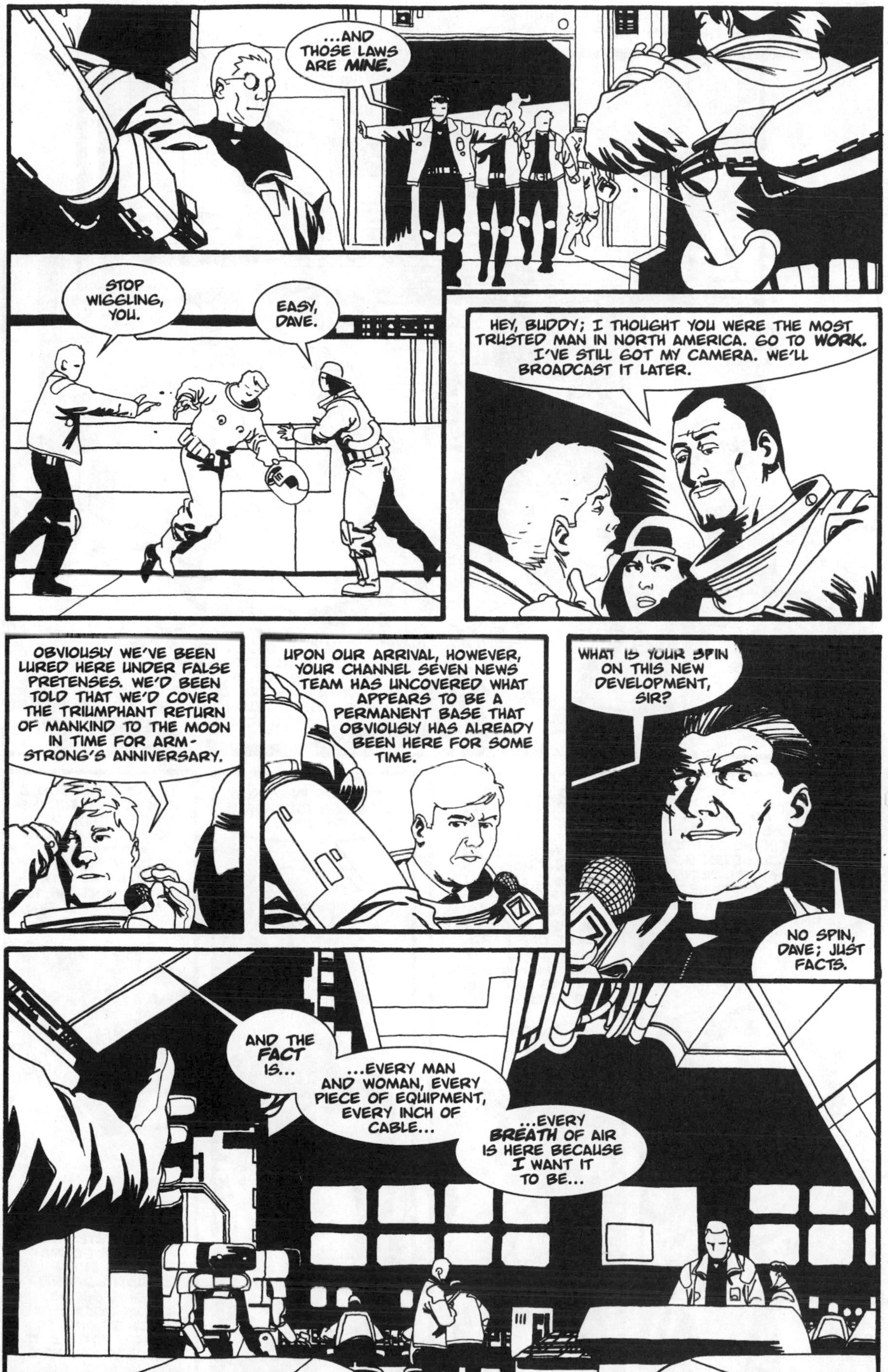
...AND THOSE LAWS ARE MINE.
STOP WIGGLING, YOU.
EASY, DAVE.
HEY, BUDDY; I THOUGHT YOU WERE THE MOST TRUSTED MAN IN NORTH AMERICA. GO TO WORK. I'VE STILL GOT MY CAMERA. WE'LL BROADCAST IT LATER.
OBVIOUSLY WE'VE BEEN LURED HERE UNDER FALSE PRETENSES. WE'D BEEN TOLD THAT WE'D COVER THE TRIUMPHANT RETURN OF MANKIND TO THE MOON IN TIME FOR ARM-STRONG'S ANNIVERSARY.
UPON OUR ARRIVAL, HOWEVER, YOUR CHANNEL SEVEN NEWS TEAM HAS UNCOVERED WHAT APPEARS TO BE A PERMANENT BASE THAT OBVIOUSLY HAS ALREADY BEEN HERE FOR SOME TIME.
WHAT IS YOUR SPIN ON THIS NEW DEVELOPMENT, SIR?
NO SPIN, DAVE; JUST FACTS.
AND THE FACT IS...
...EVERY MAN AND WOMAN, EVERY PIECE OF EQUIPMENT, EVERY INCH OF CABLE...
...EVERY BREATH OF AIR IS HERE BECAUSE I WANT IT TO BE...

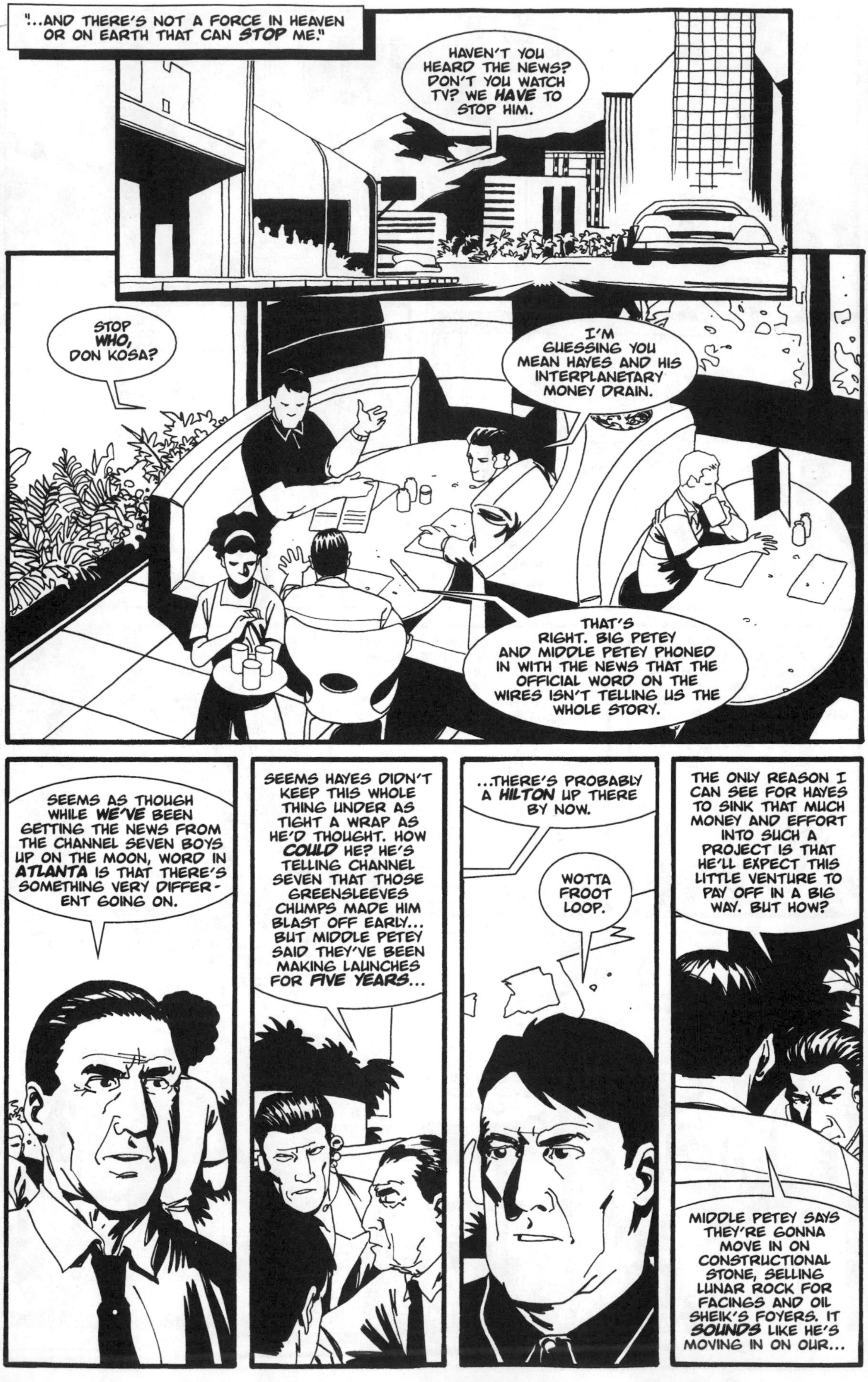
"...AND THERE'S NOT A FORCE IN HEAVEN OR ON EARTH THAT CAN STOP ME."
HAVEN'T YOU HEARD THE NEWS? DON'T YOU WATCH TV? WE HAVE TO STOP HIM.
STOP WHO, DON KOSA?
I'M GUESSING YOU MEAN HAYES AND HIS INTERPLANETARY MONEY DRAIN.
THAT'S RIGHT. BIG PETEY AND MIDDLE PETEY PHONED IN WITH THE NEWS THAT THE OFFICIAL WORD ON THE WIRES ISN'T TELLING US THE WHOLE STORY.
SEEMS AS THOUGH WHILE WE'VE BEEN GETTING THE NEWS FROM THE CHANNEL SEVEN BOYS UP ON THE MOON, WORD IN ATLANTA IS THAT THERE'S SOMETHING VERY DIFFER-ENT GOING ON.
SEEMS HAYES DIDN'T KEEP THIS WHOLE THING UNDER AS TIGHT A WRAP AS HE'D THOUGHT. HOW COULD HE? HE'S TELLING CHANNEL SEVEN THAT THOSE GREENSLEEVES CHUMPS MADE HIM BLAST OFF EARLY... BUT MIDDLE PETEY SAID THEY'VE BEEN MAKING LAUNCHES FOR FIVE YEARS...
...THERE'S PROBABLY A HILTON UP THERE BY NOW.
WOTTA FROOT LOOP.
THE ONLY REASON I CAN SEE FOR HAYES TO SINK THAT MUCH MONEY AND EFFORT INTO SUCH A PROJECT IS THAT HE'LL EXPECT THIS LITTLE VENTURE TO PAY OFF IN A BIG WAY. BUT HOW?
MIDDLE PETEY SAYS THEY'RE GONNA MOVE IN ON CONSTRUCTIONAL STONE, SELLING LUNAR ROCK FOR FACINGS AND OIL SHEIK'S FOYERS. IT SOUNDS LIKE HE'S MOVING IN ON OUR...

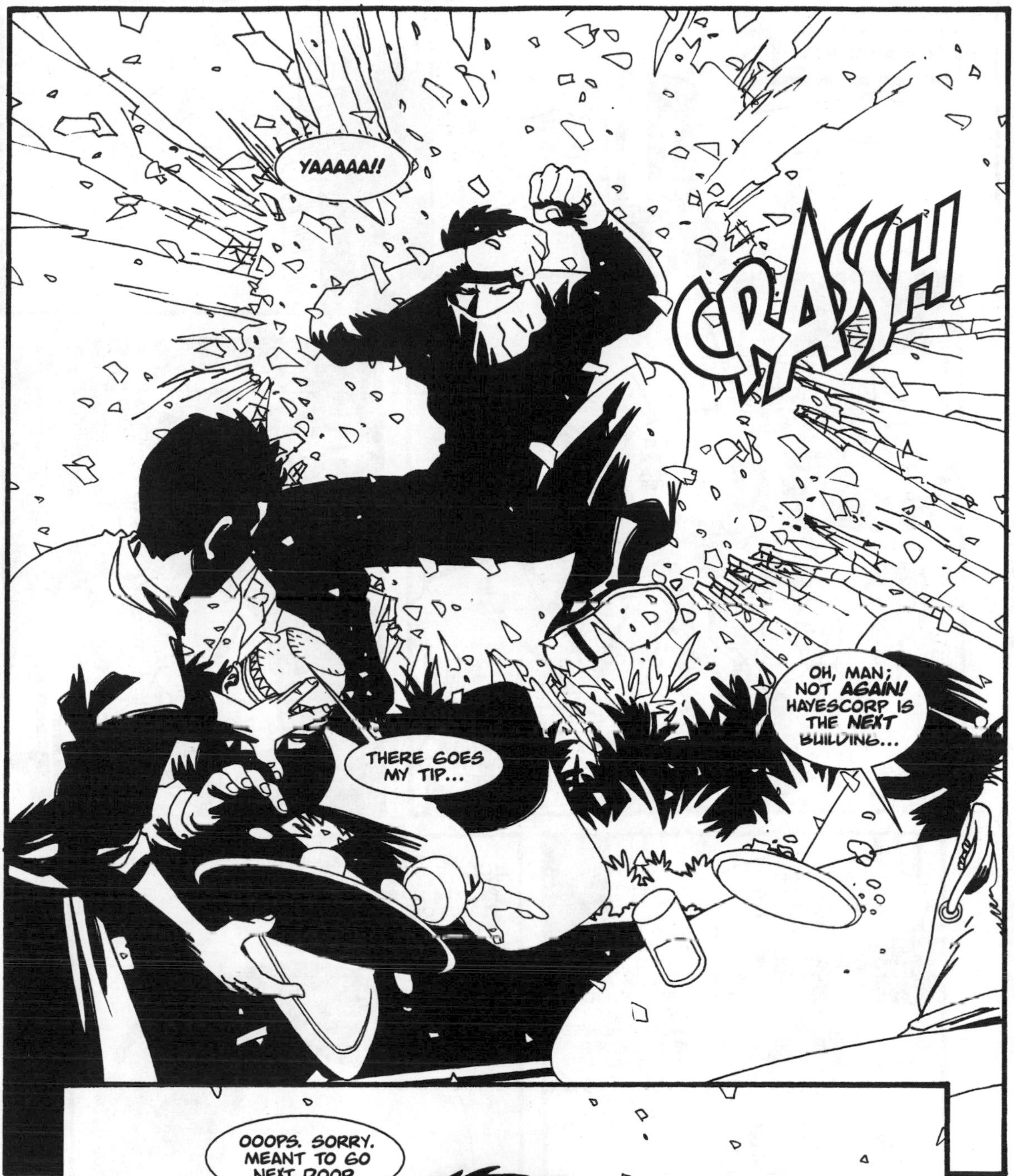
YAAAAA!!
CRASH
OH, MAN; NOT AGAIN! HAYESCORP IS THE NEXT BUILDING...
THERE GOES MY TIP...

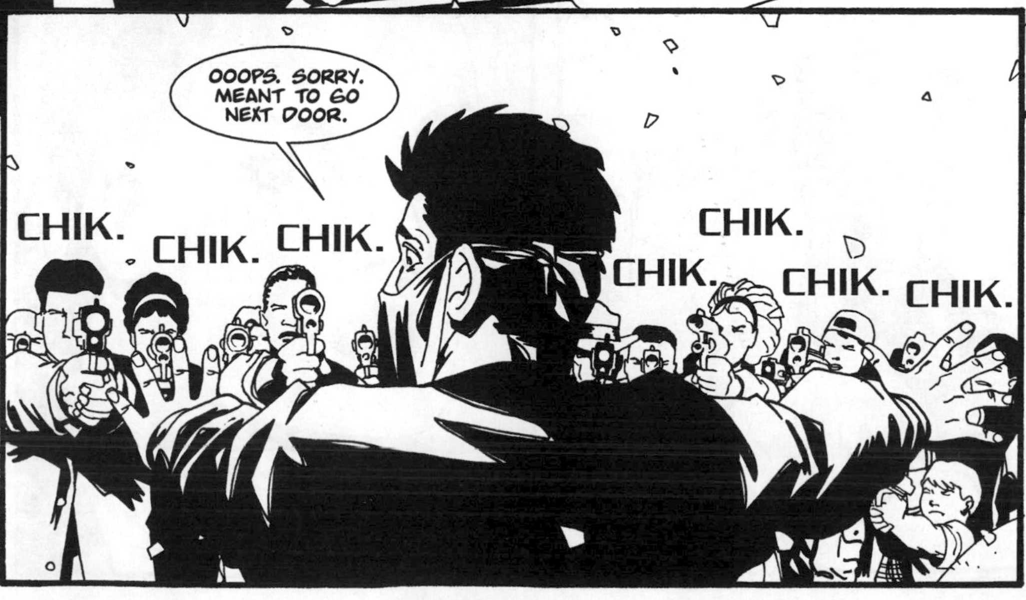
OOOPS. SORRY. MEANT TO GO NEXT DOOR.
CHIK. CHIK. CHIK. CHIK. CHIK. CHIK. CHIK.

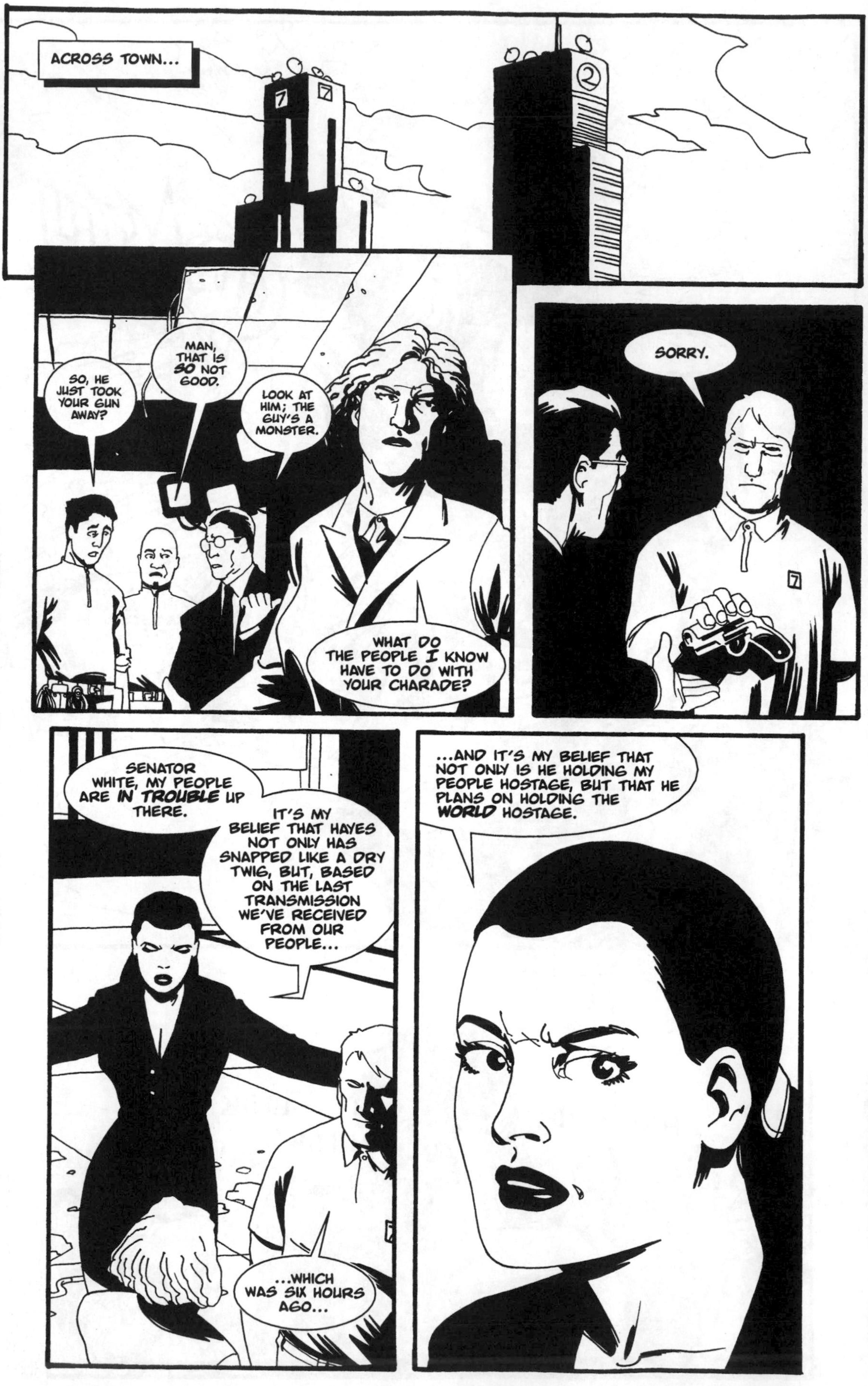
ACROSS TOWN...
SO, HE JUST TOOK YOUR GUN AWAY?
MAN, THAT IS SO NOT GOOD.
LOOK AT HIM; THE GUY'S A MONSTER.
WHAT DO THE PEOPLE I KNOW HAVE TO DO WITH YOUR CHARADE?
SORRY.
SENATOR WHITE, MY PEOPLE ARE IN TROUBLE UP THERE.
IT'S MY BELIEF THAT HAYES NOT ONLY HAS SNAPPED LIKE A DRY TWIG, BUT, BASED ON THE LAST TRANSMISSION WE'VE RECEIVED FROM OUR PEOPLE...
...WHICH WAS SIX HOURS AGO...
...AND IT'S MY BELIEF THAT NOT ONLY IS HE HOLDING MY PEOPLE HOSTAGE, BUT THAT HE PLANS ON HOLDING THE WORLD HOSTAGE.

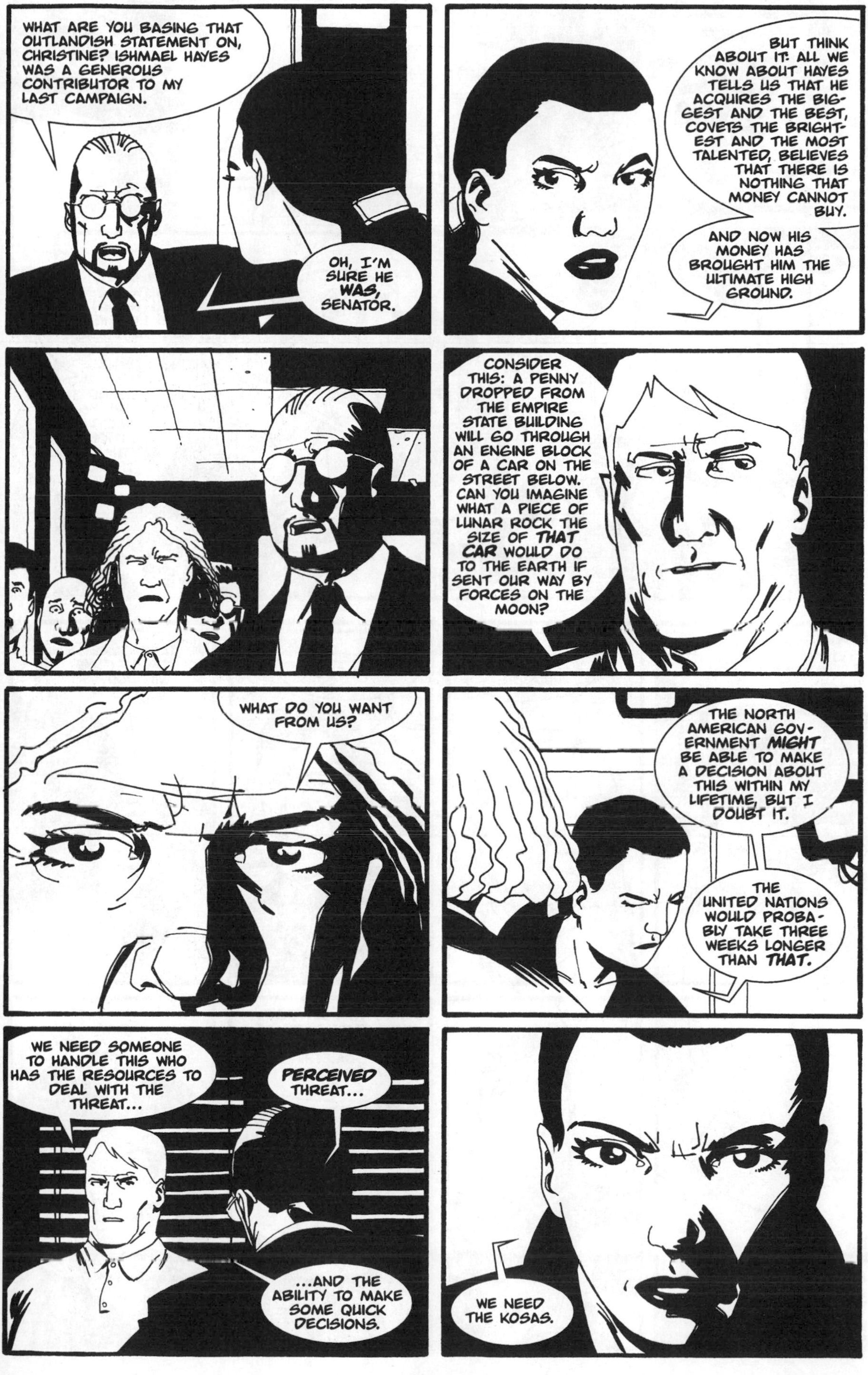
WHAT ARE YOU BASING THAT OUTLANDISH STATEMENT ON, CHRISTINE? ISHMAEL HAYES WAS A GENEROUS CONTRIBUTOR TO MY LAST CAMPAIGN.
OH, I'M SURE HE WAS, SENATOR.
BUT THINK ABOUT IT: ALL WE KNOW ABOUT HAYES TELLS US THAT HE ACQUIRES THE BIGGEST AND THE BEST, COVETS THE BRIGHTEST AND THE MOST TALENTED, BELIEVES THAT THERE IS NOTHING THAT MONEY CANNOT BUY.
AND NOW HIS MONEY HAS BROUGHT HIM THE ULTIMATE HIGH GROUND.
CONSIDER THIS: A PENNY DROPPED FROM THE EMPIRE STATE BUILDING WILL GO THROUGH AN ENGINE BLOCK OF A CAR ON THE STREET BELOW. CAN YOU IMAGINE WHAT A PIECE OF LUNAR ROCK THE SIZE OF THAT CAR WOULD DO TO THE EARTH IF SENT OUR WAY BY FORCES ON THE MOON?
WHAT DO YOU WANT FROM US?
THE NORTH AMERICAN GOVERNMENT MIGHT BE ABLE TO MAKE A DECISION ABOUT THIS WITHIN MY LIFETIME, BUT I DOUBT IT.
THE UNITED NATIONS WOULD PROBABLY TAKE THREE WEEKS LONGER THAN THAT.
WE NEED SOMEONE TO HANDLE THIS WHO HAS THE RESOURCES TO DEAL WITH THE THREAT...
PERCEIVED THREAT...
...AND THE ABILITY TO MAKE SOME QUICK DECISIONS.
WE NEED THE KOSAS.

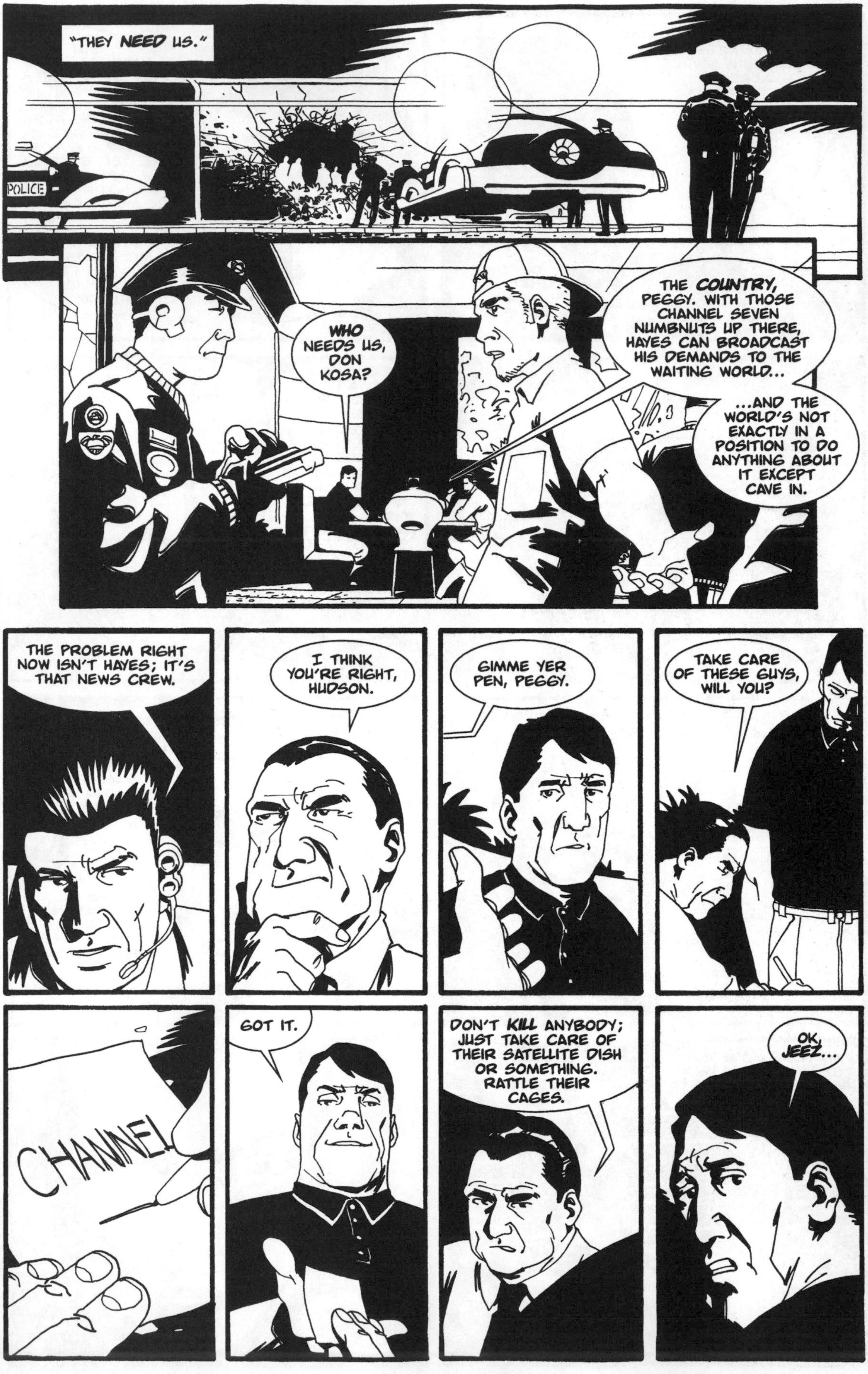
"THEY NEED US."
POLICE
WHO NEEDS US, DON KOSA?
THE COUNTRY, PEGGY. WITH THOSE CHANNEL SEVEN NUMBNUTS UP THERE, HAYES CAN BROADCAST HIS DEMANDS TO THE WAITING WORLD...
...AND THE WORLD'S NOT EXACTLY IN A POSITION TO DO ANYTHING ABOUT IT EXCEPT CAVE IN.
THE PROBLEM RIGHT NOW ISN'T HAYES; IT'S THAT NEWS CREW.
I THINK YOU'RE RIGHT, HUDSON.
GIMME YER PEN, PEGGY.
TAKE CARE OF THESE GUYS, WILL YOU?
CHANNEL
GOT IT.
DON'T KILL ANYBODY; JUST TAKE CARE OF THEIR SATELLITE DISH OR SOMETHING. RATTLE THEIR CAGES.
OK, JEEZ...

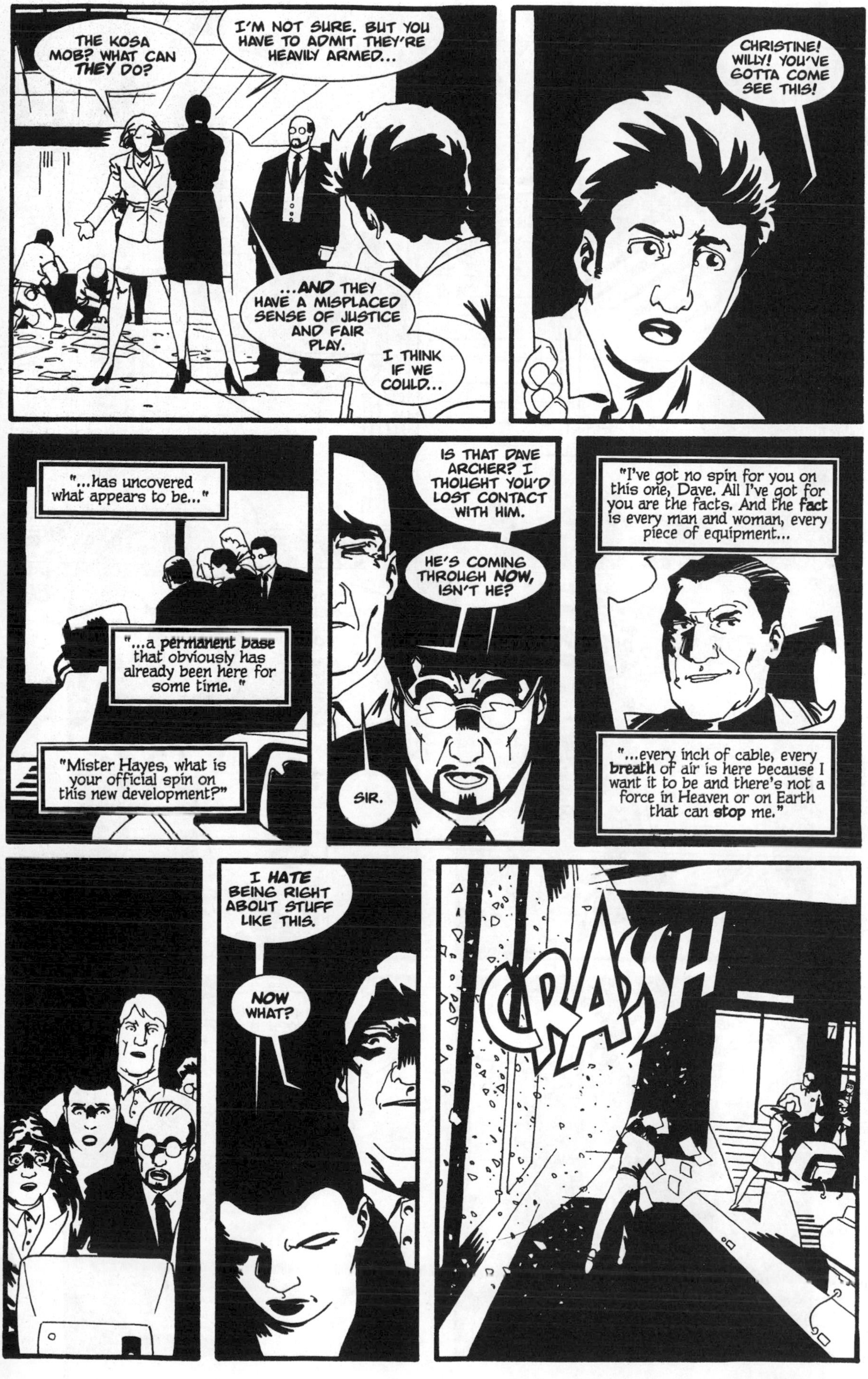
THE KOSA MOB? WHAT CAN THEY DO?
I'M NOT SURE. BUT YOU HAVE TO ADMIT THEY'RE HEAVILY ARMED...
...AND THEY HAVE A MISPLACED SENSE OF JUSTICE AND FAIR PLAY.
I THINK IF WE COULD...
CHRISTINE! WILLY! YOU'VE GOTTA COME SEE THIS!
"...has uncovered what appears to be..."
"...a permanent base that obviously has already been here for some time."
"Mister Hayes, what is your official spin on this new development?"
IS THAT DAVE ARCHER? I THOUGHT YOU'D LOST CONTACT WITH HIM.
HE'S COMING THROUGH NOW, ISN'T HE?
SIR.
"I've got no spin for you on this one, Dave. All I've got for you are the facts. And the fact is every man and woman, every piece of equipment..."
"...every inch of cable, every breath of air is here because I want it to be and there's not a force in Heaven or on Earth that can stop me."
I HATE BEING RIGHT ABOUT STUFF LIKE THIS.
NOW WHAT?
CRASH

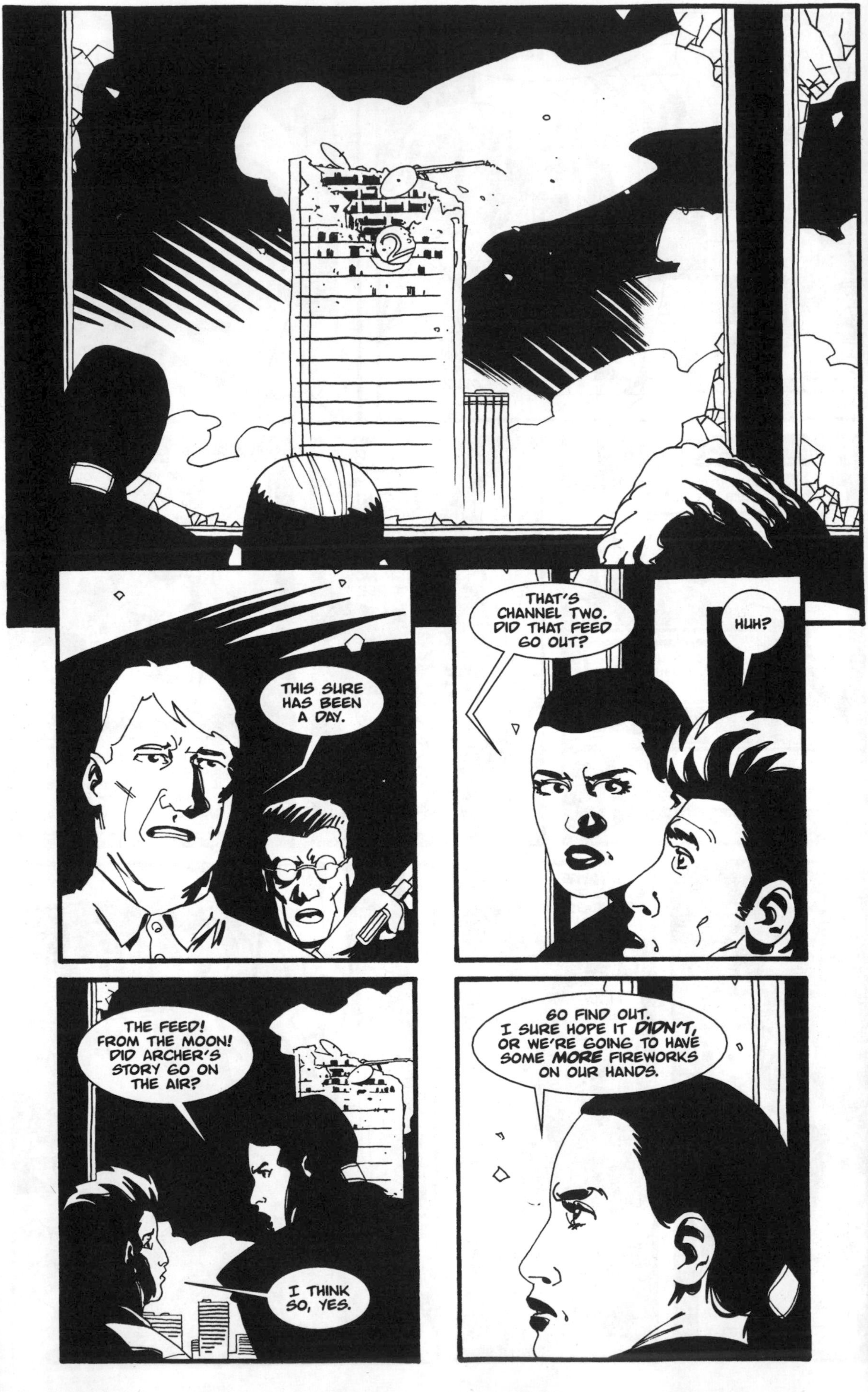
THIS SURE HAS BEEN A DAY.
THAT'S CHANNEL TWO. DID THAT FEED GO OUT?
HUH?
THE FEED! FROM THE MOON! DID ARCHER'S STORY GO ON THE AIR?
I THINK SO, YES.
GO FIND OUT. I SURE HOPE IT *DIDN'T*, OR WE'RE GOING TO HAVE SOME *MORE* FIREWORKS ON OUR HANDS.

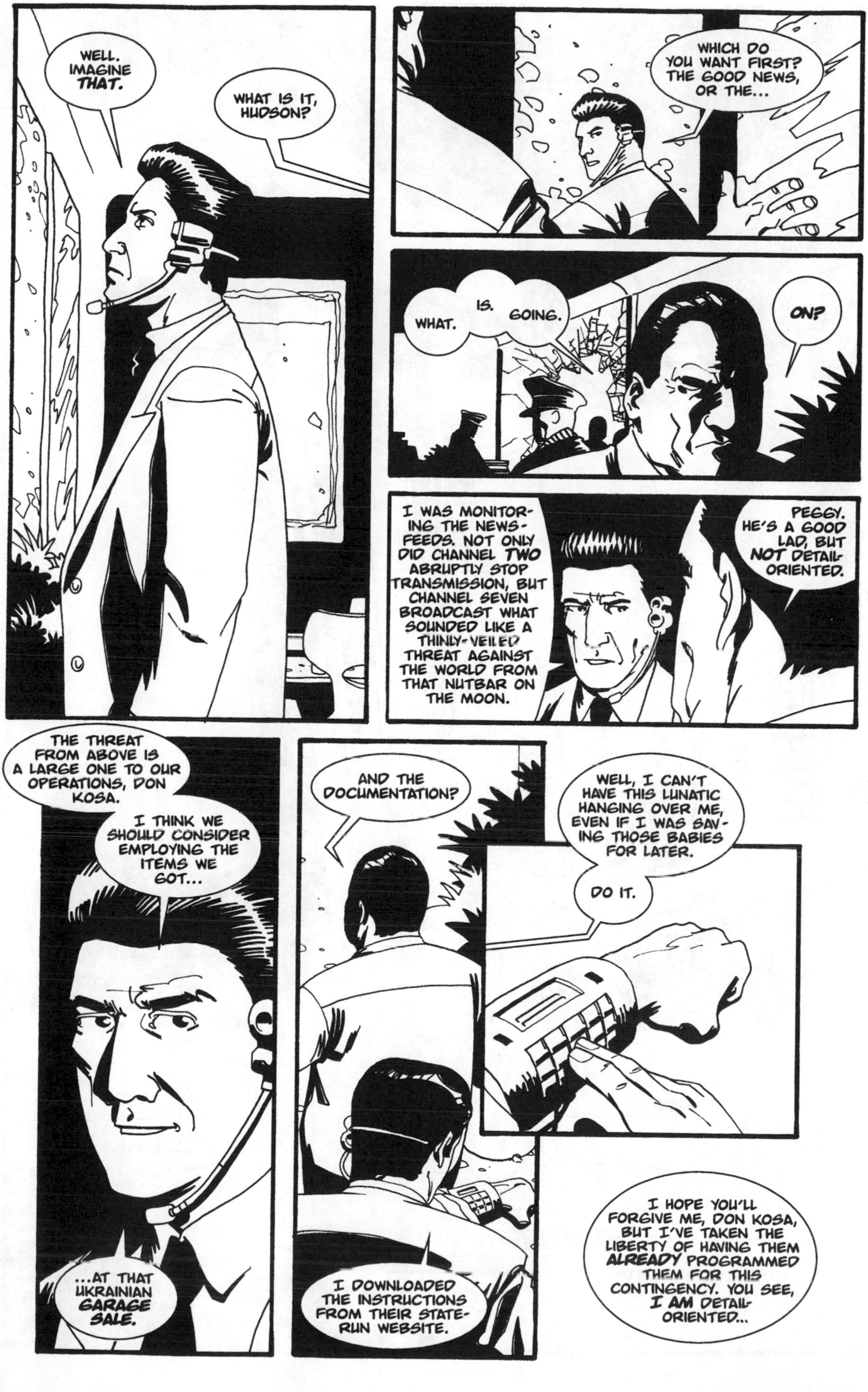

WELL. IMAGINE THAT.
WHAT IS IT, HUDSON?
WHICH DO YOU WANT FIRST? THE GOOD NEWS, OR THE...
WHAT. IS. GOING.
ON?
I WAS MONITORING THE NEWS-FEEDS. NOT ONLY DID CHANNEL TWO ABRUPTLY STOP TRANSMISSION, BUT CHANNEL SEVEN BROADCAST WHAT SOUNDED LIKE A THINLY-VEILED THREAT AGAINST THE WORLD FROM THAT NUTBAR ON THE MOON.
PEGGY. HE'S A GOOD LAD, BUT NOT DETAIL-ORIENTED.
THE THREAT FROM ABOVE IS A LARGE ONE TO OUR OPERATIONS, DON KOSA.
I THINK WE SHOULD CONSIDER EMPLOYING THE ITEMS WE GOT...
...AT THAT UKRAINIAN GARAGE SALE.
AND THE DOCUMENTATION?
I DOWNLOADED THE INSTRUCTIONS FROM THEIR STATE-RUN WEBSITE.
WELL, I CAN'T HAVE THIS LUNATIC HANGING OVER ME, EVEN IF I WAS SAVING THOSE BABIES FOR LATER.
DO IT.
I HOPE YOU'LL FORGIVE ME, DON KOSA, BUT I'VE TAKEN THE LIBERTY OF HAVING THEM ALREADY PROGRAMMED THEM FOR THIS CONTINGENCY. YOU SEE, I AM DETAIL-ORIENTED...

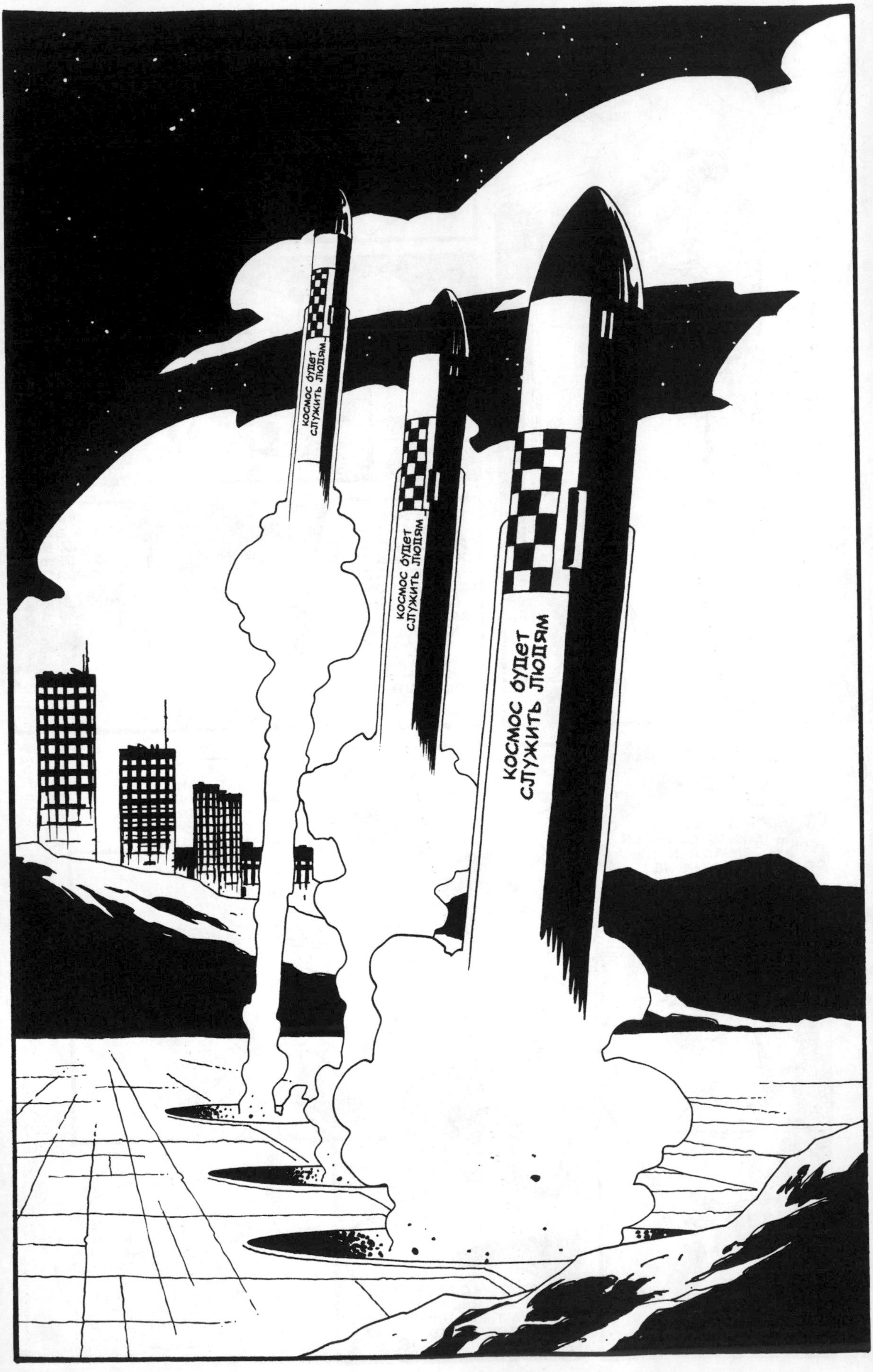
КОСМОС БУДЕТ СЛУЖИТЬ ЛЮДЯМ
КОСМОС БУДЕТ СЛУЖИТЬ ЛЮДЯМ
КОСМОС БУДЕТ СЛУЖИТЬ ЛЮДЯМ

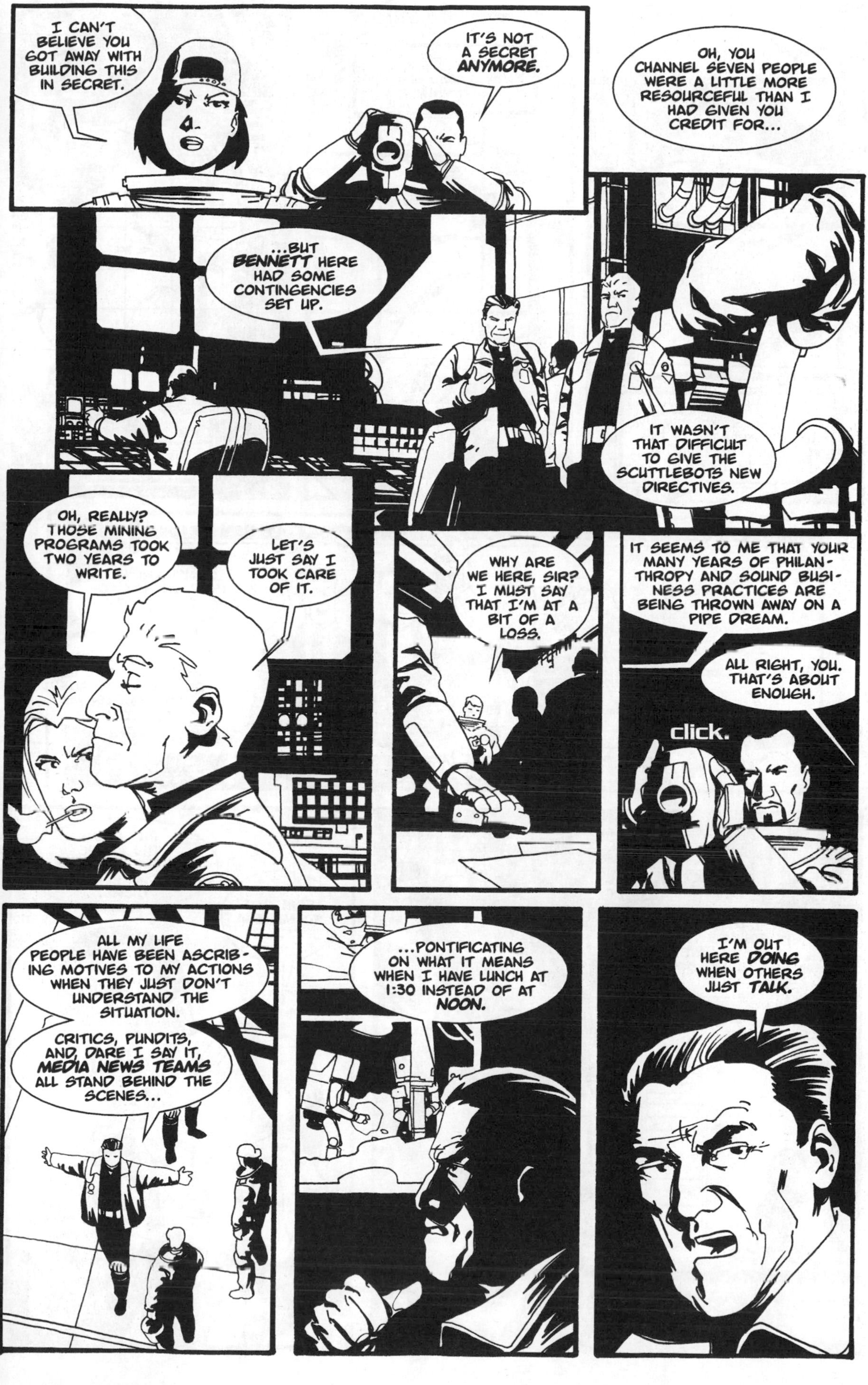
I CAN'T BELIEVE YOU GOT AWAY WITH BUILDING THIS IN SECRET.
IT'S NOT A SECRET ANYMORE.
OH, YOU CHANNEL SEVEN PEOPLE WERE A LITTLE MORE RESOURCEFUL THAN I HAD GIVEN YOU CREDIT FOR...
...BUT BENNETT HERE HAD SOME CONTINGENCIES SET UP.
IT WASN'T THAT DIFFICULT TO GIVE THE SCUTTLEBOTS NEW DIRECTIVES.
OH, REALLY? THOSE MINING PROGRAMS TOOK TWO YEARS TO WRITE.
LET'S JUST SAY I TOOK CARE OF IT.
WHY ARE WE HERE, SIR? I MUST SAY THAT I'M AT A BIT OF A LOSS.
IT SEEMS TO ME THAT YOUR MANY YEARS OF PHILAN-THROPY AND SOUND BUSI-NESS PRACTICES ARE BEING THROWN AWAY ON A PIPE DREAM.
ALL RIGHT, YOU. THAT'S ABOUT ENOUGH.
click.
ALL MY LIFE PEOPLE HAVE BEEN ASCRIB-ING MOTIVES TO MY ACTIONS WHEN THEY JUST DON'T UNDERSTAND THE SITUATION.
CRITICS, PUNDITS, AND, DARE I SAY IT, MEDIA NEWS TEAMS ALL STAND BEHIND THE SCENES...
...PONTIFICATING ON WHAT IT MEANS WHEN I HAVE LUNCH AT 1:30 INSTEAD OF AT NOON.
I'M OUT HERE DOING WHEN OTHERS JUST TALK.

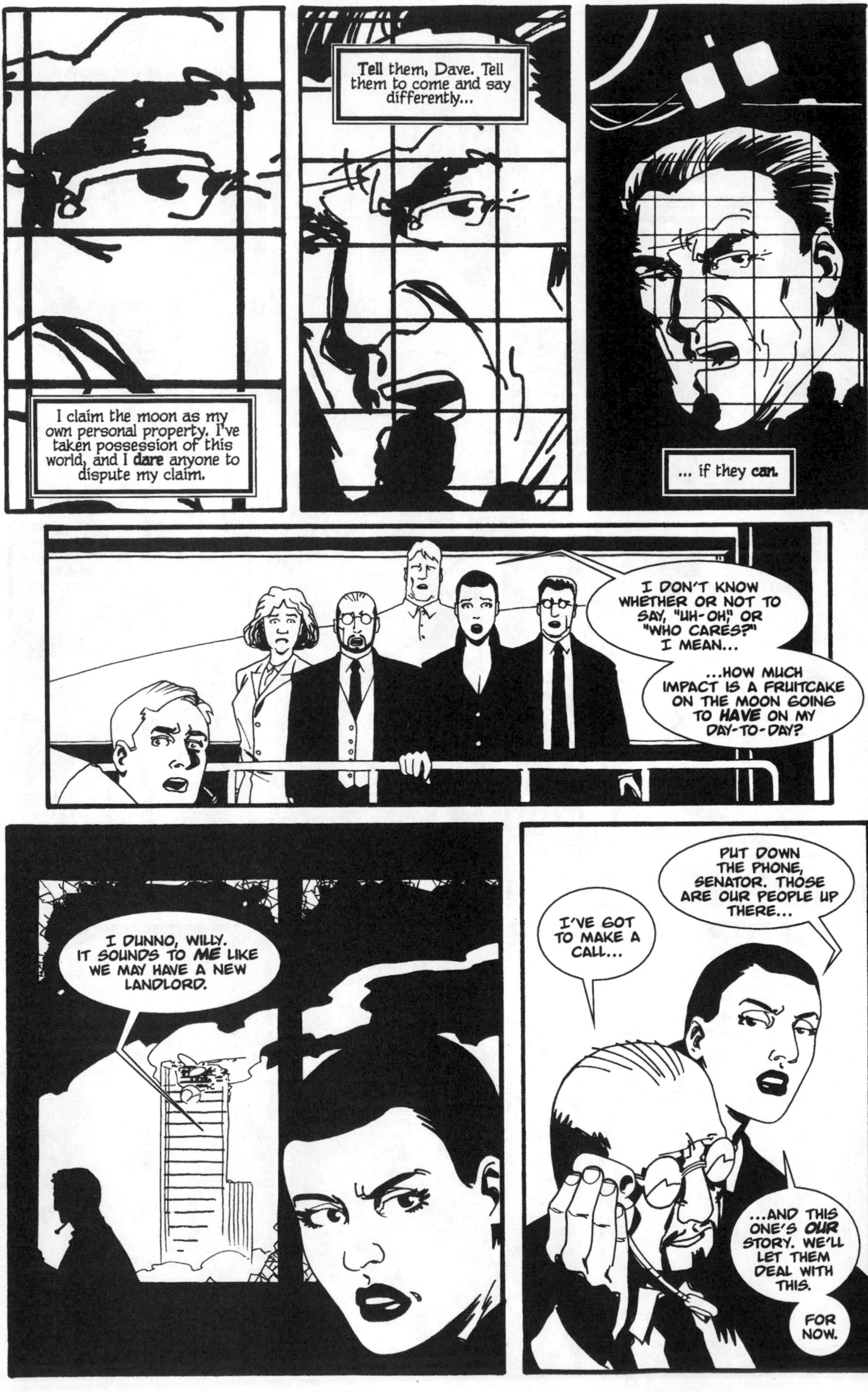

I claim the moon as my own personal property. I've taken possession of this world, and I dare anyone to dispute my claim.
Tell them, Dave. Tell them to come and say differently...
... if they can.
I DON'T KNOW WHETHER OR NOT TO SAY, "UH-OH," OR "WHO CARES?" I MEAN...
...HOW MUCH IMPACT IS A FRUITCAKE ON THE MOON GOING TO HAVE ON MY DAY-TO-DAY?
I DUNNO, WILLY. IT SOUNDS TO ME LIKE WE MAY HAVE A NEW LANDLORD.
I'VE GOT TO MAKE A CALL...
PUT DOWN THE PHONE, SENATOR. THOSE ARE OUR PEOPLE UP THERE...
...AND THIS ONE'S OUR STORY. WE'LL LET THEM DEAL WITH THIS.
FOR NOW.

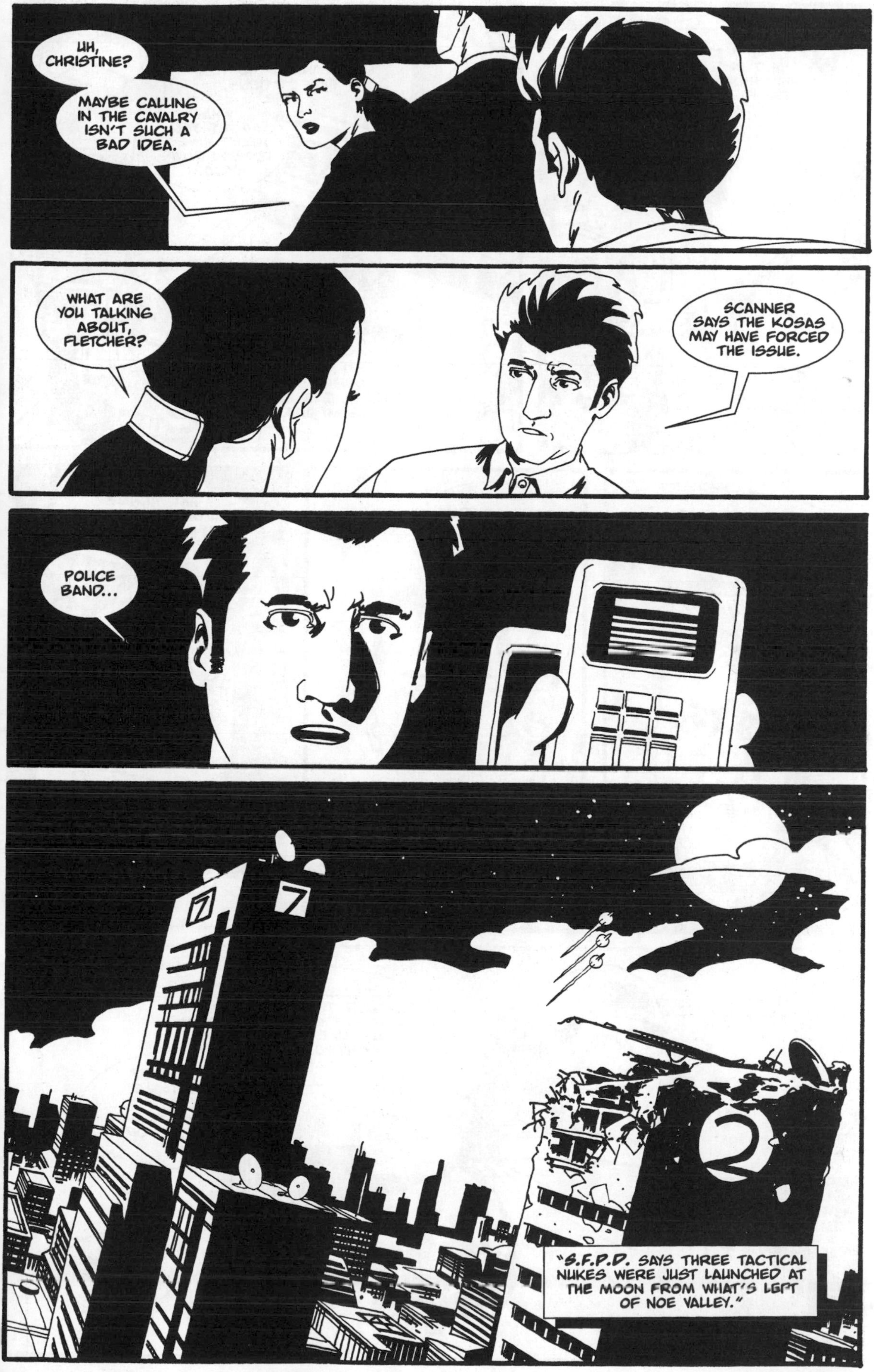
UH, CHRISTINE?
MAYBE CALLING IN THE CAVALRY ISN'T SUCH A BAD IDEA.
WHAT ARE YOU TALKING ABOUT, FLETCHER?
SCANNER SAYS THE KOSAS MAY HAVE FORCED THE ISSUE.
POLICE BAND...
7
7
2
"S.F.P.D. SAYS THREE TACTICAL NUKES WERE JUST LAUNCHED AT THE MOON FROM WHAT'S LEFT OF NOE VALLEY."

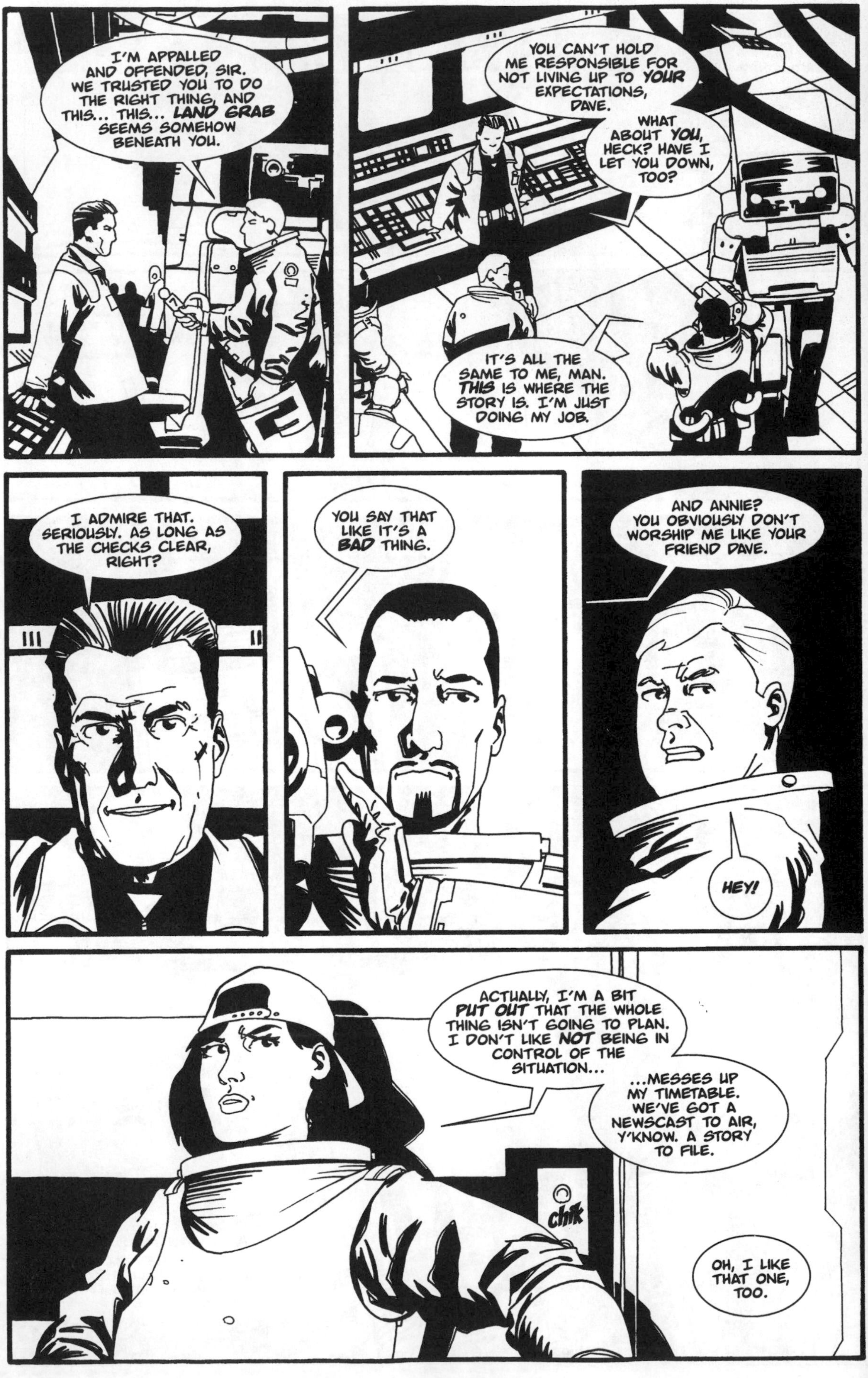
I'M APPALLED AND OFFENDED, SIR. WE TRUSTED YOU TO DO THE RIGHT THING, AND THIS... THIS... LAND GRAB SEEMS SOMEHOW BENEATH YOU.
YOU CAN'T HOLD ME RESPONSIBLE FOR NOT LIVING UP TO YOUR EXPECTATIONS, DAVE.
WHAT ABOUT YOU, HECK? HAVE I LET YOU DOWN, TOO?
IT'S ALL THE SAME TO ME, MAN. THIS IS WHERE THE STORY IS. I'M JUST DOING MY JOB.
I ADMIRE THAT. SERIOUSLY. AS LONG AS THE CHECKS CLEAR, RIGHT?
YOU SAY THAT LIKE IT'S A BAD THING.
AND ANNIE? YOU OBVIOUSLY DON'T WORSHIP ME LIKE YOUR FRIEND DAVE.
HEY!
ACTUALLY, I'M A BIT PUT OUT THAT THE WHOLE THING ISN'T GOING TO PLAN. I DON'T LIKE NOT BEING IN CONTROL OF THE SITUATION...
...MESSES UP MY TIMETABLE. WE'VE GOT A NEWSCAST TO AIR, Y'KNOW. A STORY TO FILE.
chik
OH, I LIKE THAT ONE, TOO.

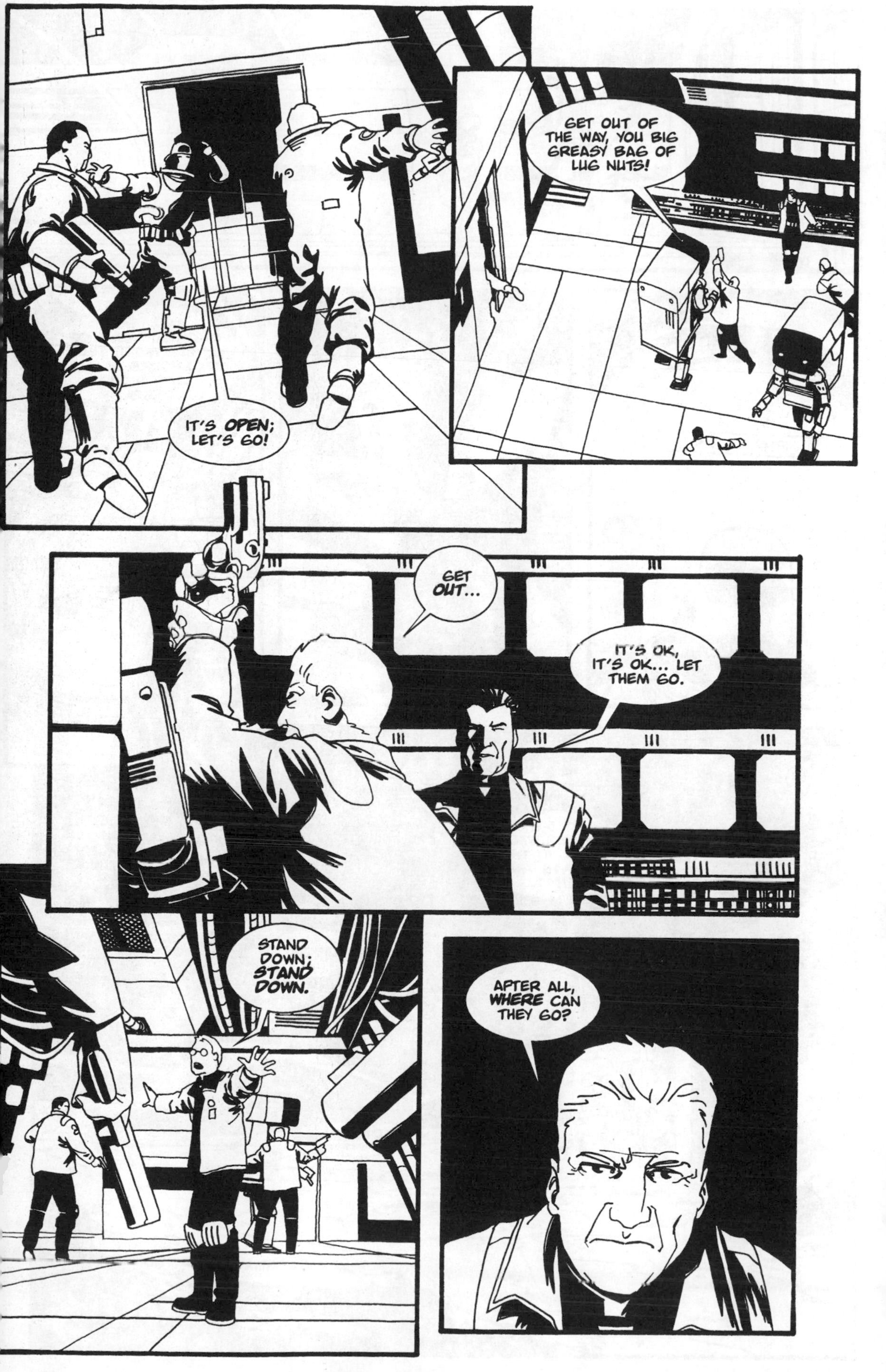
IT'S OPEN; LET'S GO!
GET OUT OF THE WAY, YOU BIG GREASY BAG OF LUG NUTS!
GET OUT...
IT'S OK, IT'S OK... LET THEM GO.
STAND DOWN; STAND DOWN.
AFTER ALL, WHERE CAN THEY GO?

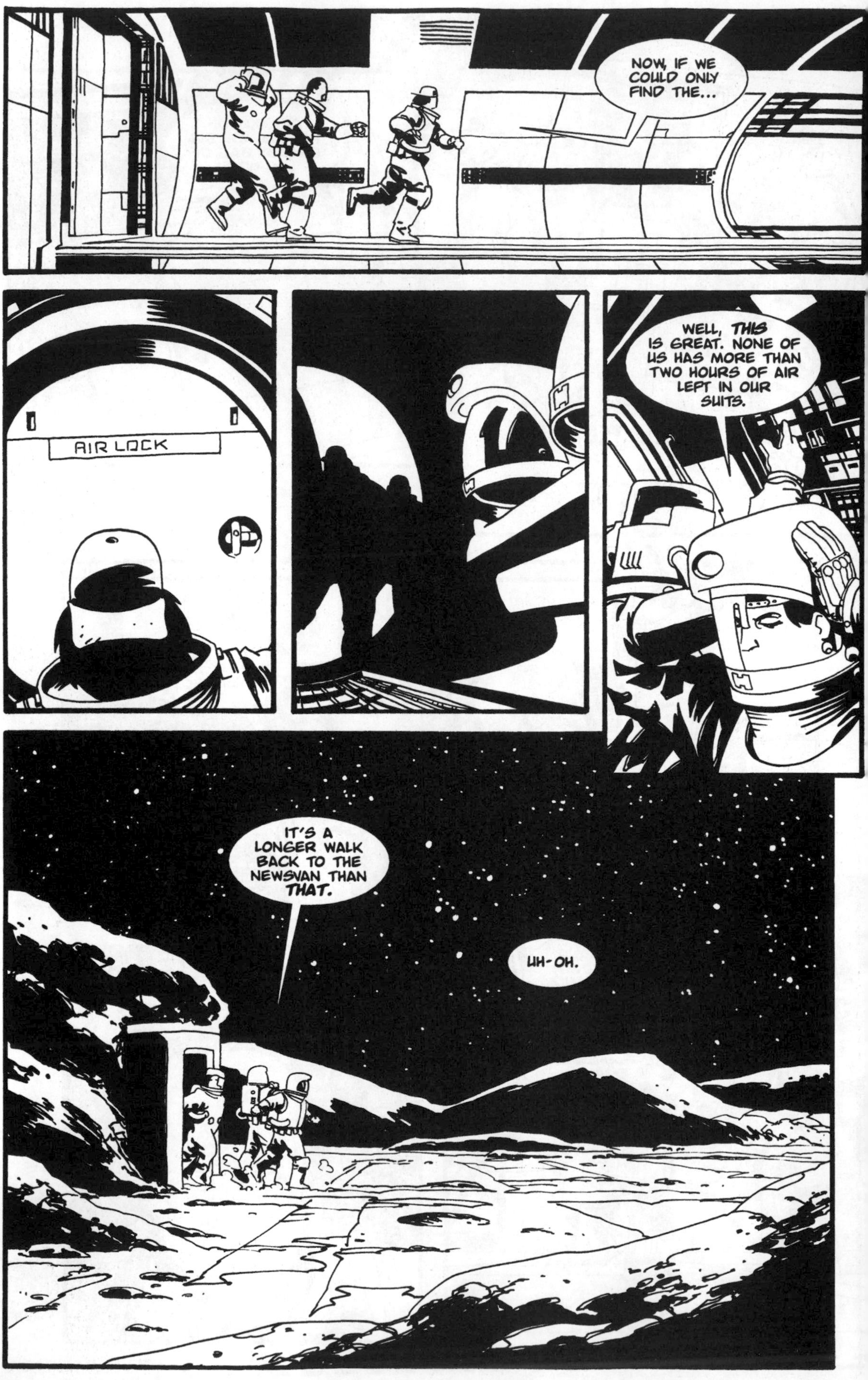
NOW, IF WE COULD ONLY FIND THE...
AIR LOCK
WELL, THIS IS GREAT. NONE OF US HAS MORE THAN TWO HOURS OF AIR LEFT IN OUR SUITS.
IT'S A LONGER WALK BACK TO THE NEWSVAN THAN THAT.
UH-OH.

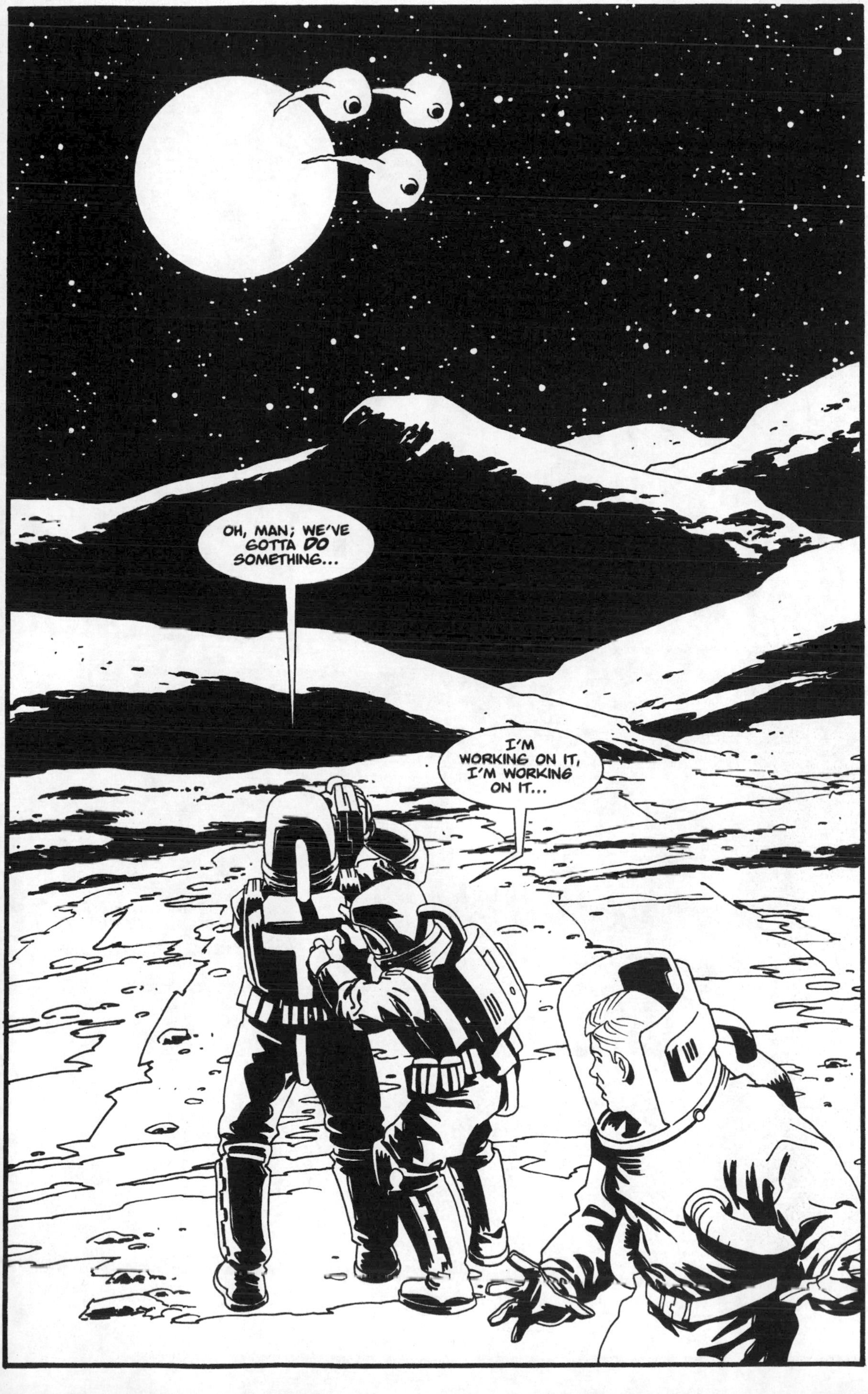
OH, MAN; WE'VE GOTTA *DO* SOMETHING...
I'M WORKING ON IT, I'M WORKING ON IT...

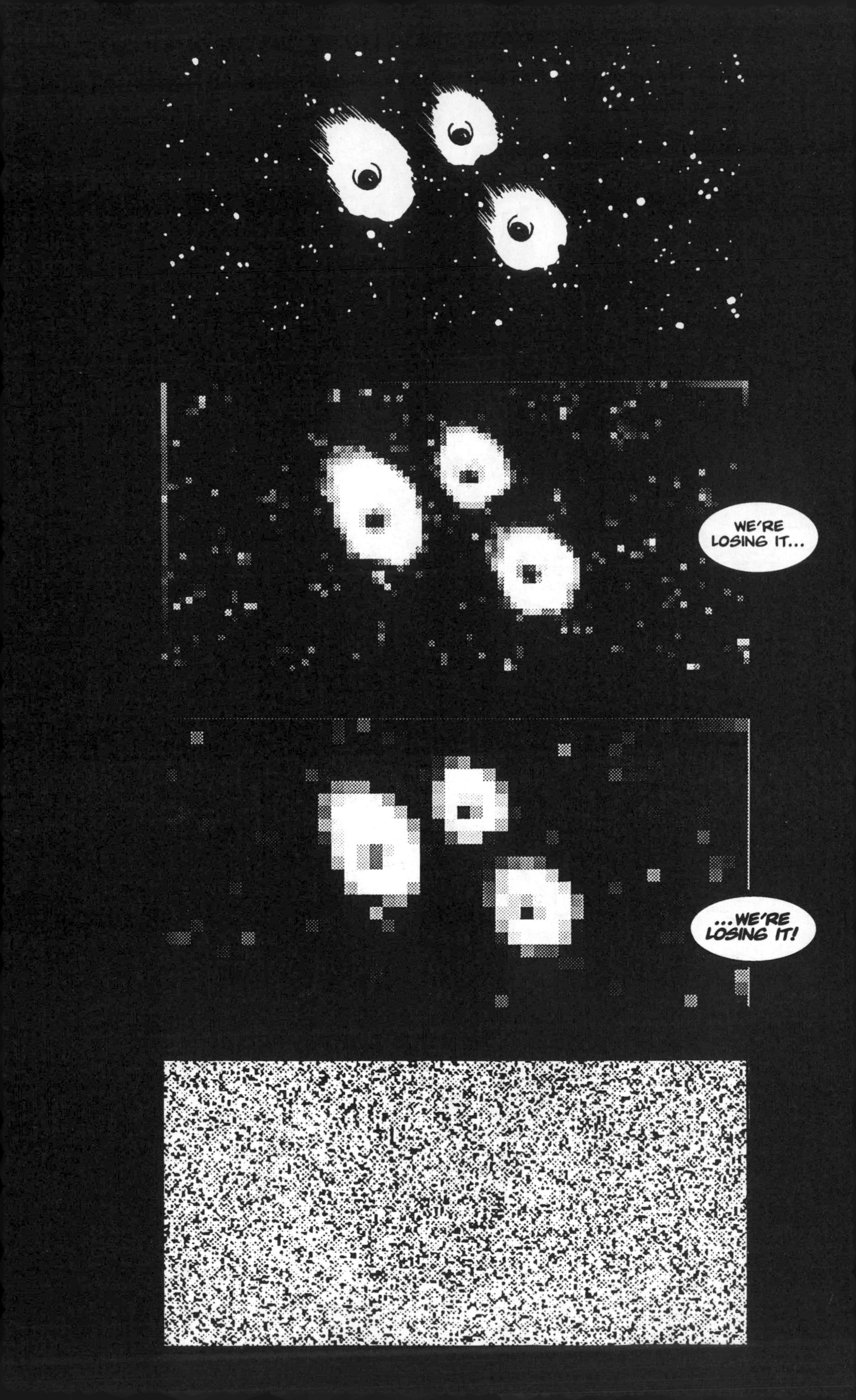
WE'RE LOSING IT...
...WE'RE LOSING IT!

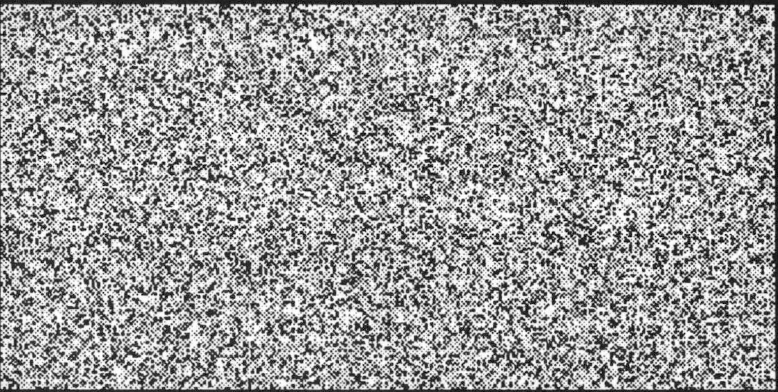
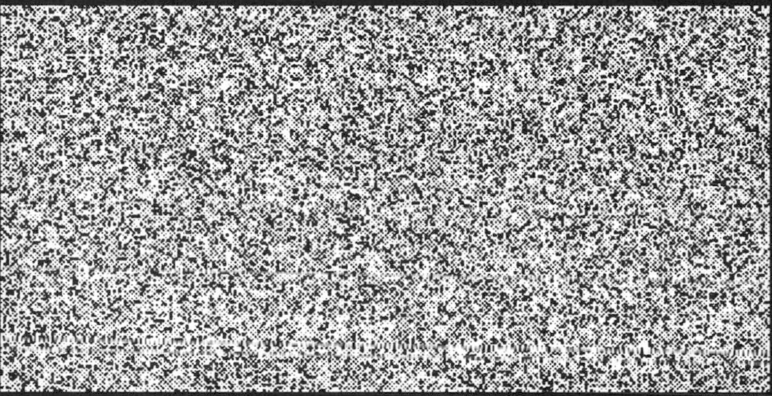
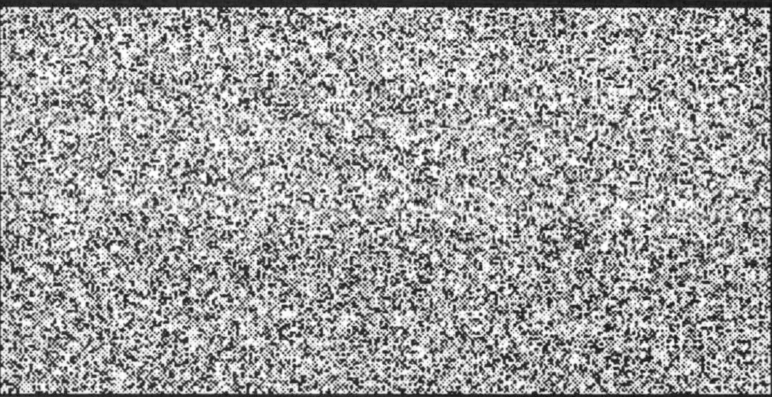
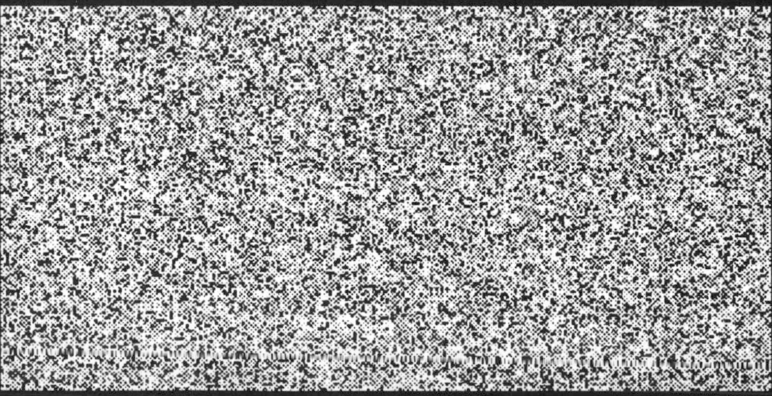

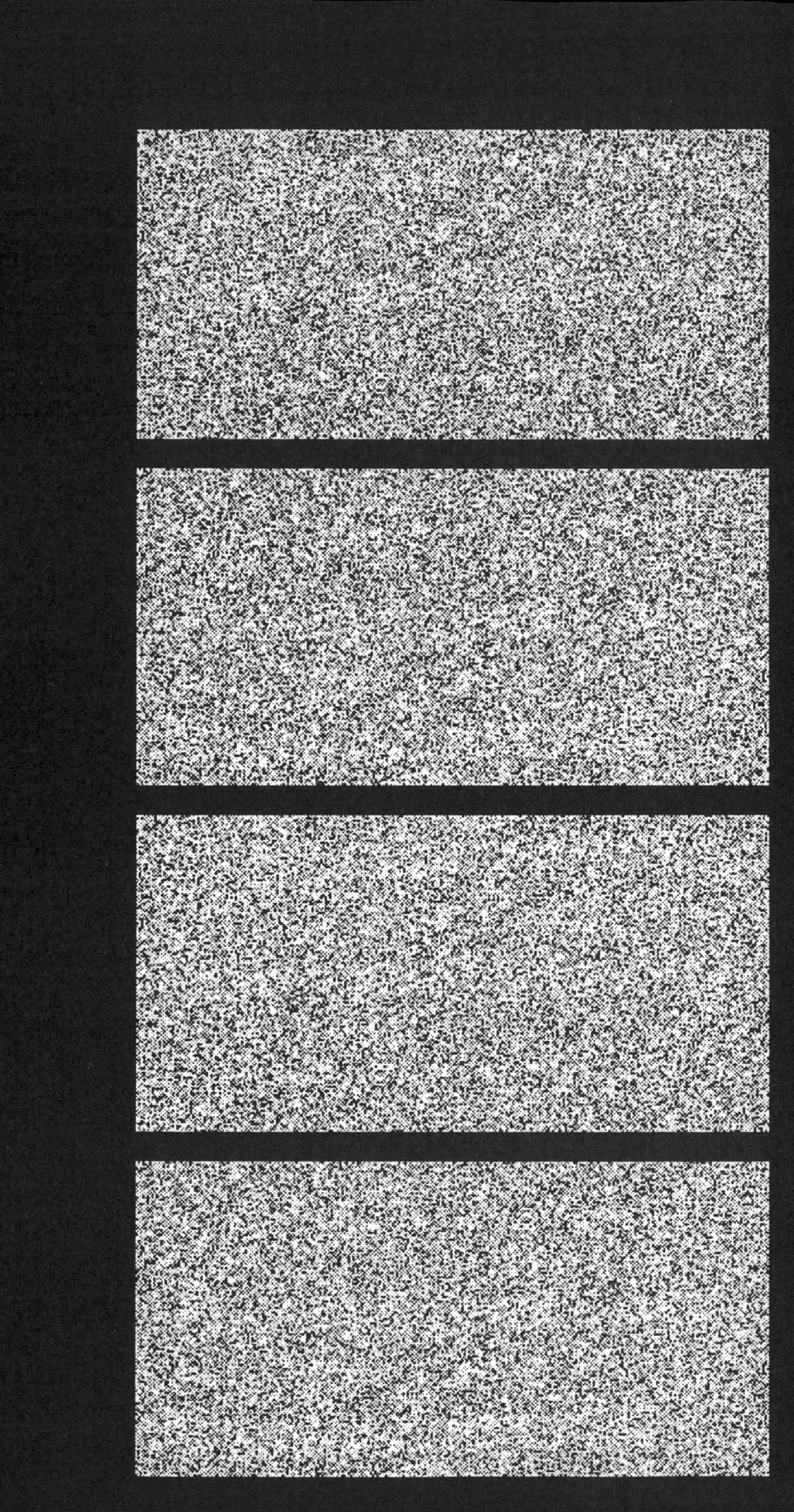

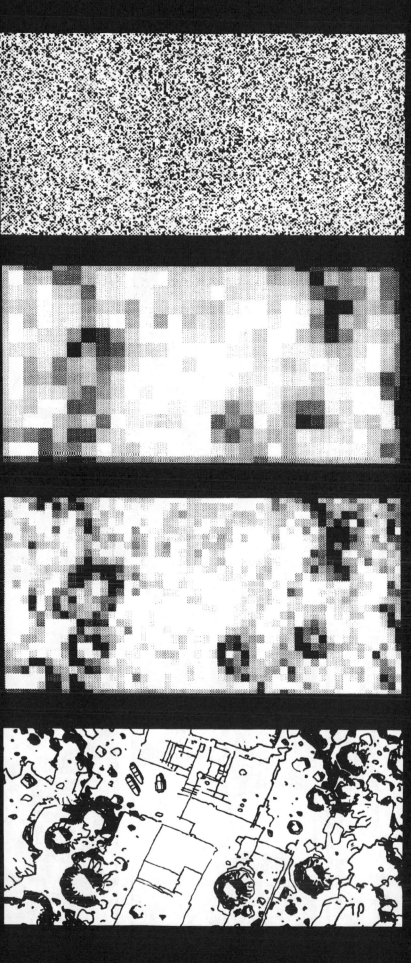

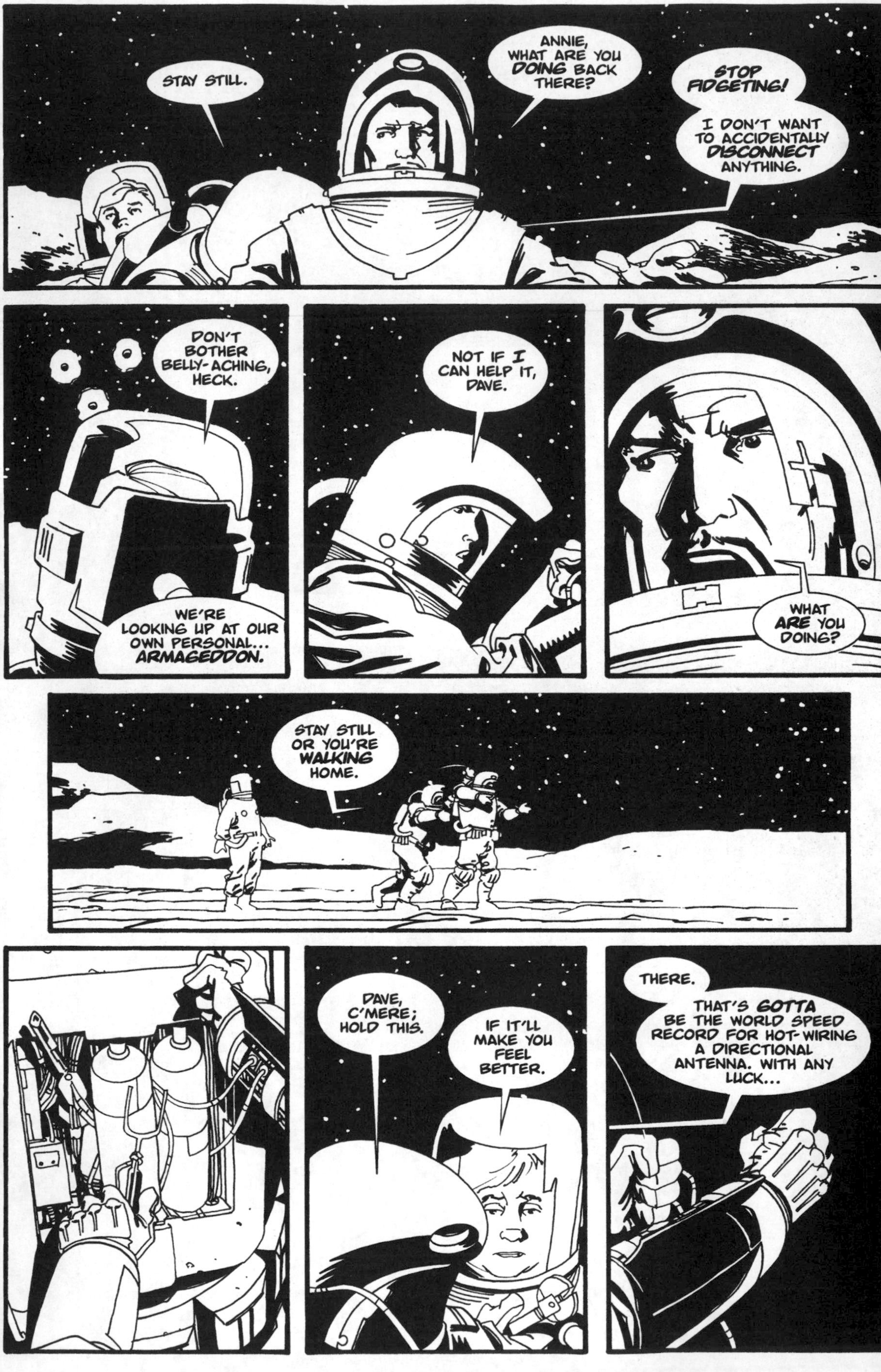
STAY STILL.
ANNIE, WHAT ARE YOU DOING BACK THERE?
STOP FIDGETING!
I DON'T WANT TO ACCIDENTALLY DISCONNECT ANYTHING.
DON'T BOTHER BELLY-ACHING, HECK.
WE'RE LOOKING UP AT OUR OWN PERSONAL... ARMAGEDDON.
NOT IF I CAN HELP IT, DAVE.
WHAT ARE YOU DOING?
STAY STILL OR YOU'RE WALKING HOME.
DAVE, C'MERE; HOLD THIS.
IF IT'LL MAKE YOU FEEL BETTER.
THERE.
THAT'S GOTTA BE THE WORLD SPEED RECORD FOR HOT-WIRING A DIRECTIONAL ANTENNA. WITH ANY LUCK...

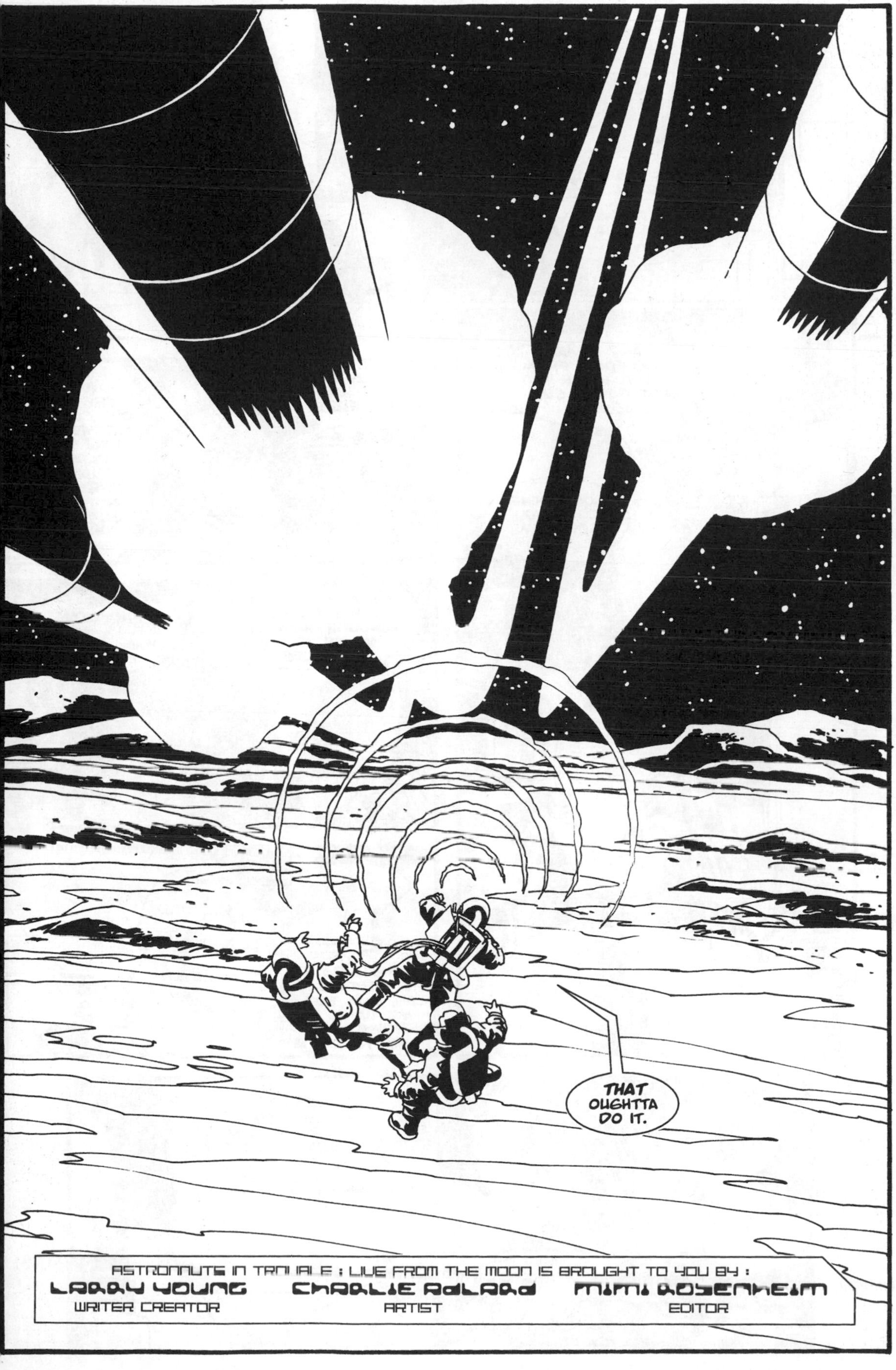
THAT OUGHTTA DO IT.
ASTRONAUTS IN TROUBLE: LIVE FROM THE MOON IS BROUGHT TO YOU BY:
LARRY YOUNG
WRITER CREATOR
CHARLIE ADLARD
ARTIST
MIMI ROSENHEIM
EDITOR

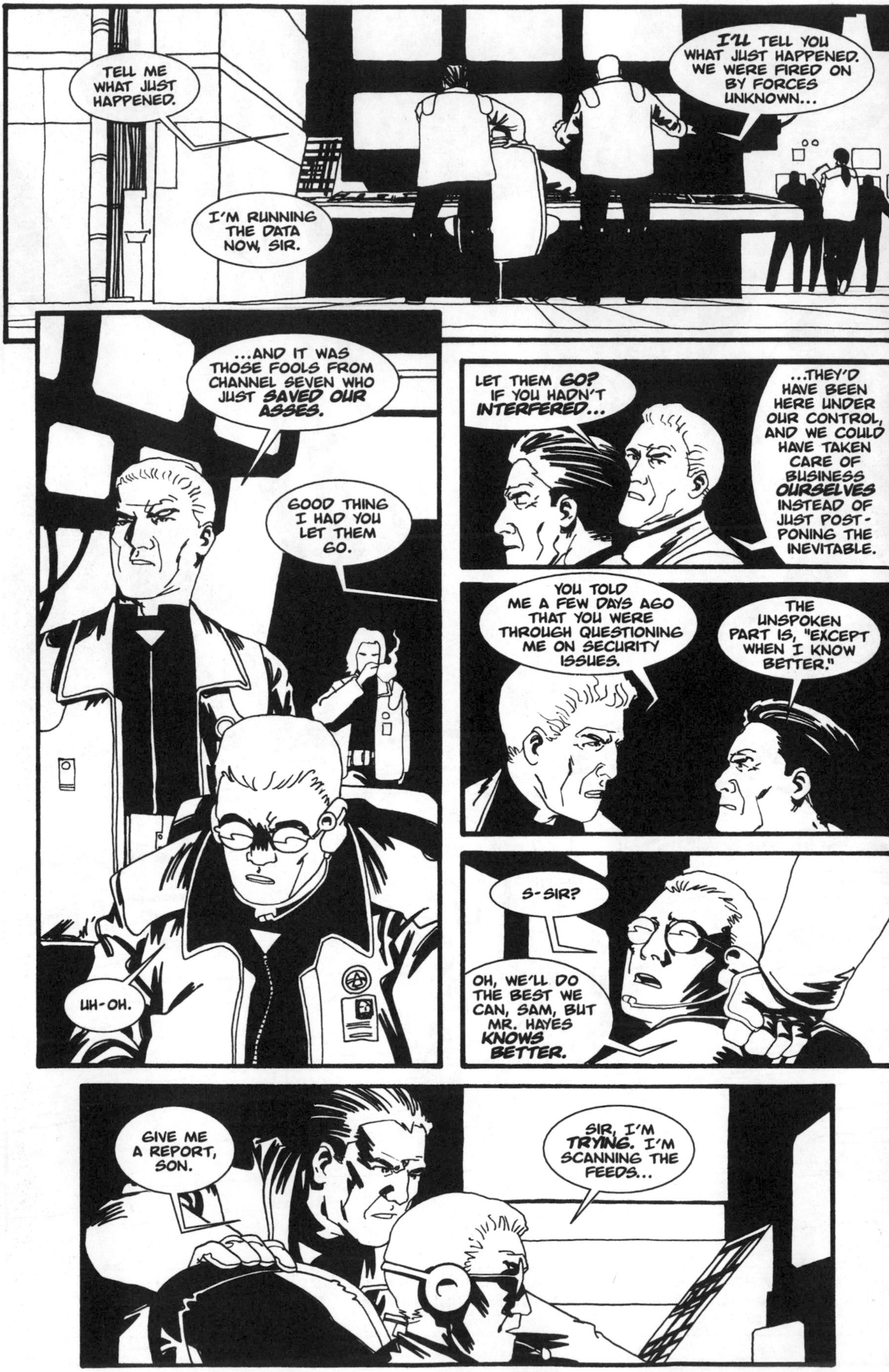
TELL ME WHAT JUST HAPPENED.
I'LL TELL YOU WHAT JUST HAPPENED. WE WERE FIRED ON BY FORCES UNKNOWN...
I'M RUNNING THE DATA NOW, SIR.
...AND IT WAS THOSE FOOLS FROM CHANNEL SEVEN WHO JUST SAVED OUR ASSES.
GOOD THING I HAD YOU LET THEM GO.
UH-OH.
LET THEM GO? IF YOU HADN'T INTERFERED...
...THEY'D HAVE BEEN HERE UNDER OUR CONTROL, AND WE COULD HAVE TAKEN CARE OF BUSINESS OURSELVES INSTEAD OF JUST POST-PONING THE INEVITABLE.
YOU TOLD ME A FEW DAYS AGO THAT YOU WERE THROUGH QUESTIONING ME ON SECURITY ISSUES.
THE UNSPOKEN PART IS, "EXCEPT WHEN I KNOW BETTER."
S-SIR?
OH, WE'LL DO THE BEST WE CAN, SAM, BUT MR. HAYES KNOWS BETTER.
GIVE ME A REPORT, SON.
SIR, I'M TRYING. I'M SCANNING THE FEEDS...

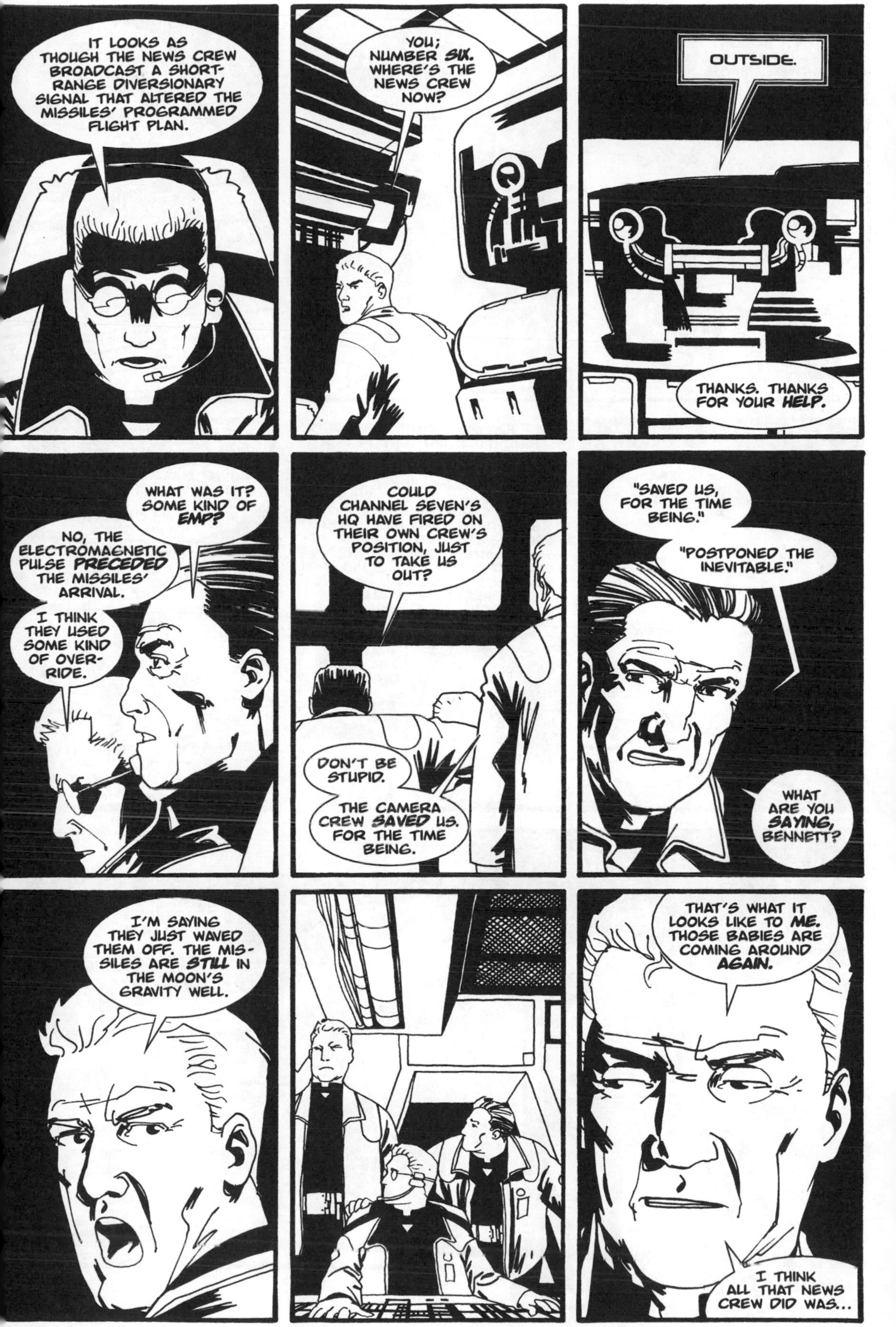
IT LOOKS AS THOUGH THE NEWS CREW BROADCAST A SHORT-RANGE DIVERSIONARY SIGNAL THAT ALTERED THE MISSILES' PROGRAMMED FLIGHT PLAN.
YOU; NUMBER SIX. WHERE'S THE NEWS CREW NOW?
OUTSIDE.
THANKS. THANKS FOR YOUR HELP.
WHAT WAS IT? SOME KIND OF EMP?
NO, THE ELECTROMAGNETIC PULSE PRECEDED THE MISSILES' ARRIVAL.
I THINK THEY USED SOME KIND OF OVER-RIDE.
COULD CHANNEL SEVEN'S HQ HAVE FIRED ON THEIR OWN CREW'S POSITION, JUST TO TAKE US OUT?
DON'T BE STUPID.
THE CAMERA CREW SAVED US. FOR THE TIME BEING.
"SAVED US, FOR THE TIME BEING."
"POSTPONED THE INEVITABLE."
WHAT ARE YOU SAYING, BENNETT?
I'M SAYING THEY JUST WAVED THEM OFF. THE MIS-SILES ARE STILL IN THE MOON'S GRAVITY WELL.
THAT'S WHAT IT LOOKS LIKE TO ME. THOSE BABIES ARE COMING AROUND AGAIN.
I THINK ALL THAT NEWS CREW DID WAS...

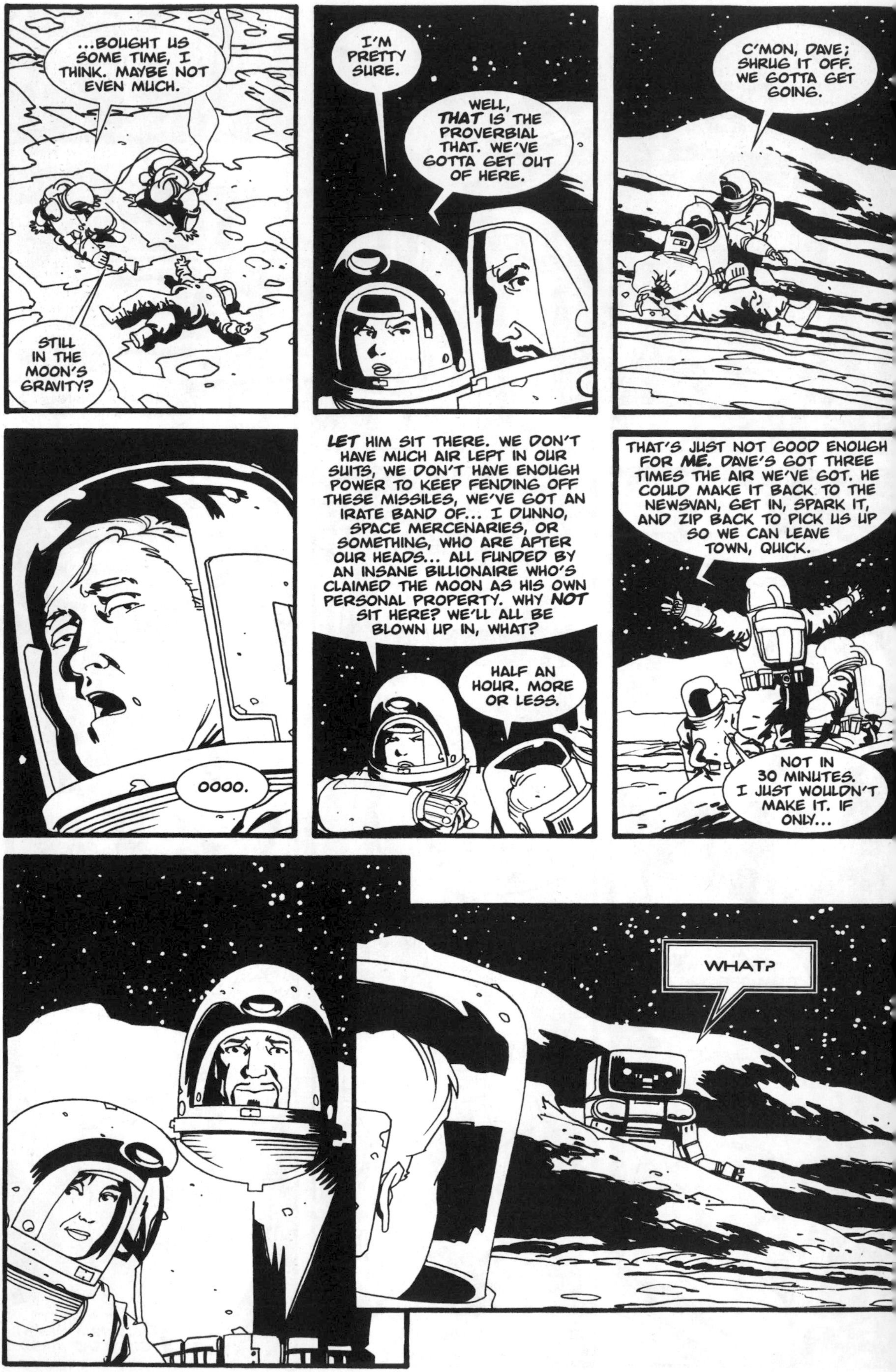
...BOUGHT US SOME TIME, I THINK. MAYBE NOT EVEN MUCH.
STILL IN THE MOON'S GRAVITY?
I'M PRETTY SURE.
WELL, THAT IS THE PROVERBIAL THAT. WE'VE GOTTA GET OUT OF HERE.
C'MON, DAVE; SHRUG IT OFF. WE GOTTA GET GOING.
OOOO.
LET HIM SIT THERE. WE DON'T HAVE MUCH AIR LEFT IN OUR SUITS, WE DON'T HAVE ENOUGH POWER TO KEEP FENDING OFF THESE MISSILES, WE'VE GOT AN IRATE BAND OF... I DUNNO, SPACE MERCENARIES, OR SOMETHING, WHO ARE AFTER OUR HEADS... ALL FUNDED BY AN INSANE BILLIONAIRE WHO'S CLAIMED THE MOON AS HIS OWN PERSONAL PROPERTY. WHY NOT SIT HERE? WE'LL ALL BE BLOWN UP IN, WHAT?
HALF AN HOUR. MORE OR LESS.
THAT'S JUST NOT GOOD ENOUGH FOR ME. DAVE'S GOT THREE TIMES THE AIR WE'VE GOT. HE COULD MAKE IT BACK TO THE NEWSVAN, GET IN, SPARK IT, AND ZIP BACK TO PICK US UP SO WE CAN LEAVE TOWN, QUICK.
NOT IN 30 MINUTES. I JUST WOULDN'T MAKE IT. IF ONLY...
WHAT?

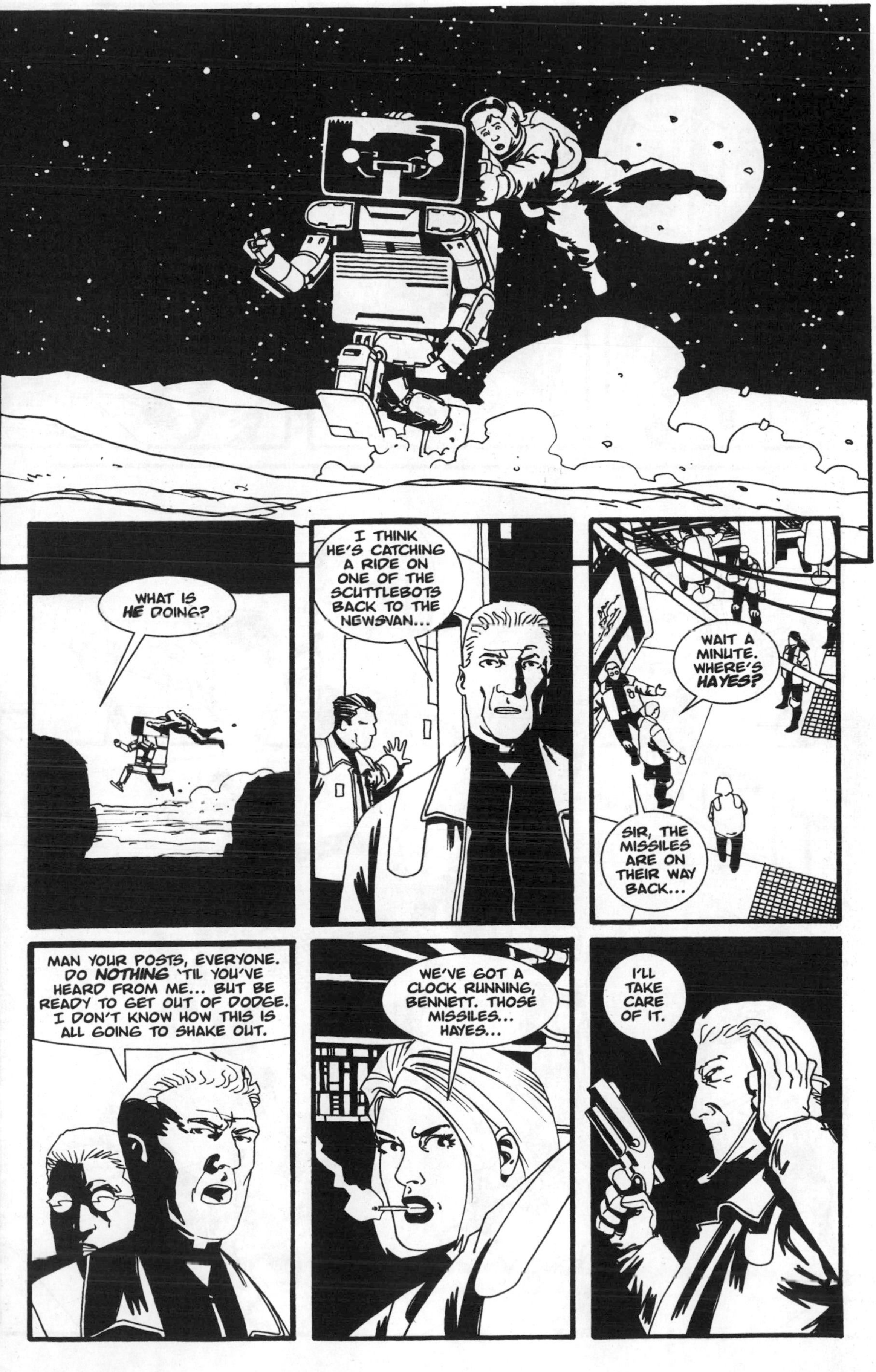
WHAT IS HE DOING?
I THINK HE'S CATCHING A RIDE ON ONE OF THE SCUTTLEBOTS BACK TO THE NEWSVAN...
WAIT A MINUTE. WHERE'S HAYES?
SIR, THE MISSILES ARE ON THEIR WAY BACK...
MAN YOUR POSTS, EVERYONE. DO NOTHING 'TIL YOU'VE HEARD FROM ME... BUT BE READY TO GET OUT OF DODGE. I DON'T KNOW HOW THIS IS ALL GOING TO SHAKE OUT.
WE'VE GOT A CLOCK RUNNING, BENNETT. THOSE MISSILES... HAYES...
I'LL TAKE CARE OF IT.

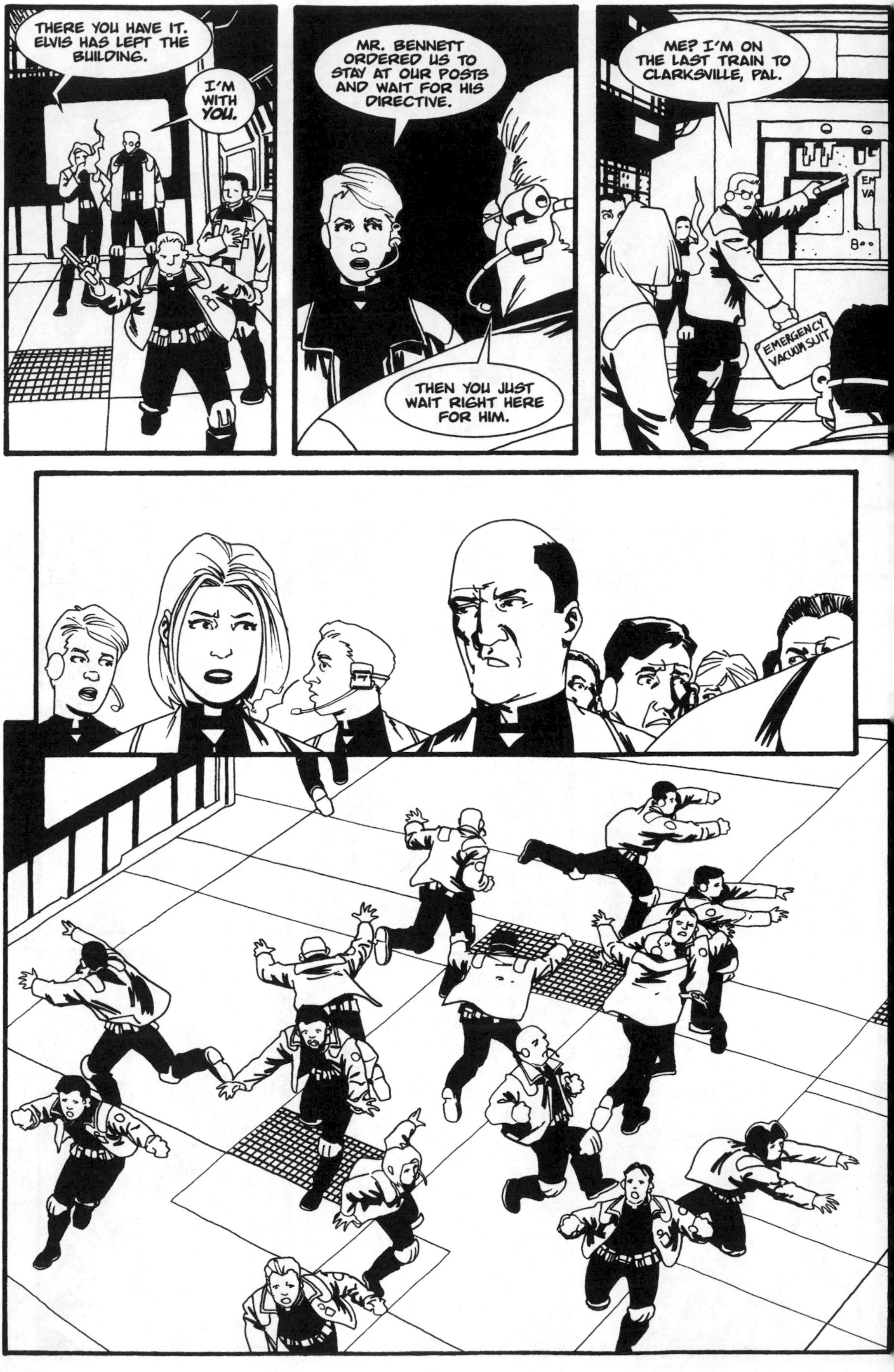
THERE YOU HAVE IT. ELVIS HAS LEFT THE BUILDING.
I'M WITH YOU.
MR. BENNETT ORDERED US TO STAY AT OUR POSTS AND WAIT FOR HIS DIRECTIVE.
THEN YOU JUST WAIT RIGHT HERE FOR HIM.
ME? I'M ON THE LAST TRAIN TO CLARKSVILLE, PAL.
EMERGENCY VACUUM SUIT

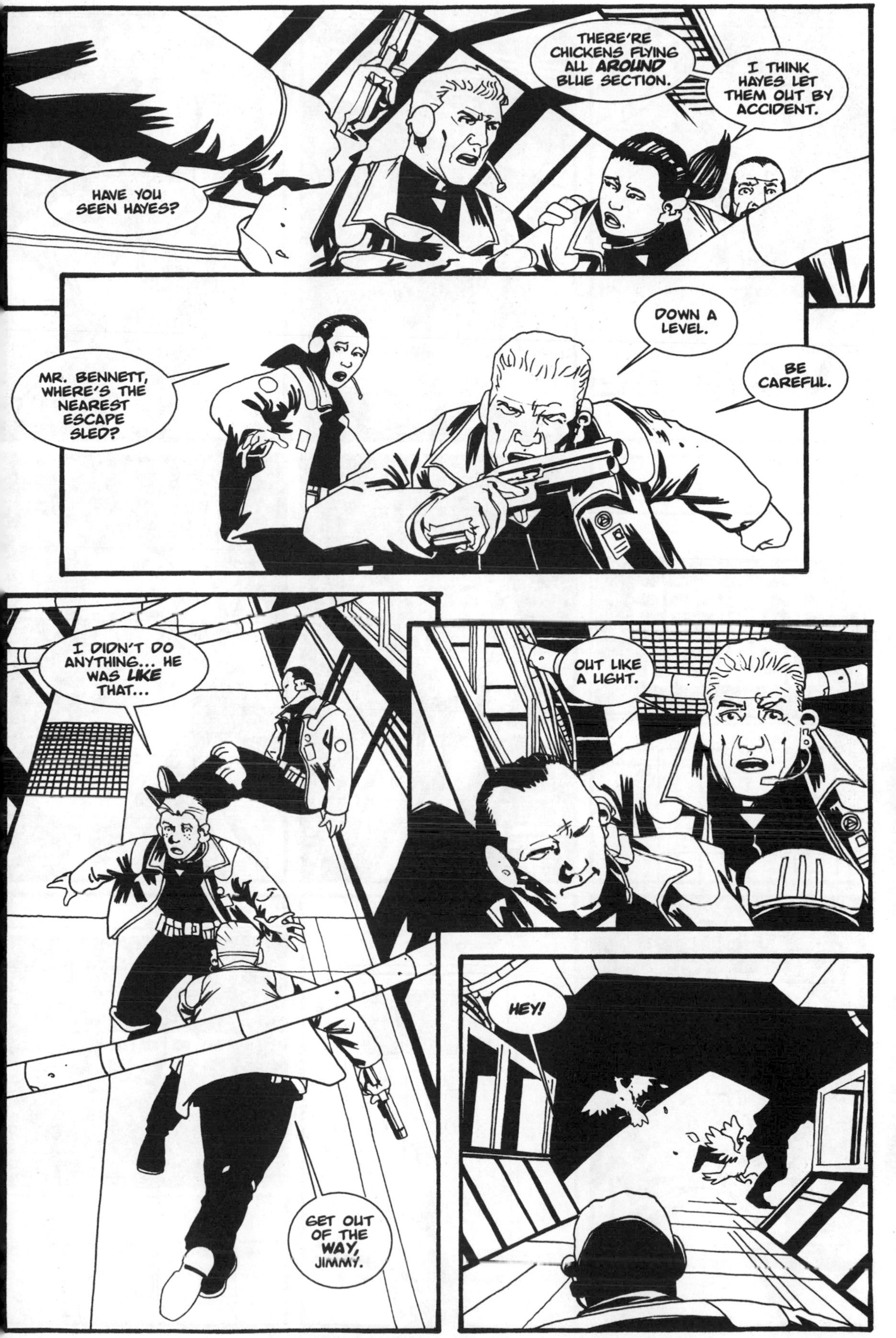
HAVE YOU SEEN HAYES?
THERE'RE CHICKENS FLYING ALL AROUND BLUE SECTION.
I THINK HAYES LET THEM OUT BY ACCIDENT.
MR. BENNETT, WHERE'S THE NEAREST ESCAPE SLED?
DOWN A LEVEL.
BE CAREFUL.
I DIDN'T DO ANYTHING... HE WAS LIKE THAT...
GET OUT OF THE WAY, JIMMY.
OUT LIKE A LIGHT.
HEY!

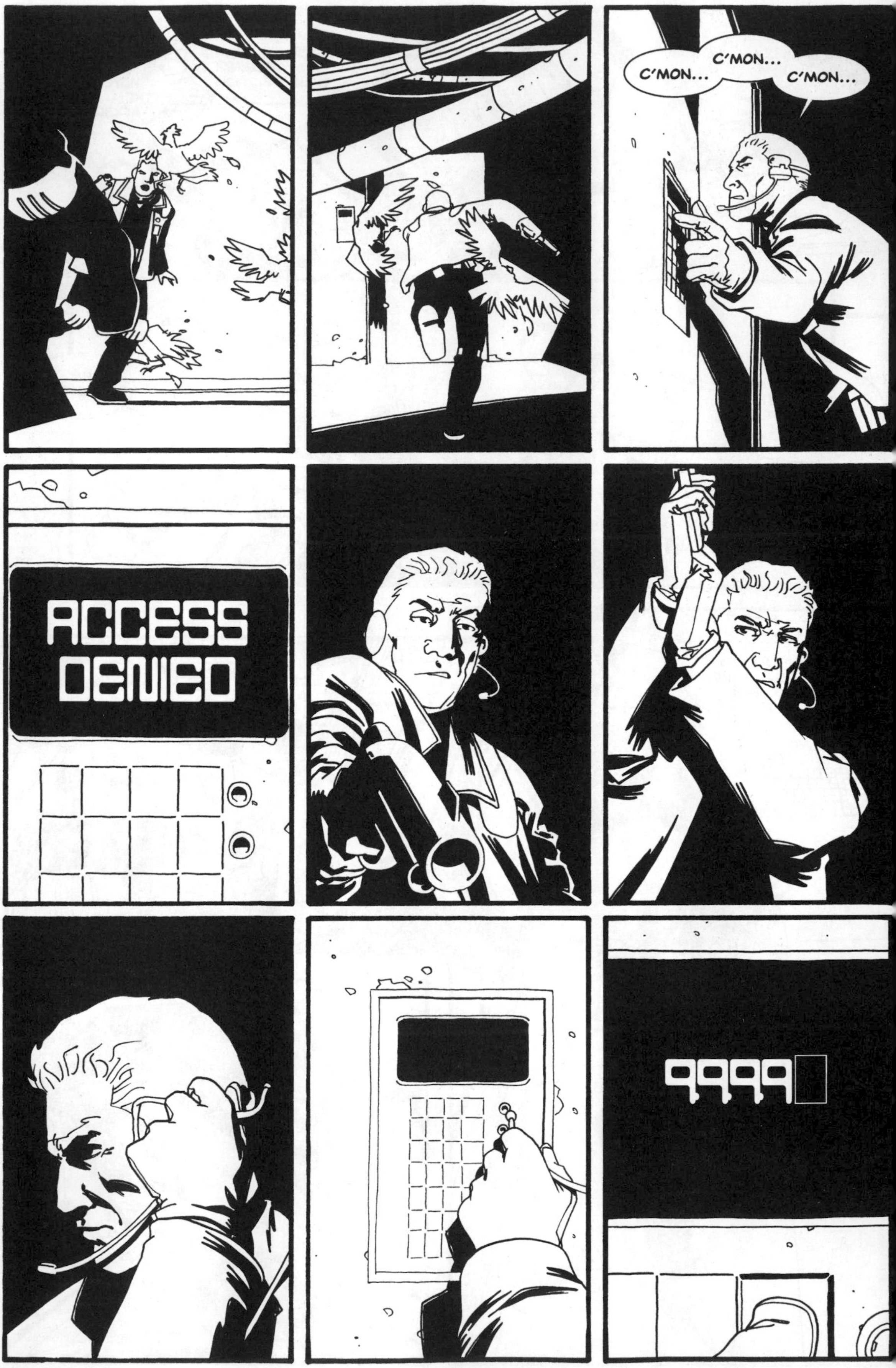
C'MON...
C'MON...
C'MON...
ACCESS
DENIED
9999

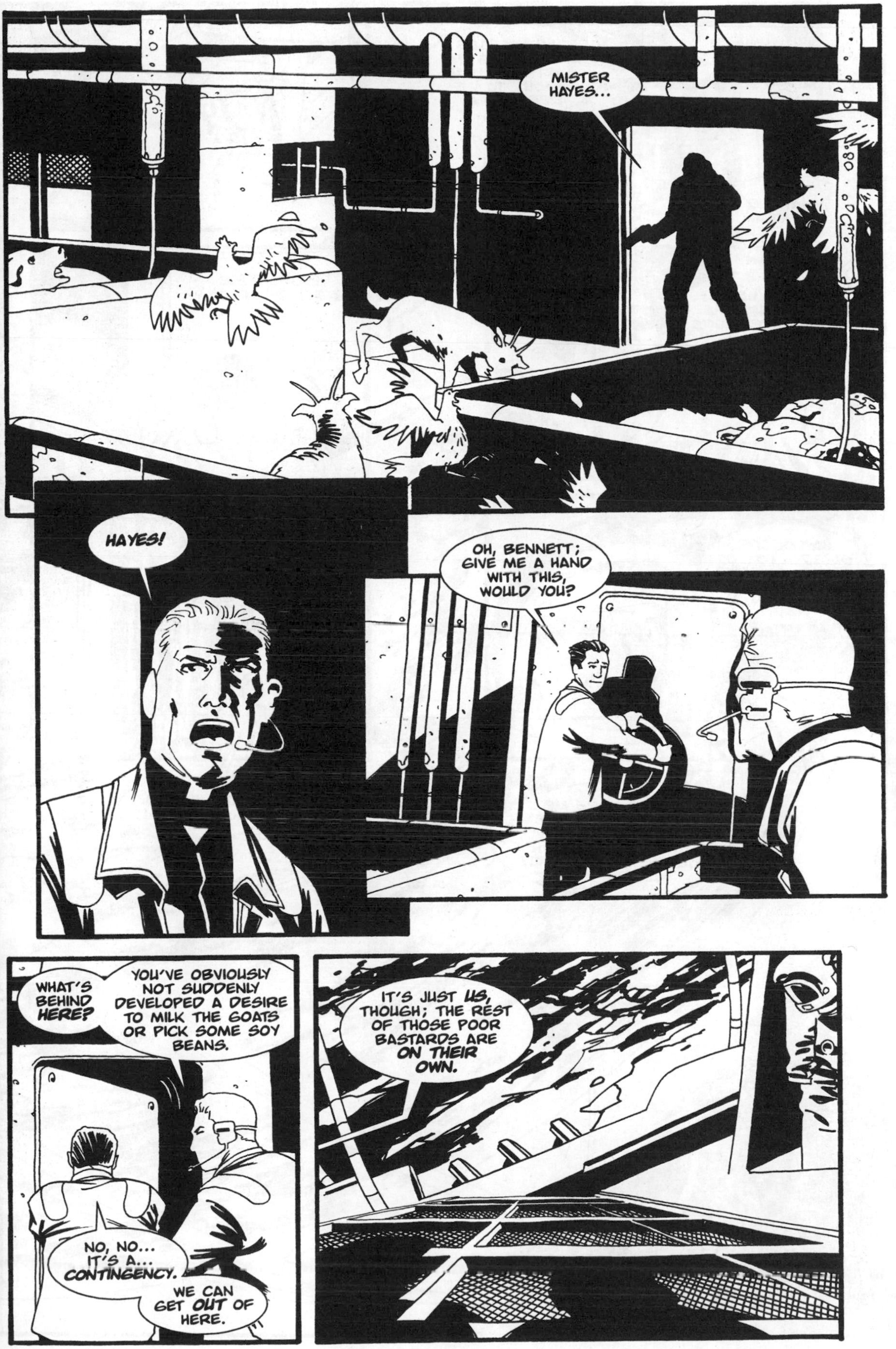
MISTER HAYES...
HAYES!
OH, BENNETT; GIVE ME A HAND WITH THIS, WOULD YOU?
WHAT'S BEHIND HERE?
YOU'VE OBVIOUSLY NOT SUDDENLY DEVELOPED A DESIRE TO MILK THE GOATS OR PICK SOME SOY BEANS.
NO, NO... IT'S A... CONTINGENCY.
WE CAN GET OUT OF HERE.
IT'S JUST US, THOUGH; THE REST OF THOSE POOR BASTARDS ARE ON THEIR OWN.

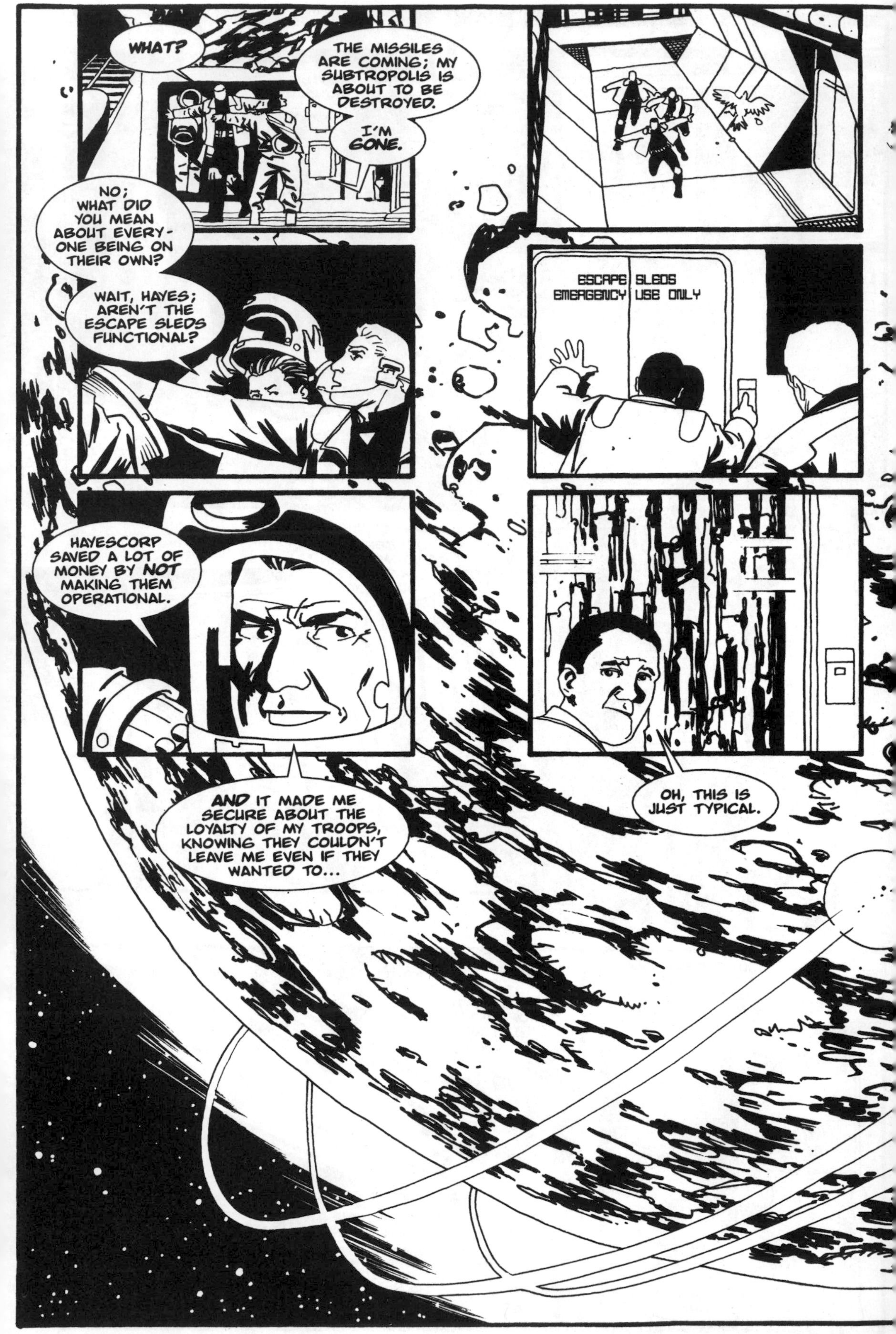
WHAT?
THE MISSILES ARE COMING; MY SUBTROPOLIS IS ABOUT TO BE DESTROYED.
I'M GONE.
NO; WHAT DID YOU MEAN ABOUT EVERY-ONE BEING ON THEIR OWN?
WAIT, HAYES; AREN'T THE ESCAPE SLEDS FUNCTIONAL?
ESCAPE SLEDS EMERGENCY USE ONLY
HAYESCORP SAVED A LOT OF MONEY BY NOT MAKING THEM OPERATIONAL.
AND IT MADE ME SECURE ABOUT THE LOYALTY OF MY TROOPS, KNOWING THEY COULDN'T LEAVE ME EVEN IF THEY WANTED TO...
OH, THIS IS JUST TYPICAL.

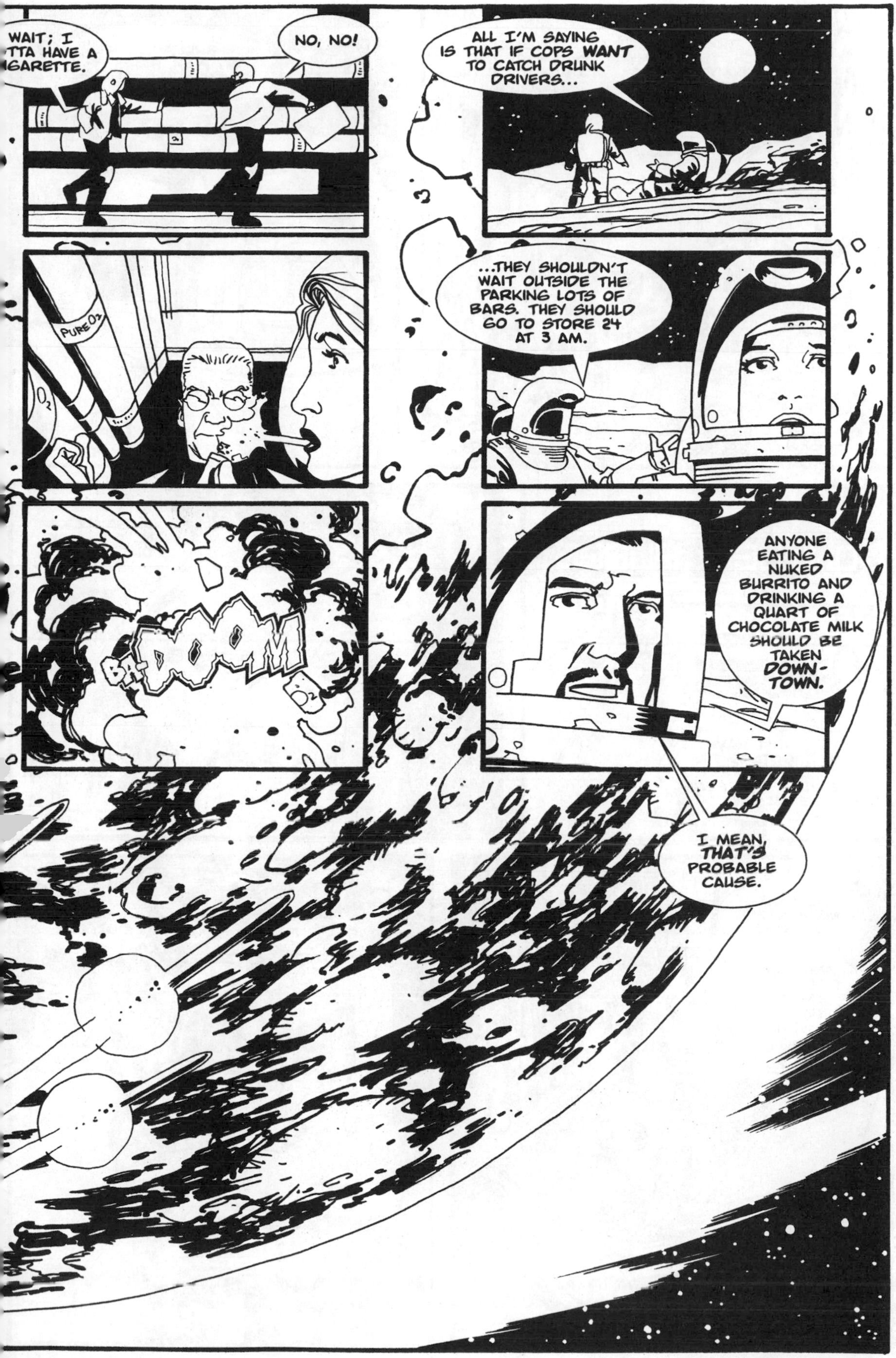
WAIT; I TTA HAVE A GARETTE.
NO, NO!
ALL I'M SAYING IS THAT IF COPS WANT TO CATCH DRUNK DRIVERS...
...THEY SHOULDN'T WAIT OUTSIDE THE PARKING LOTS OF BARS. THEY SHOULD GO TO STORE 24 AT 3 AM.
PURE O2
O2
B-DOOM
O2
ANYONE EATING A NUKED BURRITO AND DRINKING A QUART OF CHOCOLATE MILK SHOULD BE TAKEN DOWN-TOWN.
I MEAN, THAT'S PROBABLE CAUSE.

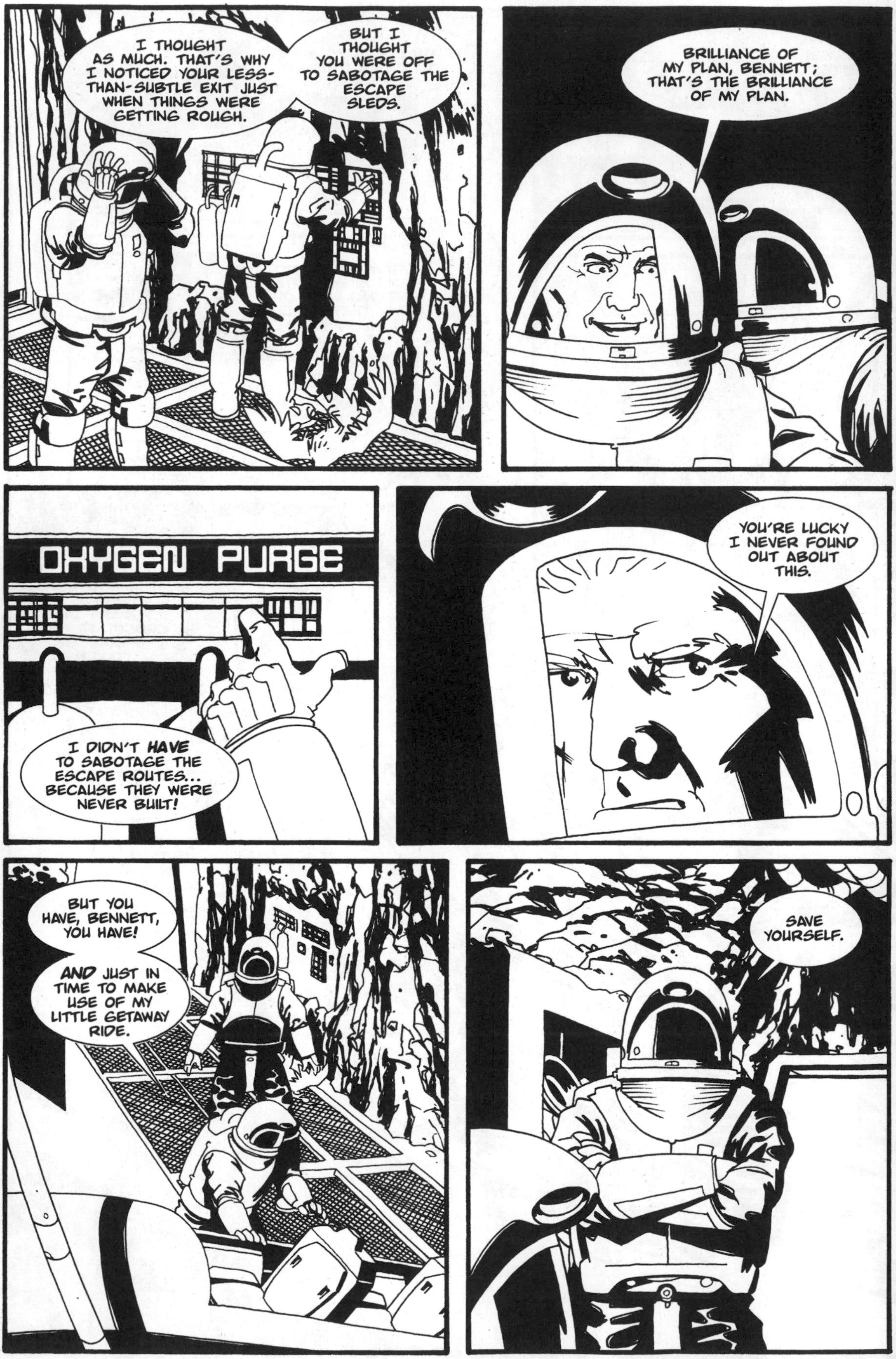
I THOUGHT AS MUCH. THAT'S WHY I NOTICED YOUR LESS-THAN-SUBTLE EXIT JUST WHEN THINGS WERE GETTING ROUGH.
BUT I THOUGHT YOU WERE OFF TO SABOTAGE THE ESCAPE SLEDS.
BRILLIANCE OF MY PLAN, BENNETT; THAT'S THE BRILLIANCE OF MY PLAN.
OXYGEN PURGE
I DIDN'T HAVE TO SABOTAGE THE ESCAPE ROUTES... BECAUSE THEY WERE NEVER BUILT!
YOU'RE LUCKY I NEVER FOUND OUT ABOUT THIS.
BUT YOU HAVE, BENNETT, YOU HAVE!
AND JUST IN TIME TO MAKE USE OF MY LITTLE GETAWAY RIDE.
SAVE YOURSELF.

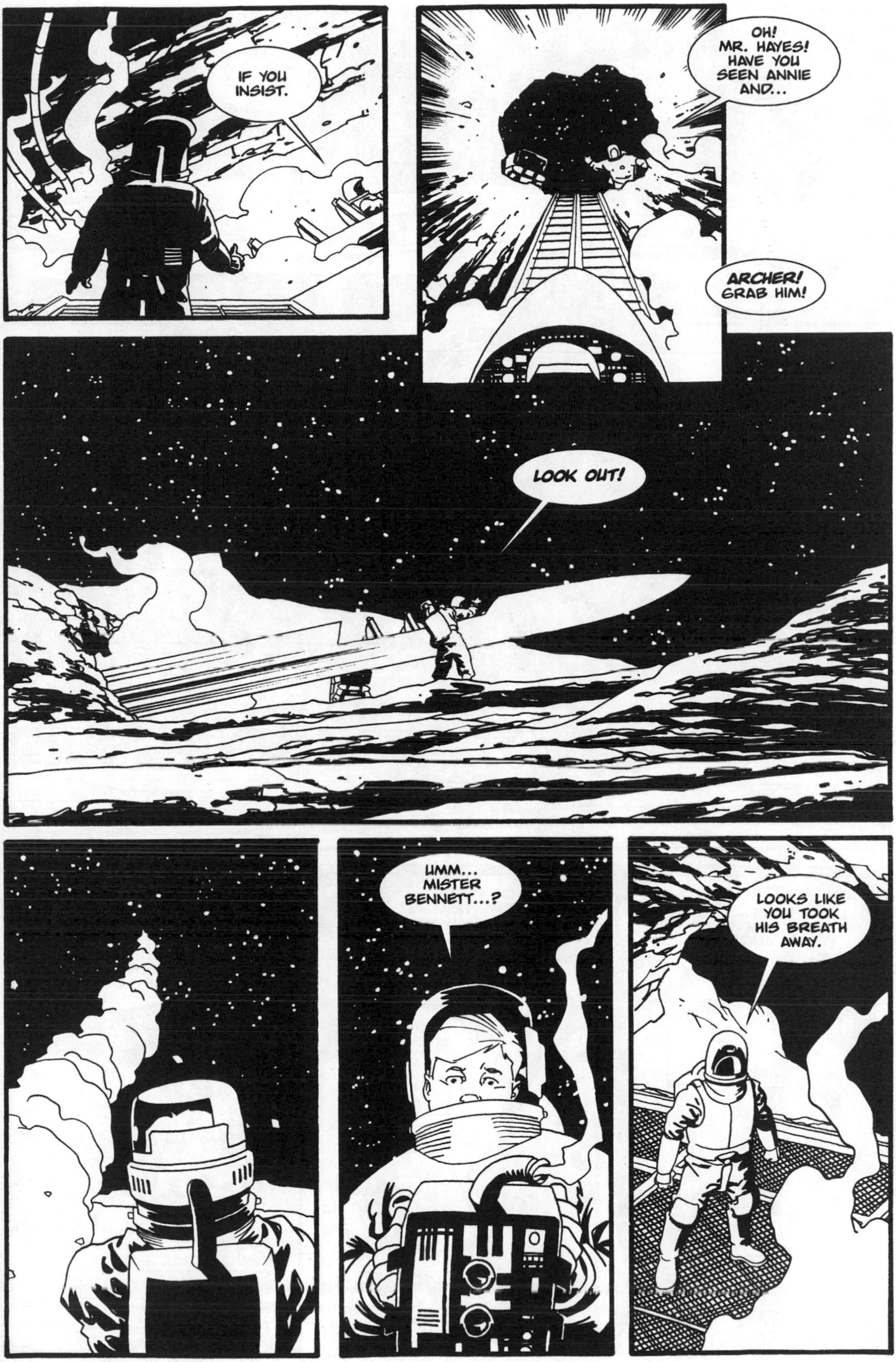
IF YOU INSIST.
OH! MR. HAYES! HAVE YOU SEEN ANNIE AND...
ARCHER! GRAB HIM!
LOOK OUT!
UMM... MISTER BENNETT...?
LOOKS LIKE YOU TOOK HIS BREATH AWAY.

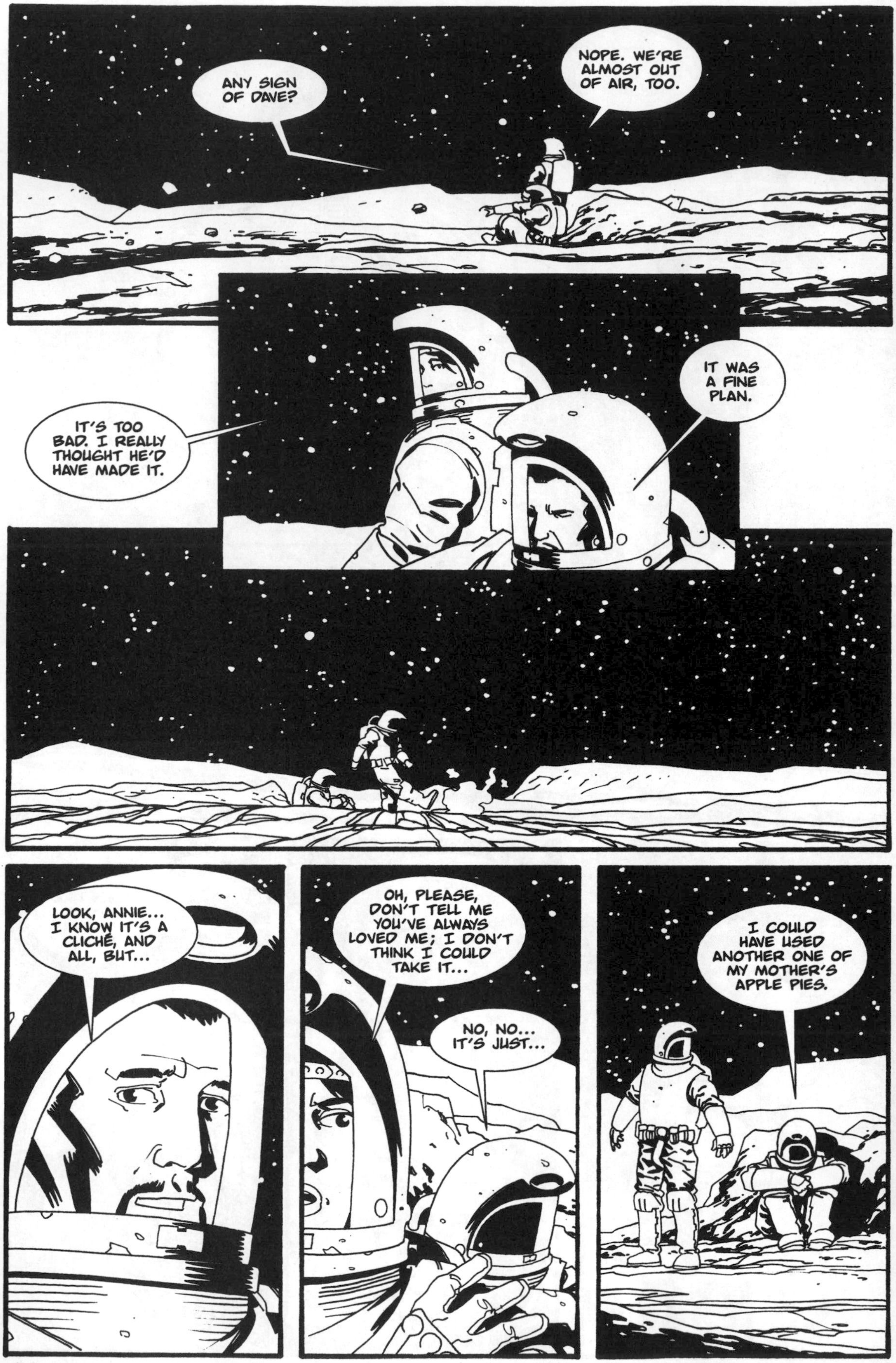
ANY SIGN OF DAVE?
NOPE. WE'RE ALMOST OUT OF AIR, TOO.
IT'S TOO BAD. I REALLY THOUGHT HE'D HAVE MADE IT.
IT WAS A FINE PLAN.
LOOK, ANNIE... I KNOW IT'S A CLICHÉ, AND ALL, BUT...
OH, PLEASE, DON'T TELL ME YOU'VE ALWAYS LOVED ME; I DON'T THINK I COULD TAKE IT...
NO, NO... IT'S JUST...
I COULD HAVE USED ANOTHER ONE OF MY MOTHER'S APPLE PIES.

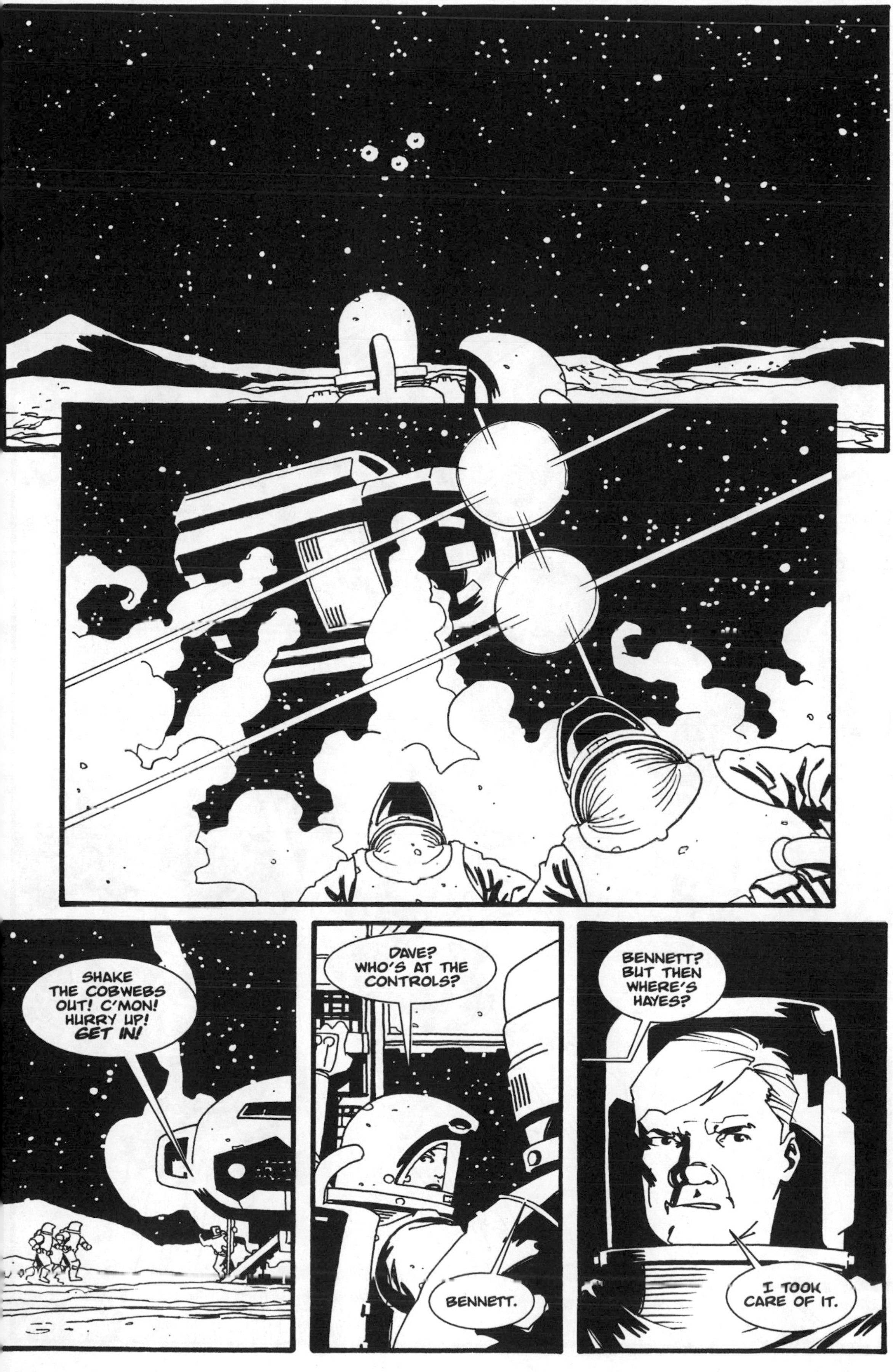
SHAKE THE COBWEBS OUT! C'MON! HURRY UP! GET IN!
DAVE? WHO'S AT THE CONTROLS?
BENNETT.
BENNETT? BUT THEN WHERE'S HAYES?
I TOOK CARE OF IT.

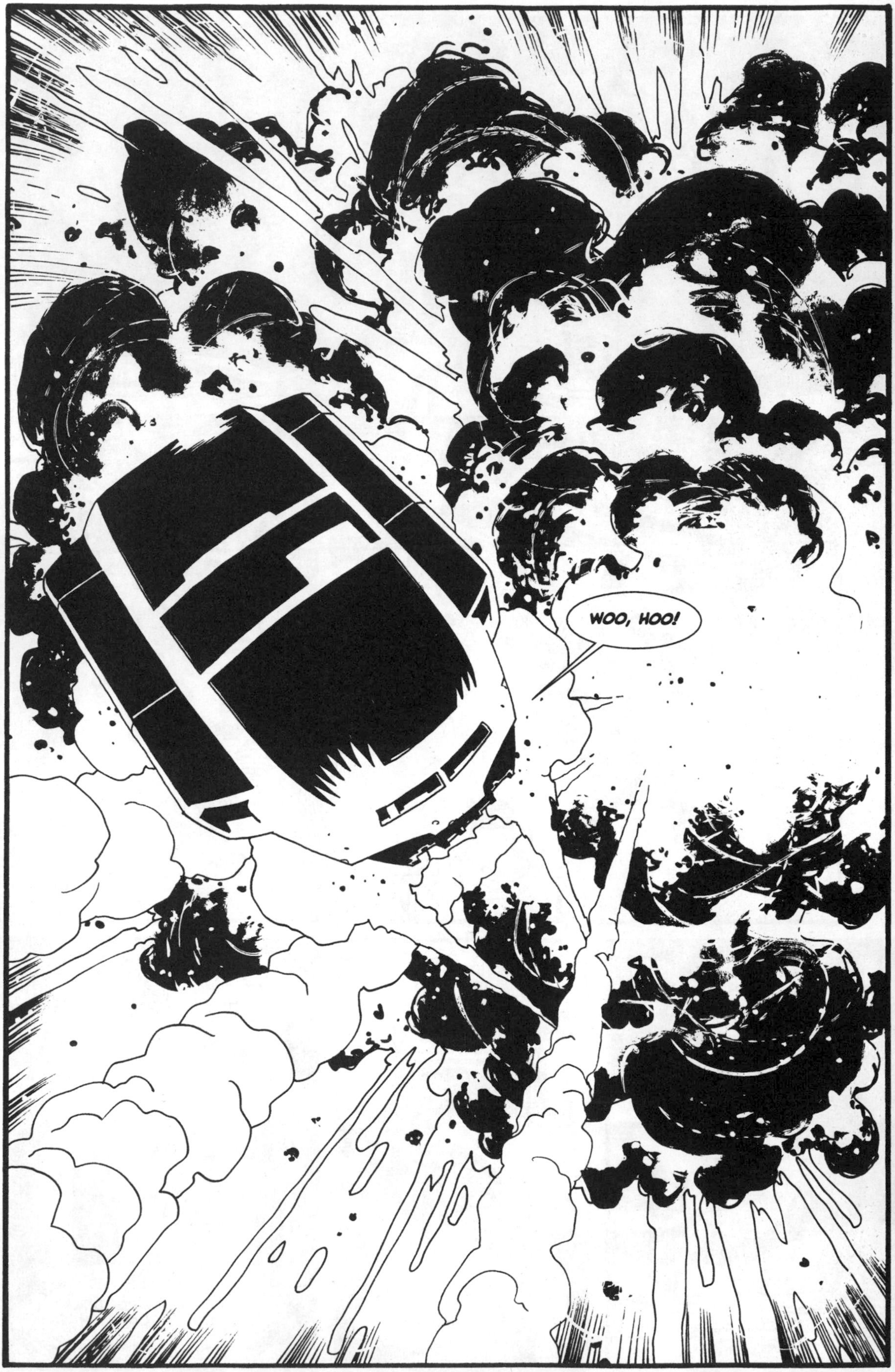
WOO, HOO!

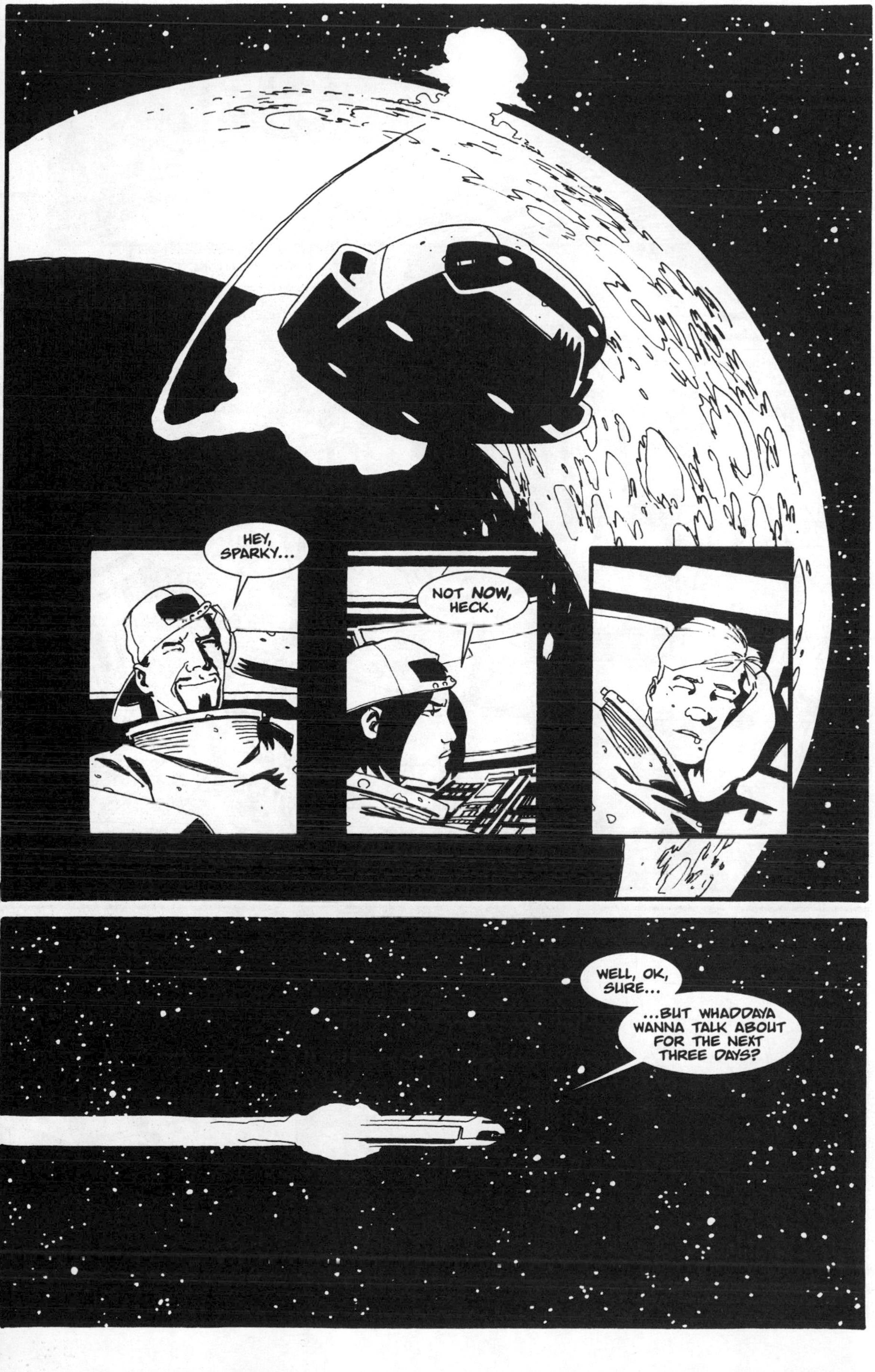
HEY, SPARKY...
NOT NOW, HECK.
WELL, OK, SURE...
...BUT WHADDAYA WANNA TALK ABOUT FOR THE NEXT THREE DAYS?

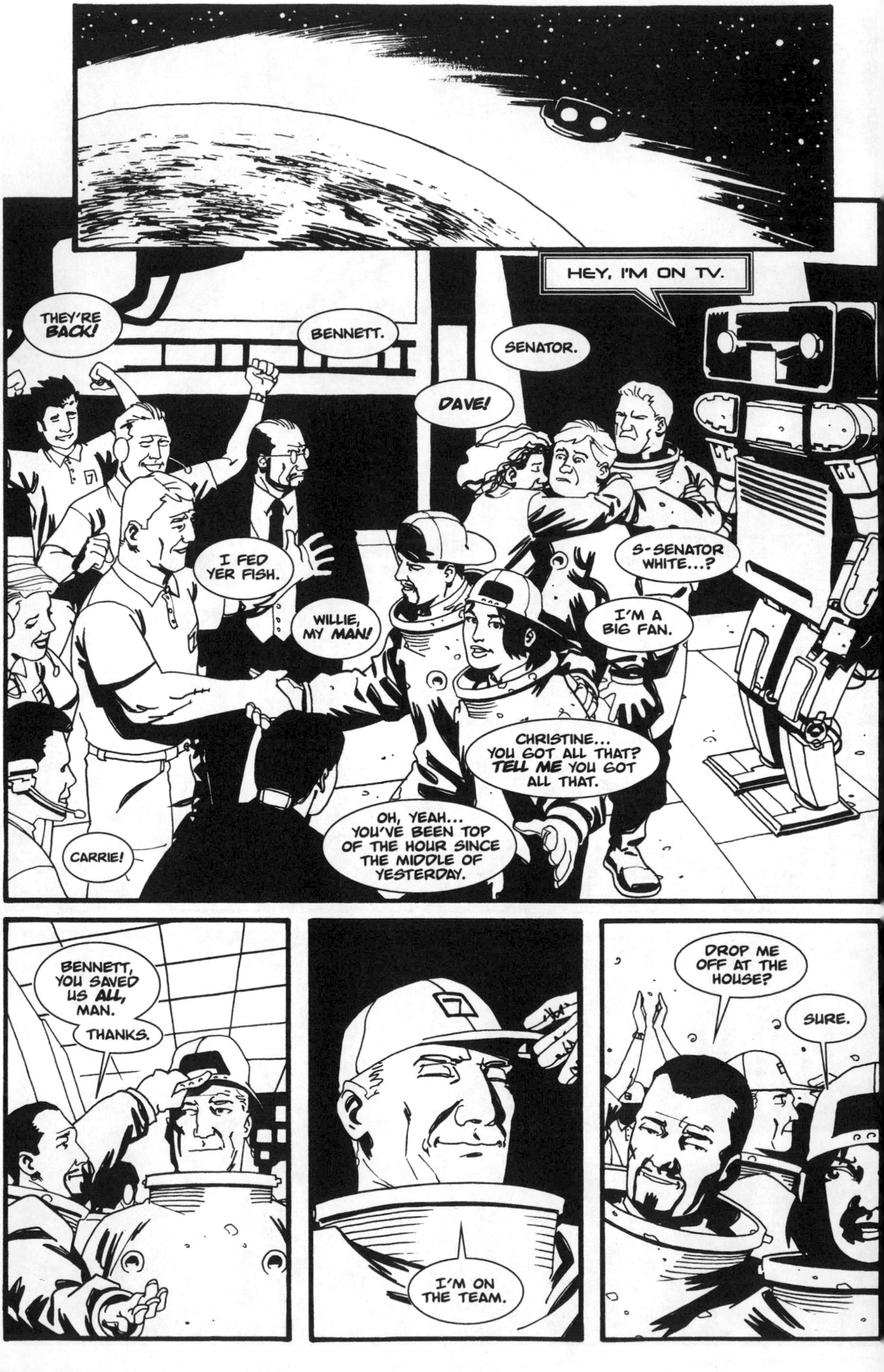
HEY, I'M ON TV.
THEY'RE BACK!
BENNETT.
SENATOR.
DAVE!
I FED YER FISH.
WILLIE, MY MAN!
S-SENATOR WHITE...?
I'M A BIG FAN.
CHRISTINE... YOU GOT ALL THAT? TELL ME YOU GOT ALL THAT.
OH, YEAH... YOU'VE BEEN TOP OF THE HOUR SINCE THE MIDDLE OF YESTERDAY.
CARRIE!
BENNETT, YOU SAVED US ALL, MAN.
THANKS.
I'M ON THE TEAM.
DROP ME OFF AT THE HOUSE?
SURE.

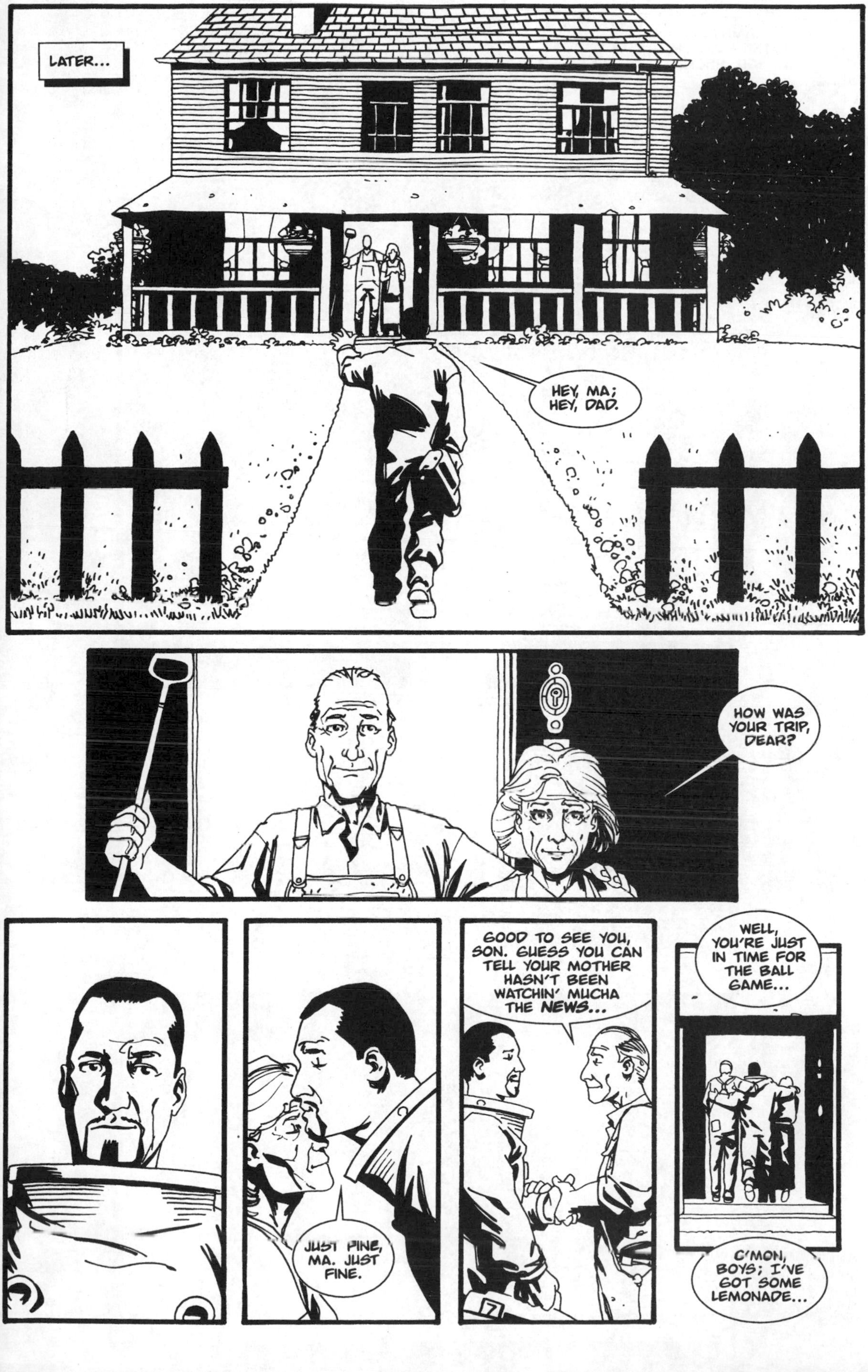
LATER...
HEY, MA; HEY, DAD.
HOW WAS YOUR TRIP, DEAR?
JUST FINE, MA. JUST FINE.
GOOD TO SEE YOU, SON. GUESS YOU CAN TELL YOUR MOTHER HASN'T BEEN WATCHIN' MUCHA THE NEWS...
WELL, YOU'RE JUST IN TIME FOR THE BALL GAME...
C'MON, BOYS; I'VE GOT SOME LEMONADE...

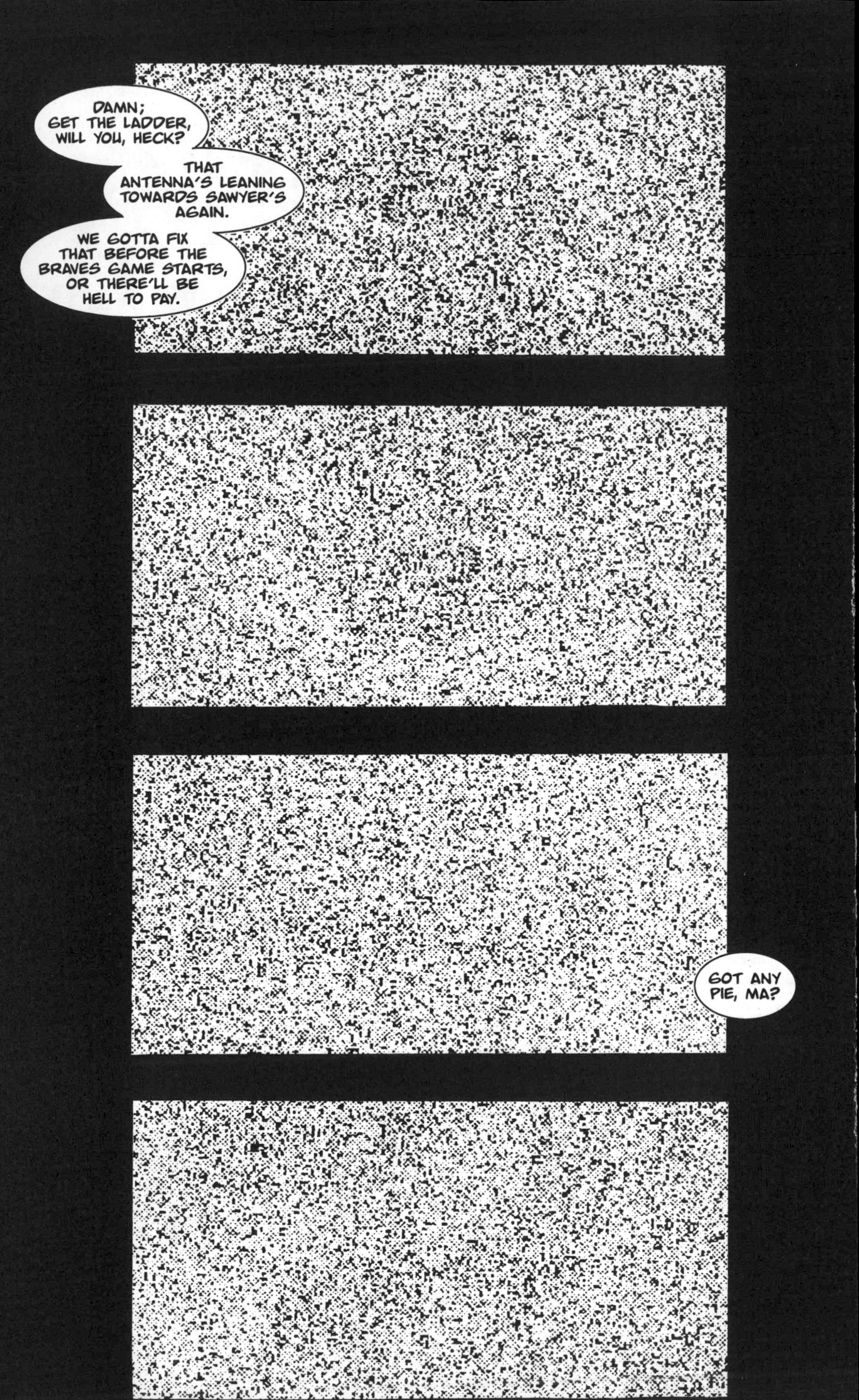
DAMN; GET THE LADDER, WILL YOU, HECK?
THAT ANTENNA'S LEANING TOWARDS SAWYER'S AGAIN.
WE GOTTA FIX THAT BEFORE THE BRAVES GAME STARTS, OR THERE'LL BE HELL TO PAY.
GOT ANY PIE, MA?

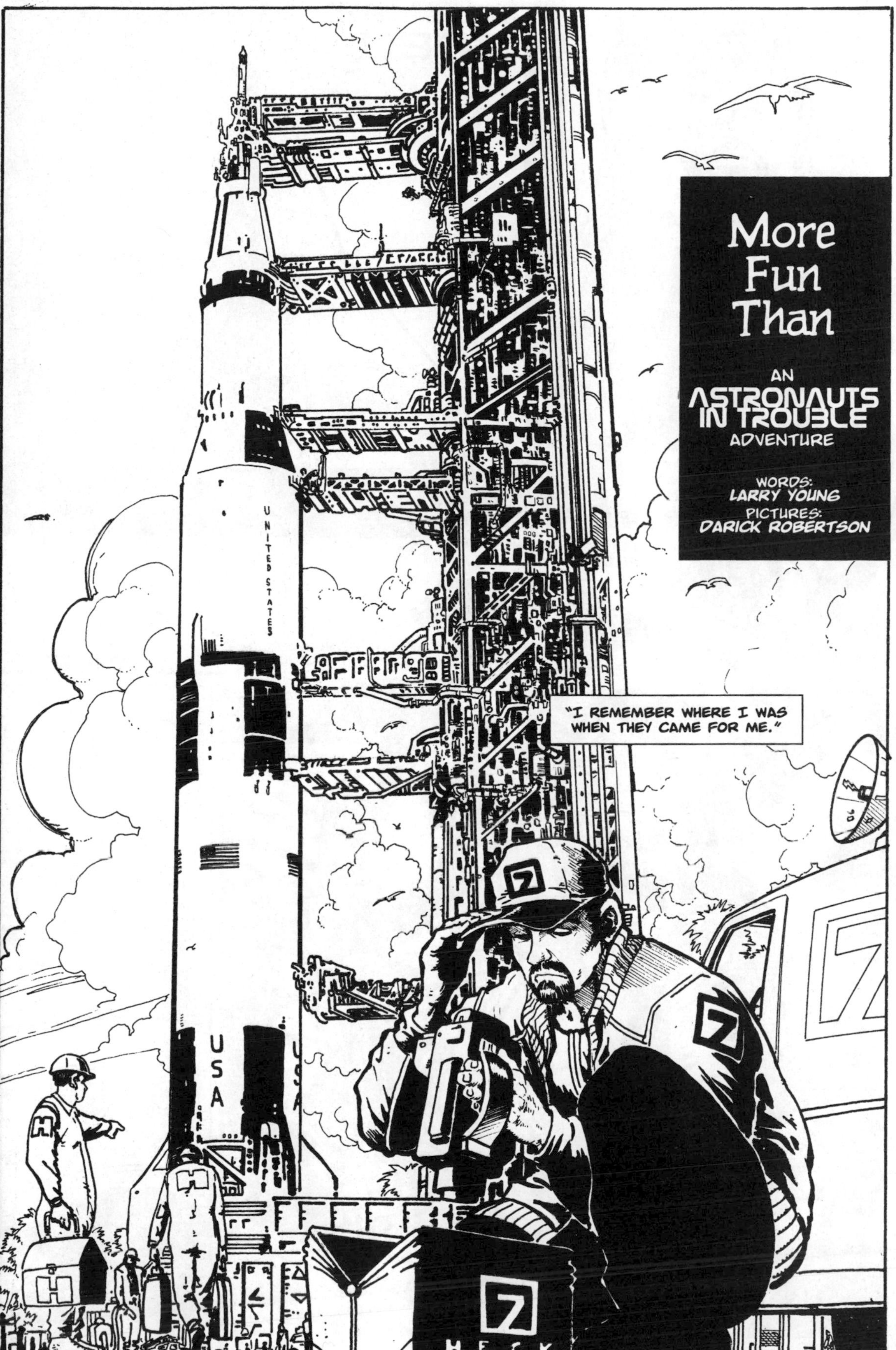
More Fun Than
AN ASTRONAUTS IN TROUBLE ADVENTURE
WORDS: LARRY YOUNG
PICTURES: DARICK ROBERTSON
"I REMEMBER WHERE I WAS WHEN THEY CAME FOR ME."
UNITED STATES
USA
HECK

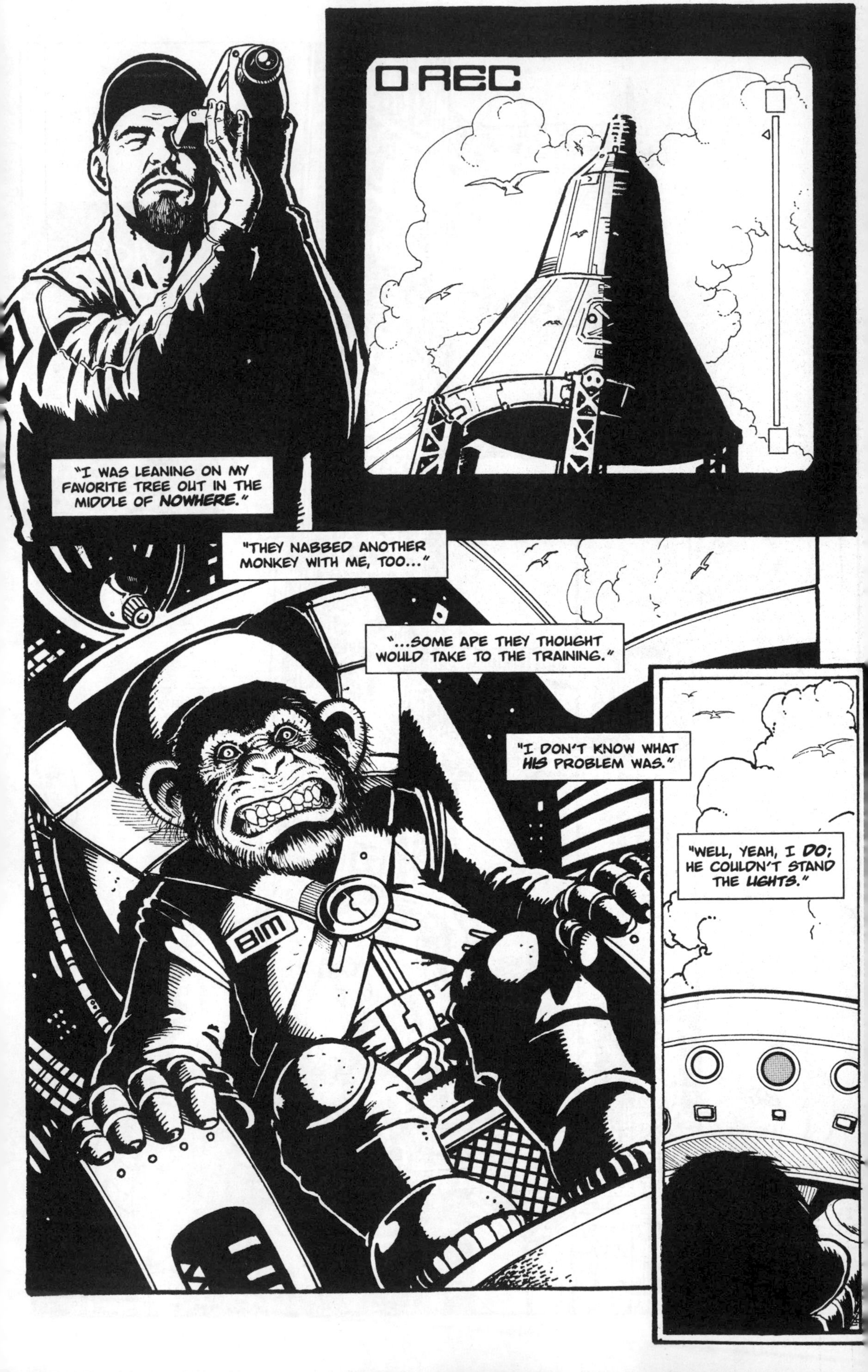
O REC
"I WAS LEANING ON MY FAVORITE TREE OUT IN THE MIDDLE OF NOWHERE."
"THEY NABBED ANOTHER MONKEY WITH ME, TOO..."
"...SOME APE THEY THOUGHT WOULD TAKE TO THE TRAINING."
BIM
"I DON'T KNOW WHAT HIS PROBLEM WAS."
"WELL, YEAH, I DO; HE COULDN'T STAND THE LIGHTS."

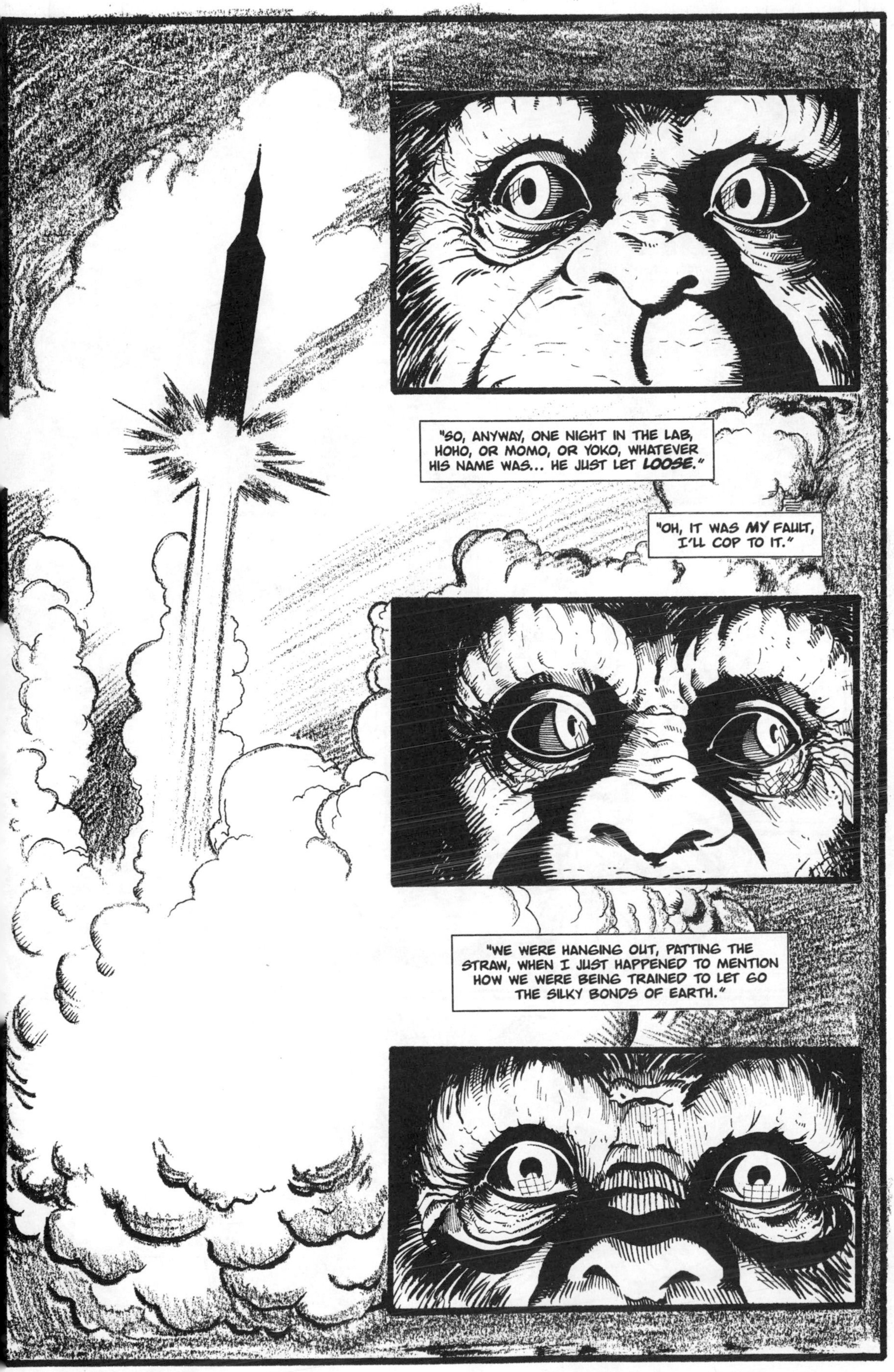

"SO, ANYWAY, ONE NIGHT IN THE LAB, HOHO, OR MOMO, OR YOKO, WHATEVER HIS NAME WAS... HE JUST LET LOOSE."
"OH, IT WAS MY FAULT, I'LL COP TO IT."
"WE WERE HANGING OUT, PATTING THE STRAW, WHEN I JUST HAPPENED TO MENTION HOW WE WERE BEING TRAINED TO LET GO THE SILKY BONDS OF EARTH."

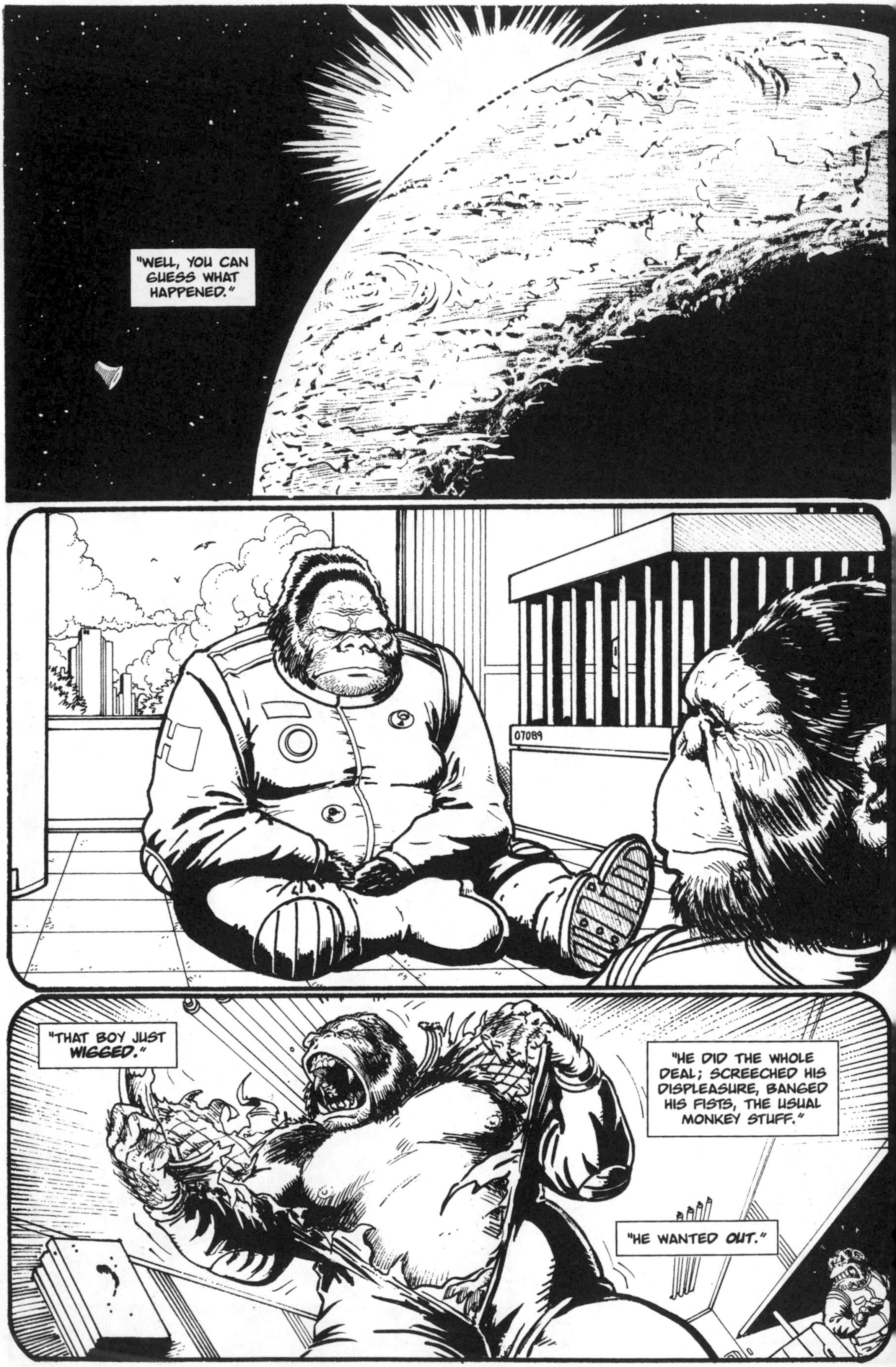
"WELL, YOU CAN GUESS WHAT HAPPENED."
07089
"THAT BOY JUST WIGGED."
"HE DID THE WHOLE DEAL; SCREECHED HIS DISPLEASURE, BANGED HIS FISTS, THE USUAL MONKEY STUFF."
"HE WANTED OUT."

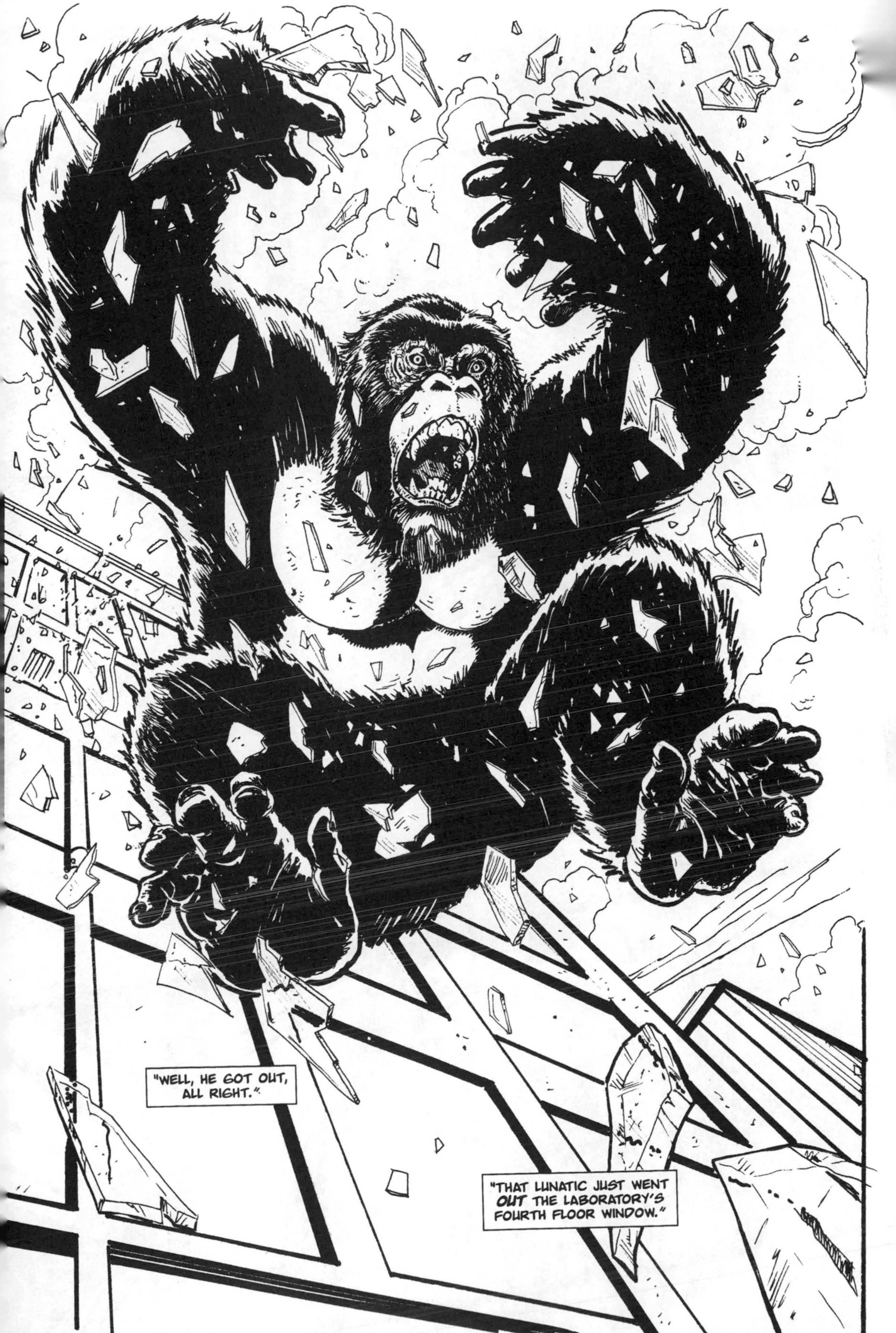
"WELL, HE GOT OUT, ALL RIGHT."
"THAT LUNATIC JUST WENT OUT THE LABORATORY'S FOURTH FLOOR WINDOW."

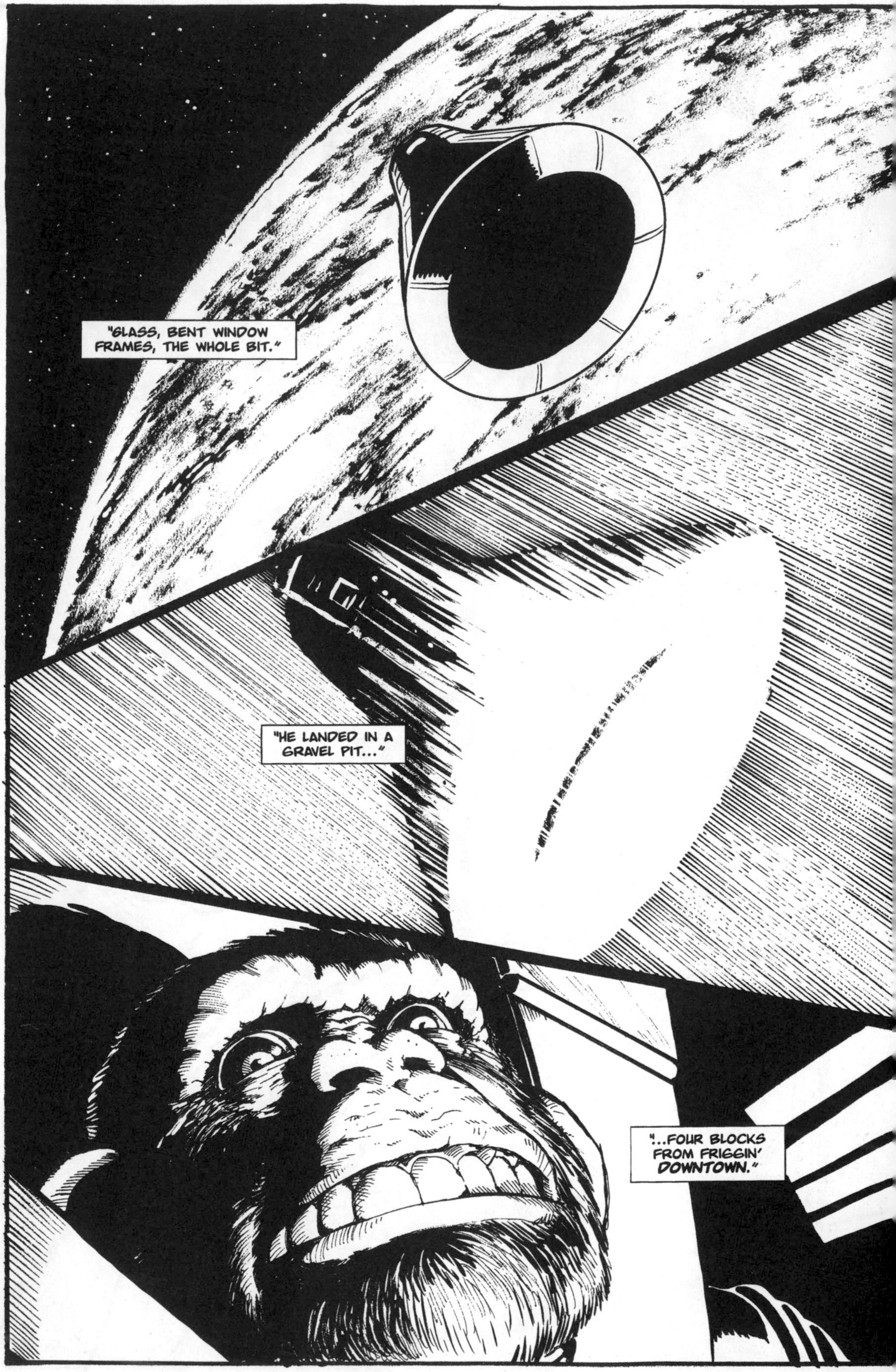
"GLASS, BENT WINDOW FRAMES, THE WHOLE BIT."
"HE LANDED IN A GRAVEL PIT..."
"...FOUR BLOCKS FROM FRIGGIN' DOWNTOWN."

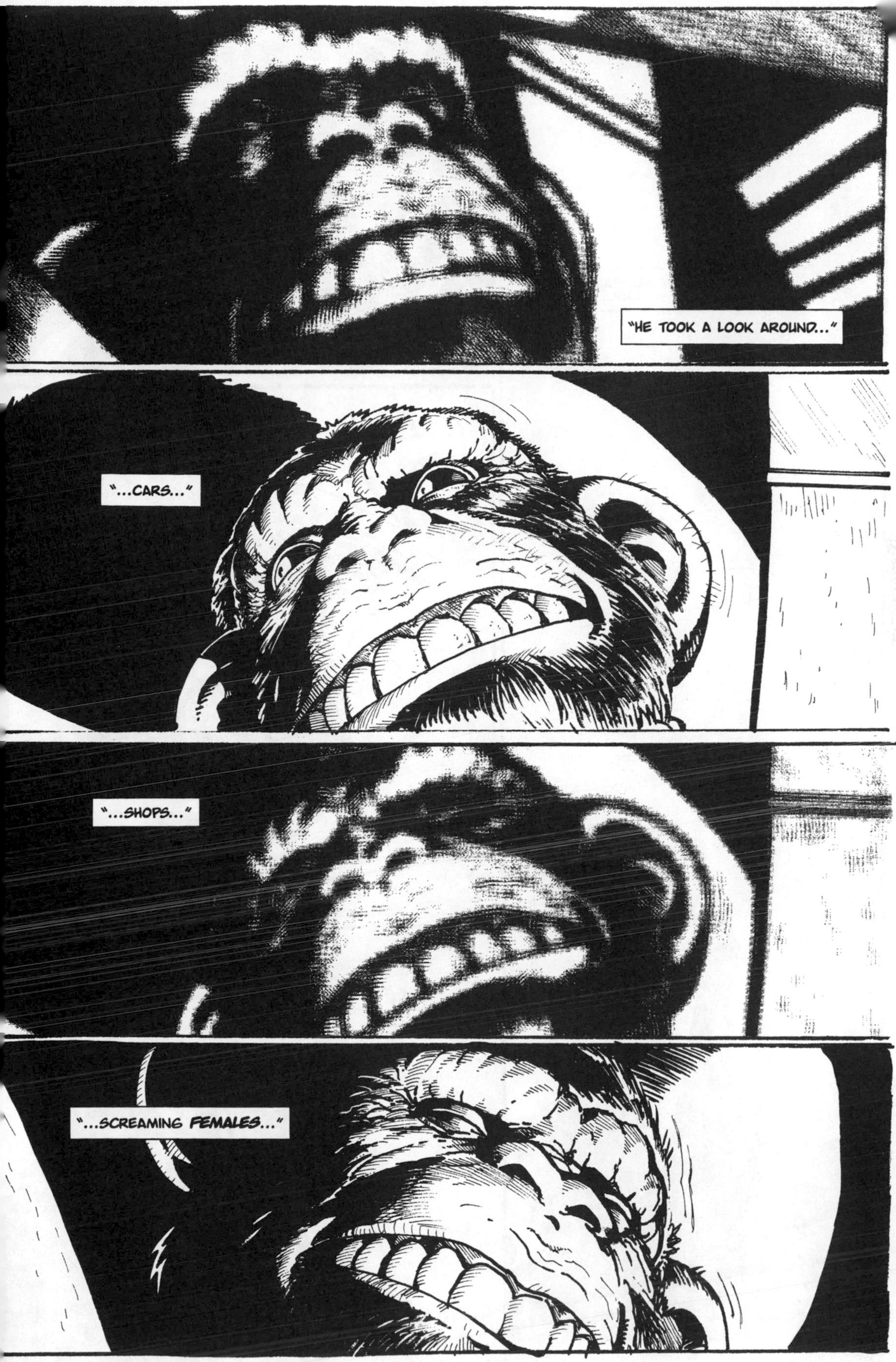
"HE TOOK A LOOK AROUND..."
"...CARS..."
"...SHOPS..."
"...SCREAMING FEMALES..."

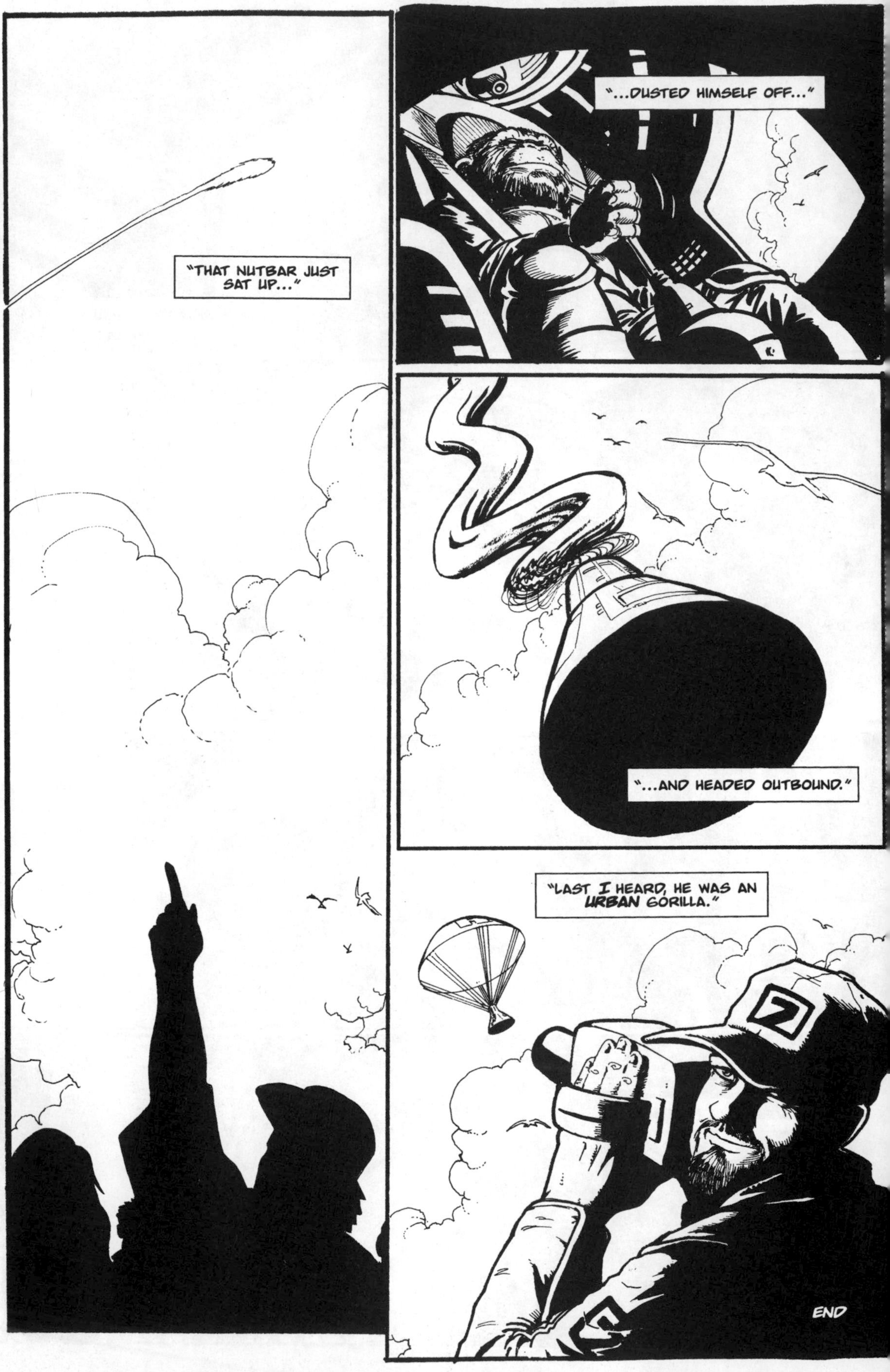
"THAT NUTBAR JUST SAT UP..."
"...DUSTED HIMSELF OFF..."
"...AND HEADED OUTBOUND."
"LAST I HEARD, HE WAS AN URBAN GORILLA."
END

On the following pages are a few pieces of art
from the AiT/Planet Lar astronaut archives.

Due to scheduling conflicts, Matt Smith was
unable to finish the final chapters of the series,
although he had started a few pages of chapter
four. Above is the splash page; on the following
pages are two more finished pages and an
unused cover.

If you're interested in a more in-depth peek
behind the scenes, look for *The Making of
Astronauts in Trouble* ISBN 0-9676848-0-6

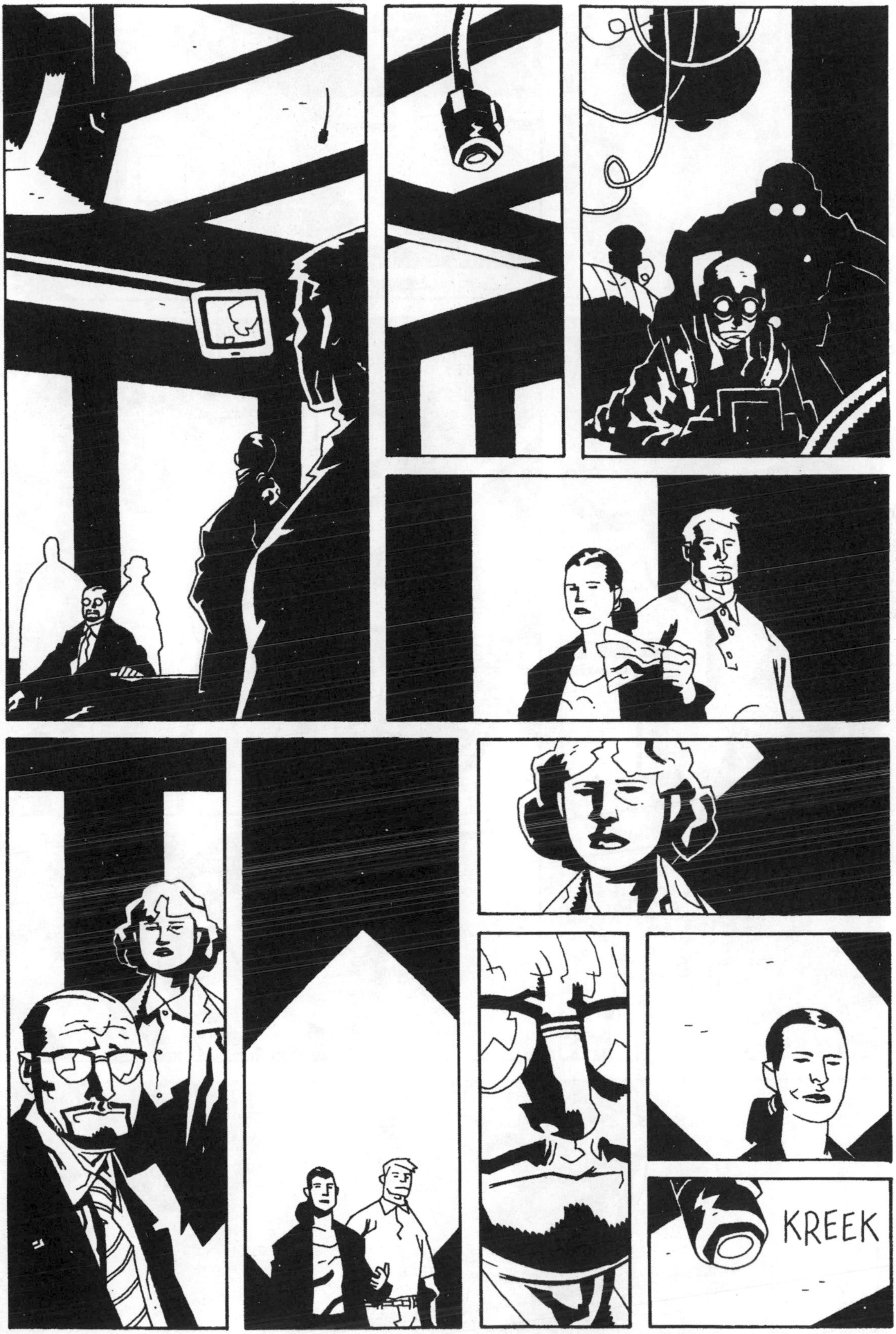
KREEK

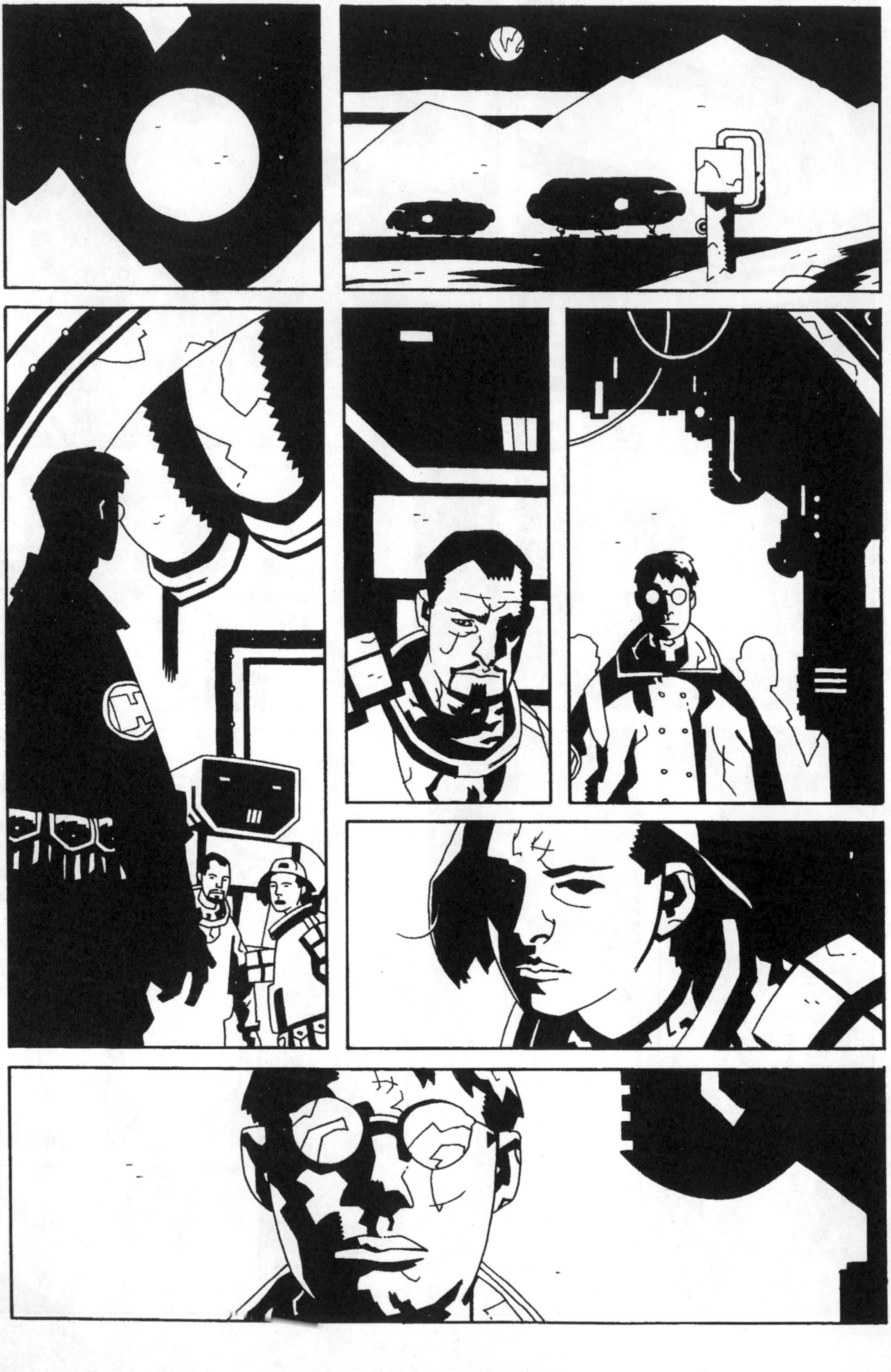

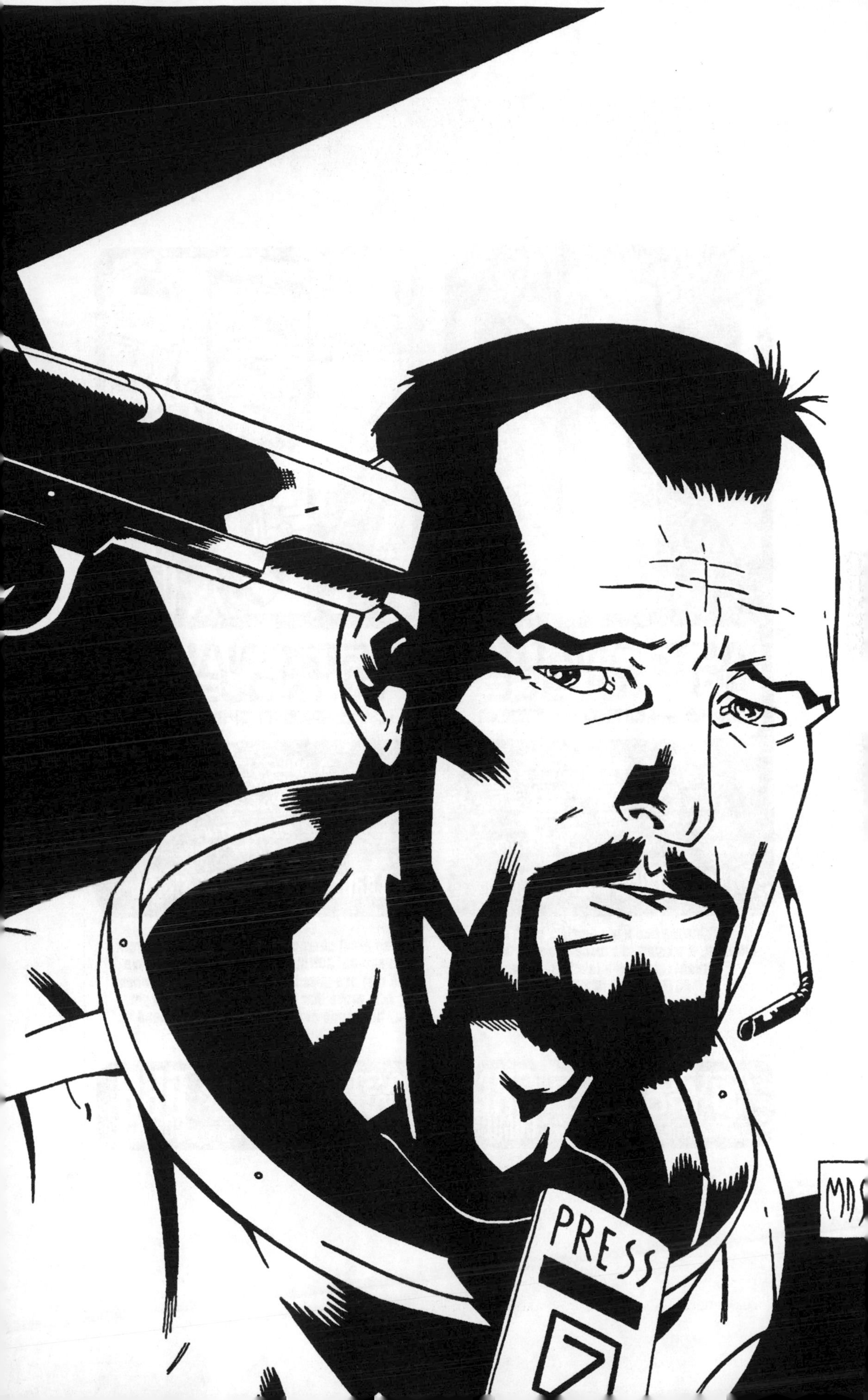
PRESS
7
MDS

ASTRONAUTS IN TROUBLE
LIVE FROM THE MOON
FIFTY YEARS AFTER ARMSTRONG'S ONE SMALL STEP, THE WORLD'S RICHEST MAN CLAIMS THE MOON AS HIS OWN PERSONAL PROPERTY...
...AND CHANNEL SEVEN IS THERE.
LARRY YOUNG • MATT SMITH
"It moves like a big movie... but it's different. It's smart. It's funny. It's entertaining without requiring a lobotomy. What ASTRONAUTS IN TROUBLE is, I swear to God, is an intelligent summer blockbuster."
--Warren Ellis
ASTRONAUTS IN TROUBLE
COMING THIS MARCH FROM
GUN DOG COMICS

ASTRONAUTS IN TROUBLE
LIVE FROM THE MOON
A WILD PILOT. A FAST SHIP. CHEAP BEER. AND SPACESUITS.
THE RIGHT STUFF AT THE RIGHT TIME.
LARRY YOUNG • MATT SMITH
"The great characters and nice, clean artwork make ASTRONAUTS IN TROUBLE a cut above the rest. It's guys like Larry Young and company who prove that this industry's not dead yet. Buy his comic or I'll kick your #@$%! head in."
--Garth Ennis
ASTRONAUTS IN TROUBLE
COMING THIS APRIL FROM
GUN DOG COMICS

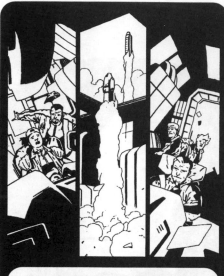

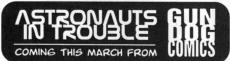

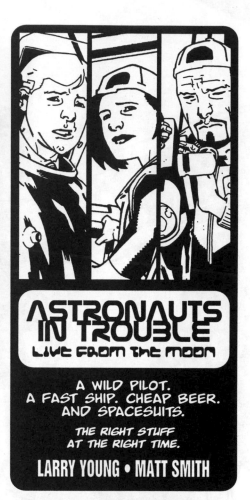

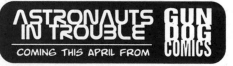

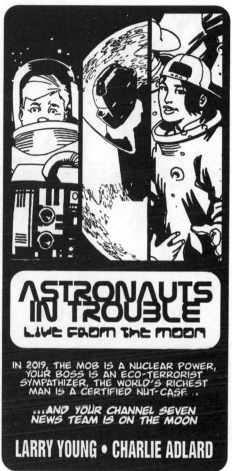

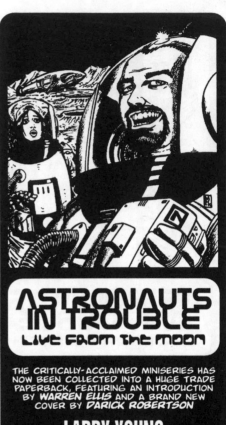

HELP MAKE SURE THIS DOESN'T HAPPEN IN 2019

(copy and mail)

The Comic Book Legal Defense Fund is a non-profit, tax-exempt organization dedicated to defending the First Amendment rights exclusively for comic book professionals and in comic books. If you are against censorship, especially in comics, say so by sending in your individual expression of Freedom of Speech in "dollars" to the CBLDF. Tell 'em you heard it from the Channel Seven News Team... *Live From the Moon.*

_____Yes! I want to help fight censorship in the comic book industry. Enclosed is my tax-deductible contribution of:

_____ $15	_____ $50	
_____ $25	_____ other	

Mail donations and inquiries to:
CBLDF • P.O. Box 693-AiT
Northampton, MA 01061
1-800-992-2533
www.cbldf.org

ASTRONAUTS IN TROUBLE

STUFF!

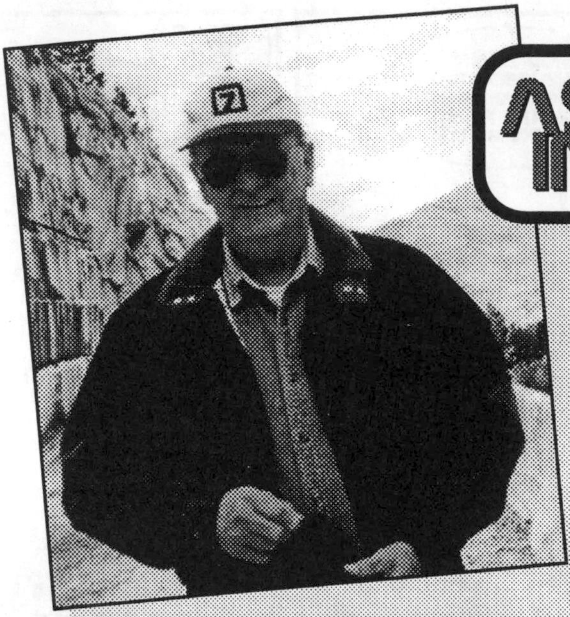

What's the rough-and-tumble man-on-the-go wearing today? Why, the official CHANNEL SEVEN baseball cap, that's what!

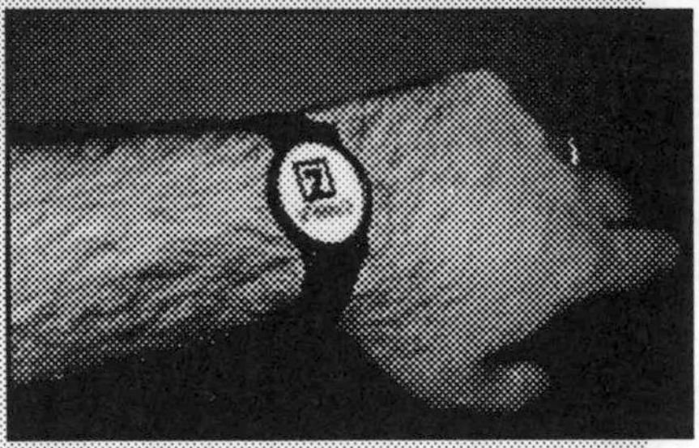

The CHANNEL SEVEN logo wristwatch tells perfect time *and* sports a real leather strap

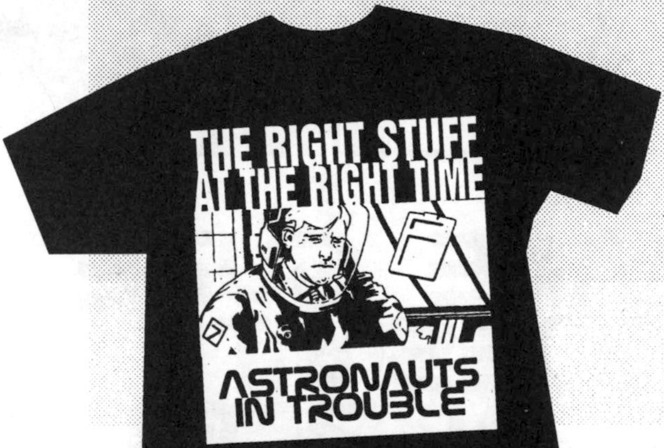
THE RIGHT STUFF
AT THE RIGHT TIME
ASTRONAUTS
IN TROUBLE

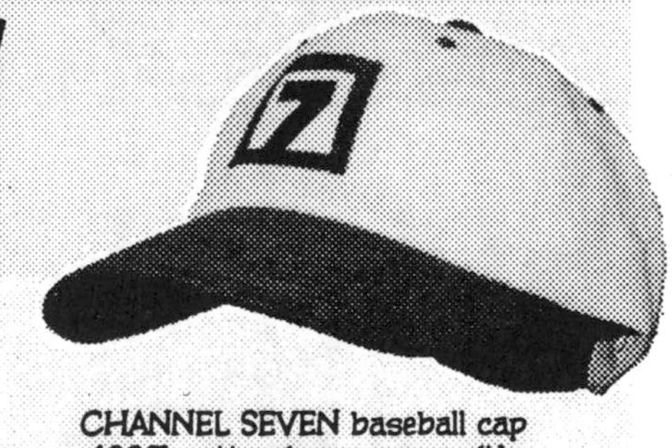

CHANNEL SEVEN baseball cap
100% cotton ivory crown with
black bill and trim
embroidered
CHANNEL SEVEN logo in front,
ASTRONAUTS IN TROUBLE logo in back
one size fits all

ASTRONAUTS IN TROUBLE:
LIVE FROM THE MOON
the official T-Shirt
art by Matt Smith • black shirt

PAYMENT CAN BE MADE BY CHECK OR MONEY ORDER

NAME ______________________

ADDRESS ______________________

CITY ______________ STATE ______ ZIP ______

QUANTITY	PRODUCT/DESCRIPTION	(please circle T-Shirt size)	PRICE	TOTAL
	CHANNEL SEVEN BASEBALL CAP	($19.95 + $2.50 shipping)	$22.45	
	ASTRONAUTS IN TROUBLE T-Shirt	($15.95 + $2.50 shipping) L • XL	$18.45	
	ASTRONAUTS IN TROUBLE Watch	($24.95 + $2.50 shipping)	$27.45	
		CALIFORNIA RESIDENTS ADD 8 1/2% SALES TAX		
			TOTAL	

AIT/plaNETLar
2034 47TH AVENUE, SAN FRANCISCO, CA 94116